Egyptian
in T

Egyptian Belly Dance in Transition

The Raqṣ Sharqī *Revolution, 1890–1930*

Heather D. Ward

McFarland & Company, Inc., Publishers
Jefferson, North Carolina

Library of Congress Cataloguing-in-Publication Data

NNames: Ward, Heather D., author.
Title: Egyptian belly dance in transition : the Raqs Sharqi revolution, 1890–1930 / Heather D. Ward.
Description: Jefferson, North Carolina : McFarland & Company, Inc., Publishers, 2018. | Includes bibliographical references and index.
Identifiers: LCCN 2017055635 | ISBN 9781476666747 (softcover : acid free paper) ♾
Subjects: LCSH: Belly dance—Egypt—History—19th century. | Belly dance—Egypt—History—20th century.
Classification: LCC GV1798.5 .W37 2018 | DDC 793.3—dc23
LC record available at https://lccn.loc.gov/2017055635

British Library cataloguing data are available

ISBN (print) 978-1-4766-6674-7
ISBN (ebook) 978-1-4766-2963-6

Front cover image: Danseuse circa 1860–1929 (G. Lékégian & Cie., photographer, New York Public Library)

Printed in the United States of America

McFarland & Company, Inc., Publishers
Box 611, Jefferson, North Carolina 28640
www.mcfarlandpub.com

Table of Contents

Preface

My involvement with *raqṣ sharqī*, i.e., belly dance, began in 1999, while I was a graduate student in anthropology at the University of Illinois at Urbana-Champaign. My story begins in a manner quite similar to that of other American women who find their way into the dance. I knew very little about it—I was primarily drawn to it for its exoticism, and because it provided me with an escape from a personal life that was in turmoil and an academic life that was stretching my coping mechanisms to their breaking point. As someone who was not particularly "at home" in my own body and who had never really felt comfortable with physical activities like dance and sport, belly dance was tremendously liberating, allowing me to connect with my body and to "claim" it, in a sense. In my mind and in my heart, the dance existed for me and for my personal fulfillment, and for the first nine months or so of private lessons, I kept my hobby a secret, even from family and close friends.

Because of the manner in which I entered the world of belly dance, my academic training and my dance training did not really intersect in any meaningful way for several years—even as my involvement with the dance deepened to the point that I began teaching classes for others. I accepted, without analysis, the information provided to me by well-meaning instructors, who proclaimed that belly dance was "by women, for women," an "ancient dance," a dance born out of a sacred connection to the mysteries of womanhood and femininity, and I gobbled up popular belly dance literature that reified these assertions. Not coincidentally, these narratives aligned well with my emotional and psychological needs at the time.

By 2005, the dance was integral to my life. It had been an anchor for me through several of the most troubling years of my life, and had helped me to emerge from the chaos a more stable and self-assured person. However, as I settled into this new era of clarity and stability, I had time to reassess my understandings of the dance that had led me to this place. Doubts about the "common knowledge" that I had long accepted began to nag at me, and for the first time, I began to apply my academic training to an examination of what I (thought I) knew. I was disturbed and distressed to find little evidential support for a lot of what I had been taught and what I had unquestioningly repeated to my own students. Moreover, I was deeply troubled by the fact that, in using belly dance to satisfy my own needs, I had carelessly embraced self-serving Orientalist narratives about the dance and its history, while neglecting the perspectives of Egyptians regarding their own dance.

As I leveraged my academic background toward a better understanding of the dance I loved, I found that my affection for belly dance became deeper, richer, and more authentic to my personality. I started to delve into what little academic work on the dance that I could find, and I discovered the reality of the dance to be even more captivating than the fantasy vision that I had previously embraced. I began listening in earnest to the voices of Egyptians and Arabs—not only professional dancers, but also ordinary individuals—in order to grasp their perspectives on belly dance, which turned out to be complex and, in many cases, conflicted. I started corresponding with Priscilla Adum and the late Dr. Hishām al-ʿAjamī, individuals who shared my interests and who inspired me to turn my attention toward exploring Arabic-language sources.

As I entered this new and exciting phase of my involvement with belly dance, I heard of a new course being offered by the well-known dancer and researcher Sahra C. Kent. This course, which she christened "Journey through Egypt," was intended to be precisely that—an academic foray into the diverse dance traditions of Egypt, combining lecture, discussion, demonstration, practice, and, ultimately, on-site study in Egypt. I was immediately interested, and I scrimped and saved in order to attend the first level of this course. In 2009, I set off to Escondido, California, nervous and unsure what to expect. When the course began, I knew I had made the right decision. I was spellbound: here we were, discussing Egyptian dances—including belly dance—from an academic, empirically-based perspective. The portions of the course that discussed the *ʿawālim* and the *ghawāzī*, Egypt's original professional dancing women, sent my mind racing with thoughts and questions regarding the history of belly dance. How and when did the dance styles of these women come to be transformed into the belly dance that I recognized? And why? I was determined to get answers to these questions.

I commenced with my own focused research into belly dance history, and I continued with Sahra's course, eventually completing levels two through four, a process that at long last brought me to Egypt. As I stood on Egyptian soil, I felt that I had found myself—I was not only a belly dancer, but I was a belly dance researcher. My academic training and my dance training had finally been woven together, and I had a clear mission—to seek out the evidence that would at long last allow an empirically based examination of the emergence of *raqṣ sharqī*.

My research interest in early *raqṣ sharqī* prompted me to dive headlong into nineteenth and early twentieth century primary sources such as turn-of-the century travel guide books and Arabic-language newspapers and magazines. It also had the side-effect of initiating my hobby of collecting period photographs, postcards, prints, and ephemera related to Egyptian entertainers and entertainment venues. These items have proven to be a boon to my investigations.

I did not initially plan to write a book based on my research. However, around five years into my investigations, I realized that I had collected sufficient information to draw the various lines of evidence together into a coherent and detailed narrative regarding the origin and early development of *raqṣ sharqī*. I began to feel a sense of obligation to share what I had learned. I recalled my own beginnings in the dance, and I realized I did not want another student to have to stumble through a forest of misinformation for years before finally arriving at some factual information about the dance. Moreover, my own early experience with belly dance reminded me how casually commonplace it has been, among non-Egyptian practitioners of this dance, to detach the dance from its cultural context and to manipulate and distort its history. I felt a responsibility to draw attention to Arabic-language primary sources, and in doing so, to the perspectives of the late nineteenth and early twentieth century Egyptians who created this dance form. For these reasons, I made the decision to start writing, and this book came to be.

I owe an incredible debt of gratitude to so many individuals and organizations for making this book possible. I first wish to thank Sahra Kent for inspiring me to embark on this journey. Without Sahra, this project would never have come to be. She has been a constant source of support and enthusiasm for my work, and for this I am sincerely grateful. I greatly appreciate the patient assistance of a number of fellow researchers, including Priscilla Adum, Aisha Ali, Frédéric Lagrange, and George Dimitri Sawa, all of whom took the time to answer my many questions and to share valuable resources with me. I am grateful to Amina

Goodyear for supporting me and for advocating for the importance of this work.

I am sincerely grateful to McFarland for taking a chance on this project, and to the external readers who took time to comment on the first draft. Additionally, I am incredibly thankful for the assistance of my permissions researcher, Margaret Gaston. I would not have been able to navigate the confusing world of copyright without her help. I appreciate the assistance of the Galerie Detaille in Marseille, who kindly granted me permission to incorporate one of their images in this text. I also owe thanks to Christine Ferhat, who took the time to proof and edit my rather rough translation of what turned out to be a very valuable French-language account.

So many individuals have assisted me with my research on-site in Egypt that I am not sure where to begin. I am deeply grateful to Sayyid Ḥankish, who time and again generously shared his wealth of knowledge and insight into the world of Egyptian music and dance, and who permitted me to share his remarkable image of Zūbah al-Klūbātīyah in this book. I wish to express my sincere appreciation and admiration for Sūsū, a retired Muḥammad 'Alī Street performer, and Khayrīyah Māzin, one of the famous Banāt Māzin of Luxor. It was an honor to have the opportunity to meet and learn from these amazing women. I thank Khālid Manṣūr and his son Bijād for tirelessly assisting me with transportation, translation, and tracking down resources. I thank 'Iṣṣām Mirsāl and his friend Muhsin Dūklah for patiently helping me with translation during interviews.

I wish to thank my friends Kathy Naylor and Andrea Menning for their advice and support. I am also grateful to all of my dance students, who have "rooted me on" during this whole process. I owe particular thanks to my student and friend Cynthia Thornbury, who generously permitted me to share one of her vintage prints in this book.

I cannot adequately convey the depth of my gratitude to my parents, Kenneth and Dianne Ward, and to my aunt, Iona Murray. Their belief in me and in my ability to succeed at this endeavor has given me the strength, confidence, and resolve necessary to carry this project through to its completion. Nor can I fully express my appreciation to Mousa Salameh, who has been a translator, a friend, a confidant, a champion, and so much more. There are no words left, but there are none needed.

I inevitably have forgotten to mention someone, so I wish to beg the apologies of anyone whose name has slipped from my memory while writing these acknowledgments; please do not let this oversight lead you to believe that I am ungrateful for your assistance.

Notes on Transcription and Translation

In general, I followed the ALA-LC (American Library Association and Library of Congress) system when transcribing Arabic terms, including the names of individuals and places. I used the anglicized spellings of well-known place names such as Alexandria and Cairo. I also used the anglicized spellings of the names of individuals who regularly employ an anglicized spelling of their own names. In quotations, I followed the transcription system of the quoted author.

Translation of Arabic sources was accomplished with the invaluable assistance of Mr. Mousa Salameh. I translated European-language sources myself, with a few exceptions which are noted in the text.

Introduction

Raqṣ sharqī ("eastern dance"), the Egyptian concert dance form commonly known as belly dance, is one of the most beguiling yet misunderstood dance forms in the world. The dance is generally performed by a solo artist, though choreographed group performances have also been part of the dance since as early as the 1930s. Most performers of *raqṣ sharqī* are female, though there are male practitioners, including several high-profile male Egyptians. The dance is characterized by a core repertoire of torso movements, including articulated hip and shoulder movements such as shimmies, circles and "figure eights" of the pelvis, and undulations of the abdomen. The movements of *raqṣ sharqī* also include an array of steps and turns that were gradually incorporated into the dance over the course of the last century. Beyond the movement vocabulary, the dance is distinguished by the significance accorded to effective musical interpretation. A skilled performer of *raqṣ sharqī* must be able to convey the rhythmic structure, instrumentation, phrasing, and feeling of Egyptian music through the dance.

Many features of *raqṣ sharqī* are shared by dance forms throughout the Middle East, North Africa, and parts of Central Asia, and in the English language, the term "belly dance" has come to be used in a broad sense to refer to this assortment of similar, but distinct, dance forms. The emergence of this term, itself a translation of the French *danse du ventre*, is touched on in Donna Carlton's *Looking for Little Egypt* (1994). The term "belly dance" is also used quite liberally to refer to a number of dance styles originating outside of the Middle East, most notably styles developed in the United States, such as American Tribal Style belly dance. These dance styles, while deriving a great deal of their foundational movements from dances such as *raqṣ sharqī*, differ markedly from the source dances in aesthetic, musical accompaniment, and costuming.

The broad usage of "belly dance" notwithstanding, it is important to note that Egyptians, when referring to *raqṣ sharqī* in English, generally call it belly dance or Oriental dance. Even for many non-Egyptian Arabs and other Middle Easterners, "belly dance" is synonymous with *raqṣ sharqī*, due in large measure to the powerful influence exerted by the Egyptian film industry throughout the Middle East. As Wood and Shay have noted: "...dancers who would be billed as belly dancers elsewhere in the world are called Egyptian dancers by Middle Easterners" (Wood and Shay 1976: 19, see also Shay 2002: 141). For these reasons, in this text, the term "belly dance" will be treated as an English-language synonym for *raqṣ sharqī* and its related Egyptian dance forms (*raqṣ baladī* and the dances of the *'awālim* and the *ghawāzī*, discussed below).

Thousands of practitioners, from casual hobbyists to dedicated professionals, have embraced *raqṣ sharqī* and its associated music and costuming. Yet, for all its popularity, the origins and history of this dance form are poorly understood and clouded in myth and hearsay. A casual search through much of the popular literature on *raqṣ sharqī* and the various other dances indiscriminately lumped under the "belly dance" umbrella reveals a broad range of "origin myths," ranging from ancient fertility cults to birthing rituals, and a common tendency to describe belly dance as "the world's oldest dance" without empirical evidence to support such a claim.[1] These unsourced, unsupported origin stories are widely circulated by instructors and aficionados of *raqṣ sharqī* and related dances, both in live classroom settings and through the Internet. Newcomers to the dance find themselves faced with a dizzying mix of fact and fiction that can be difficult to disentangle.

A fundamental source of misunderstanding in discussions regarding the history of Egyptian belly dance is a failure to distinguish between the informal, social form of the dance—what many Egyptians term *raqṣ baladī*, or indigenous dance[2]—and the professional forms of the dance, including *raqṣ sharqī*, as well as the dances of the professional entertainers known as *'awālim* and *ghawāzī*. This is a critical distinction, as these variants of belly dance occupy very different positions in Egyptian society and have followed dissimilar historical trajectories. *Raqṣ baladī*, performed for personal enjoyment in social settings, is widely accepted in Egyptian society. The various forms of professional belly dance, which involve paid performance for the entertainment of strangers, occupy a much more tenuous and ambiguous position in the culture. At festive events like wedding celebrations, multiple forms of belly dance will often be in evidence—professional belly dance performed by a professional dancer for the entertainment of the guests, and *raqṣ baladī* performed by the guests themselves for their own enjoyment. However, the same individual who would gladly hire a professional belly dancer for her daughter's wedding reception would be filled with shame if that same daughter decided to become a professional dancer herself. The complex and conflicted relationship between Egyptians and professional belly dance has been explored in detail by Karin Van Nieuwkerk (1995) in her seminal work, *A Trade Like Any Other: Female Singers and Dancers in Egypt*. More recently, Noha Roushdy has elaborated on the marginalized position of professional dancers in Egyptian society, revealing the manner in which belly dance performance embodies a "symbolic inversion" of normative femininity in Egypt (Roushdy 2009).

Raqṣ baladī may indeed be a dance form of considerable antiquity, but its exact origin and history cannot be asserted with certainty, since like so many other folk dances, it has been transmitted by generations of ordinary people through practice and imitation rather than formal documentation. By contrast, historical developments in the professional variants of belly dance are much better documented. Though it is impossible to pinpoint the precise antiquity of the dances of the *'awālim* and *ghawāzī*, their existence is chronicled in the accounts of European observers from as early as the late eighteenth century. Savary, in a letter from Cairo dated to 1785, describes the *'awālim* as an established and celebrated class of entertainers (Savary 1785: 149–156), and multiple authors offer similar accounts of the *'awālim* during the period of Napoleon's expedition to Egypt, from 1798 to 1801 (Chabrol 1822, Denon 1803, Jomard 1822, Villoteau 1809). These early accounts indicate that the *'awālim* were esteemed singers, with a command of Arabic poetry and the ability to improvise verse and melody on the spot (Chabrol 1822: 381, Savary 1785: 149–150). They were also masters of the native Egyptian dance, though they generally only performed it in the privacy of the *ḥarīm*, or women's quarters, of well-to-do Egyptian households (Savary 1785: 150–153, Villoteau 1809: 694–695). Several authors contrast a lower class of *'awālim* who were differentiated from their higher-class peers by their propensity to perform in public for the Egyptian lower classes (Chabrol 1822: 418, Jomard 1822: 733, Savary 1785: 155–156, Villoteau 1809: 694–695); Both Chabrol (1822: 418) and Villoteau (1809: 695) refer to these women as the *ghawāzī*.

The *'awālim* and the *ghawāzī* remained a source of fascination for Westerners throughout the nineteenth century, and descriptive accounts from this period are abundant. Perhaps the most referenced description of the *'awālim* and *ghawāzī* in the early decades of the nineteenth century is that of Edward Lane (Lane 1860 and 2005 [1836]). Lane expands upon earlier descriptions of these entertainers, and attempts to draw a clearer distinction between the *'awālim* and *ghawāzī*, stressing the role of *'awālim* as singers, and even going so far as to suggest that only inferior *'awālim* danced. However, Lane's sister, Sophia Lane-Poole, writing of the entertainments at the royal wedding of Zaynab Hānim (youngest daughter of Muḥammad 'Alī, the self-proclaimed Khedive, or Viceroy of Egypt), clearly indicates that esteemed *'awālim* (prestigious enough to be hired to entertain the Khedive's daughter) were also revered as excellent dancers:

> These girls were succeeded by two 'A'lmehs, the first Arab singers of Egypt; and the band struck up some beautiful Arab airs; but on that evening the 'A'lmehs did not sing; they only danced in the Arab manner, for which performance they are also celebrated as the first of their day [Lane-Poole 1846: 96].

Lane-Poole's account, though lesser known, is in many ways more valuable than that of her brother, since she had access to female-only entertainments that he did not (Fraser 2002).

Raqṣ sharqī, the concert dance now more widely identified with the term "belly dance" than either *raqṣ baladī* or *'awālim/ghawāzī* dance, emerged toward the end of the nineteenth century, during the British occupation of Egypt. There is sufficient evidence to permit a reconstruction of the development of this dance form from the *'awālim/ghawāzī* stylistic base. In spite of this, much of the current knowledge regarding the origin and history of *raqṣ sharqī* is based on group consensus among students and performers of the dance, rather than on scholarly examination of the available historical sources.

A widely-accepted explanation of the dance's origin asserts that *raqṣ sharqī* was created by Egyptians in response to Western influences and desires. The argument goes that savvy Egyptian entertainment hall owners, catering to Western audiences as well as to upper-class Egyptian audiences with Western tastes, created a dance and associated costuming style that embodied Westerners' Orientalist fantasies of Middle Eastern dance. The name that is most commonly invoked within this argument is Badī'ah Maṣābnī, the Syrian entertainer and entrepreneur who owned several entertainment halls in Cairo and Alexandria from the 1920s through the 1940s. Indeed, many aficionados of *raqṣ sharqī* believe that Badī'ah singlehandedly invented the dance.

Permutations of this narrative appear in the popular belly dance literature that is widely consumed by students, performers, and other enthusiasts of *raqṣ sharqī* (examples include Buonaventura 1998: 148–152, Dinicu 2011: 106, Zamora Chamas 2009). Perhaps the most detailed and oft-cited rendition appears in Chapter Seven of Wendy Buonaventura's *Serpent of the Nile* (1998), a lavishly illustrated yet decidedly non-academic foray into the history of belly dance. According to Buonaventura: "The cabaret style developed in the 1920s in the nightspots of Algiers, Beirut, and Cairo which sprang up, in the first instance, to satisfy the demands of a colonial audience" (Buonaventura 1998: 148). Without any empirical evidence to support her assertions, she goes on to explain how Arab dancers, "in their desire to emulate Western behaviour and modes of fashion" (1998: 149), imitated "Hollywood" fantasies of Oriental dance in technique and costuming. She accords creative primacy to Badīʿah Maṣābnī:

> The first Egyptian cabaret, the Casino Opera, was opened in 1926 in Cairo by Syrian actress-dancer Badia Masabni. Badia's offered a varied bill of all-round entertainment, including an innovatory 6 o'clock matinée for women only, which was packed out every evening. With an eye on Western entertainment, she then decided to broaden the scope of Egyptian *baladi* [1998: 149].

In reality, the Casino Opera was neither the first Egyptian cabaret, nor was it open in 1926 (the author conflates the Casino Opera with one of Badīʿah Maṣābnī's other establishments). These factual errors aside, Buonaventura's statements typify the singular importance generally accorded to Badīʿah Maṣābnī. For additional examples, see Lüscher (2000: 18–19) and Zamora Chamas (2009).

The above-described narrative is not limited to the popular literature. It also appears in scholarly treatments of *raqṣ sharqī* and related dance forms, such as in Shay and Sellers-Young's volume of essays, *Belly Dance: Orientalism, Transnationalism, and Harem Fantasy*:

> Responding to political and economic changes following World War I, Cairo also became the entertainment center as new cabarets and restaurants opened to satisfy the growing tourist industry. One of the most successful of these new nightclubs was Syrian actress-dancer Badia Masabni's Casino Opera House, which opened in 1926. An astute business woman, she offered all-round entertainment, including a daily program just for women. A woman familiar with western films, she created cabaret revues, a primary component of which was dance that would appeal to both tourists and members of the Egyptian upper class, whose tastes were increasingly dictated by America and Europe. Thus, the village dance of wedding celebrations, was transformed from a primarily stationary solo improvisational form to a floor show that borrowed freely from the all-female image of Middle Eastern dance produced by American film corporations [Shay and Sellers-Young 2005: 19–20, see also Adra 2005: 47 in the same volume].

Notably, Shay and Sellers-Young echo many of Buonaventura's egregious factual errors regarding Badīʿah Maṣābnī. Problematically, scholarly authors continue to rely on and cite questionable sources such as Buonaventura in discussions of the history of *raqṣ sharqī*. See, for example, Rousdhy (2009: 35–36) and Van Nieuwkerk (1995: 41–42).

An examination of primary sources from the nineteenth and early twentieth centuries raises two significant issues with the accepted narrative. First, the assertion that Egyptian entertainment hall owners were targeting their programs specifically to Europeans, Americans, and the colonized Egyptian elite is fundamentally flawed. Both foreign and indigenous sources from turn-of-the-century Egypt reveal that many popular venues were frequented by indigenous audiences from a broad range of social strata, and that both Egyptian and other Middle Eastern and North African entertainment was in high demand at these venues. Moreover, while Egyptian artists and entertainers were certainly open to foreign innovations, these foreign elements were invariably adapted and repurposed to suit indigenous interests and aesthetics.

Second, the overwhelming importance assigned to Badīʿah Maṣābnī ignores the history of Egyptian entertainment halls prior to the 1930s and the influence of earlier entertainers and business owners on the development of *raqṣ sharqī*, as well as on Badīʿah 's own business model. In fact, I argue that two significant features that differentiate *raqṣ sharqī* from the dances of the *ʿawālim* and *ghawāzī* —performance for the sake of performance, and performance for a primarily non-participating audience—were in place in Egyptian entertainment halls as early as the 1890s—much earlier than the grand opening of Badīʿah Maṣābnī's first establishment in 1926.

In short, the widely accepted narrative described above quickly falls apart in the face of primary source evidence. Yet, primary source materials are frequently ignored in discussions of the history of *raqṣ sharqī*. Especially problematic is the remarkable lack of attention to Arabic-language sources from the late nineteenth and early twentieth centuries. There are a handful of exceptions, such as the work of Karin Van Nieuwkerk, and more recently, Priscilla Adum. In general, however, Arabic-language primary sources are rarely invoked to support or question existing constructs of the history of *raqṣ sharqī*, and this points to the most glaring problem with these narratives: they ignore the voices of the late nineteenth/early twentieth century Egyptians who created the dance.

In reducing the Egyptian role to a response or reaction to the West, current narratives regarding the origin and development of *raqṣ sharqī* reiterate the pervasive Orientalist paradigm that so often infects European and American understandings of the Arab world. Generally speaking, Orientalism refers to a pattern of thought which creates an essentialist, stereotyped vision of the peoples and cultures of the Middle East, North Africa, and Asia—the so-called "Orient." In essence, Orientalism allows the "West" to define itself by constructing and controlling an opposing "East." The Orient is characterized by its timelessness, irrationality, disorder, and depravity; in direct contrast, the Occident is progressive, rational, orderly, and virtuous. Orientalism also provides the framework within which the advanced West deals with the backwards East. Edward Said, in his seminal work on the subject, writes:

> Taking the late eighteenth century as a very roughly defined starting point Orientalism can be discussed and analyzed as the corporate institution for dealing with the Orient—dealing with it by making statements about it, authorizing views of it, describing it, by teaching it, settling it, ruling over it: in short, Orientalism as a Western style for dominating, restructuring, and having authority over the Orient [Said 1979: 3].

The hegemonic dimension of Orientalism is crucial, as it has enabled Westerners to position themselves as the prime movers of Oriental history. As Said notes:

> So impressive have the descriptive and textual successes of Orientalism been that entire periods of the Orient's cultural, political, and social history are considered mere responses to the West. The West is the actor, the Orient a passive reactor. The West is the spectator, the judge and jury, of every facet of Oriental behavior [Said 1979: 108–109].

Within the Orientalist framework, then, the "Oriental" individual lacks agency, the capacity to act on his or her own behalf. The implication for the current discussion is clear. To suggest that Egyptians created *raqṣ sharqī* to please Westerners not only ignores the substantial primary source evidence available, but also reduces Egyptians to passive, agencyless entities who create only in response to the powerful impulse of Western influence.

The reduction of Egyptians to acquiescent, obsequious subjects fails to account for the complex negotiations and contestations of cultural identity that take place at the interface of colonizing and colonized peoples—what Homi Bhabha has called the "in-between" spaces of cultural difference. It is undeniable that *raqṣ sharqī*, like other forms of Egyptian art and entertainment at the turn of the nineteenth and twentieth centuries, incorporates some decidedly Western features (features that will be detailed later in this study). Yet, Egyptians—both historically and in the present day—view *raqṣ sharqī* as authentically Egyptian, and they claim it as part of their cultural heritage, in spite of its non-Egyptian elements. The cultural authenticity of *raqṣ sharqī* in the eyes of Egyptians themselves undermines the assertion that the dance was created with Western consumers in mind. Clearly, an examination of the emergence and development of *raqṣ sharqī* requires a more nuanced understanding of how and why the dance came to incorporate European and American cultural features, even as it was embraced by Egyptians as an authentic part of their heritage.

Of particular relevance here are the deliberate ways in which colonized peoples absorb and integrate elements of colonizing cultures into the construction of their own identities—the interrelated phenomena of mimicry and hybridity. Mimicry refers to the process of colonized peoples imitating cultural attributes of their colonizers, while hybridity describes the mixed cultural forms that result from the interaction of different cultures. Postcolonial scholar Homi Bhabha (1994) has examined how mimicry and hybridity can subvert colonial power by undermining the Self/Other binary upon which colonization depends. As Bhabha demonstrates, the colonizer actively encourages the colonized to imitate the colonizing culture—per the "civilizing mission" of colonization. At the same time, the colonizer desires—indeed, needs—the colonized subject to remain identifiably different—an Other to be dominated. From the perspective of the colonial power, "...colonial mimicry is the desire for a reformed, recognizable Other, *as a subject of a difference that is almost the same, but not quite*" (Bhabha 1994: 86). From the perspective of the colonized subject, however, mimicry becomes a mechanism for asserting presence: "As Lacan reminds us, mimicry is like camouflage, not a harmonization of repression of difference, but a form of resemblance, that differs from or defends presence by displaying it in part, metonymically" (Bhabha 1994: 90). The ambivalence thus created destabilizes colonial power by enabling hybrid cultural forms and thereby disrupting the colonizer's discourse of the Otherness of the colonized. In Bhabha's framework, hybridity is a direct threat to colonial power: "The display of hybridity—its peculiar 'replication'—terrorizes authority with the *ruse* of recognition, its mimicry, its mockery" (Bhabha 1994: 115).

The tremendous value in the phenomena of mimicry and hybridity lies in their deconstruction of essentialist cultural categories. As Said notes: "...cultural forms are hybrid, mixed, impure, and the time has come in cultural analysis to reconnect their analysis with their actuality" (Said 1994: 14). Hybridity is not a corruption or a pollution of a pure and primeval cultural identity, because there is no such thing. Rather, hybridity is itself a product of the construction, negotiation, contestation, and performance of cultural identity. Bhabha states:

> What is theoretically innovative, and politically crucial, is the need to think beyond narratives of originary and initial subjectivities and to focus on those moments or processes that are produced in the articulation of cultural differences. These 'in-between' spaces provide the terrain for elaborating strategies of selfhood—singular or communal—that initiate new signs of identity, and innovative sites of collaboration, and contestation, in the act of defining the idea of society itself [Bhabha 1994: 1–2].

Here, Bhabha echoes Stuart Hall, whose own work stresses the productive nature of cultural identity:

> Perhaps instead of thinking of identity as an already accomplished fact, which the new cultural practices then represent, we should think, instead, of identity as a 'production', which is never complete, always in process, and always constituted within, not outside, representation [Hall 1990: 222].

The phenomena of mimicry and hybridity, when seen as important aspects of cultural identity production, resolve the seeming contradiction posed by *raqṣ sharqī*: a dance form that incorporates both "Eastern" and "Western" elements, yet that has been embraced by Egyptians as an authentically Egyptian cultural expression. Within this framework, the hybrid nature of *raqṣ sharqī* can be viewed as the product of Egyptian agency, rather than a distortion of "pure" indigenous dance imposed by Westerners.

There have been few scholarly treatments of the history of *raqṣ sharqī*, let alone those that address these particular issues. Van Nieuwkerk's (1995) landmark study provides a historical overview of Egypt's female professional entertainers in order to establish a foundation for understanding the role of these women in late twentieth century Egyptian society. Her examination of nineteenth century female entertainers is particularly thorough and well-referenced. On the other hand, aspects of her treatment of Egyptian dancers and entertainment venues at the turn of the nineteenth and twentieth centuries—the crucial period in which *raqṣ sharqī* was emerging—are problematic, such as her citation of Buonaventura's wholly unsupported narrative regarding the "Hollywood" origins of the Egyptian belly dance costume (Van Nieuwkerk 1995: 42). Ultimately, Van Nieuwkerk reiterates the commonly held view that early twentieth century "nightclub" entertainment "was aimed mainly at Arabic and European tourists"—though she goes on to add that many Egyptians frequented the nightclubs as well (Van Nieuwkerk 1995: 40). In fairness to Van Nieuwkerk, elucidating the early history of *raqṣ sharqī* was not the primary goal of her work, and her study stands as an outstanding resource for understanding the complex position of female singers and dancers in late twentieth-century Egyptian society.

Kathleen Fraser (2015) provides a comprehensive analysis of the *'awālim* and *ghawāzī* in the period spanning from 1760 to 1870, based on her exhaustive study of the descriptive accounts of eighteenth and nineteenth century European observers. However, her study period ends just as the critical period for the emergence of *raqṣ sharqī* begins. Further, several issues with her study undermine its potential to provide a solid foundation for an examination of the developments in Egyptian dance immediately following her study period. A flaw in her interpretation of Arabic terminology weakens her argument regarding the relative social status of the *'awālim* and *ghawāzī* and how each was impacted by a government pronouncement in the 1830s—a critical problem in explaining ensuing developments in the dance as well as in the social status of female professional entertainers. Further, Fraser does not utilize a significant primary source available during the latter part of her period of study—photographs of Egyptian female entertainers, many of which were featured on the *cartes de visite* that were widely circulated in the 1860s and 1870s—which raises several issues with her conclusions regarding the development of costuming for belly dance. Finally, Fraser does not utilize the available documentation of Egyptian dance aesthetics and technique in the twentieth century—particularly that of the twentieth century *'awālim* and *ghawāzī*—in order to extrapolate from European textual and artistic depictions of Egyptian dance. This suggests that her reconstruction of dance technique and choreography is more reflective of meanings attributed to the dance by European observers than those espoused by the Egyptians themselves. In spite of these issues, Fraser's work is an admirable and valuable contribution to the body of knowledge regarding the early history of Egyptian belly dance.

The chapters that follow represent my own attempt to remedy the current lack of scholarly attention to this subject by providing an empirically-based examination of the origin and early history of *raqṣ sharqī* at the turn of the nineteenth and twentieth centuries. In this study, I approach *raqṣ sharqī* as a hybrid cultural expression emerging from the process of Egyptian cultural and national identity production. I position the emergence and development of *raqṣ sharqī* within the context of larger trends in the contemporary Egyptian arts and entertainment milieu. In doing so, I demonstrate that the early history of *raqṣ sharqī* parallels early developments in other forms of Egyptian arts and entertainment, where foreign ideas and influences were embraced, but always on Egyptian terms and toward Egyptian ends. I reveal how these processes were enabled and nurtured by the emergence of formalized performance spaces in nineteenth century Egypt, and by the growing nationalist sentiment among the Egyptian populace. *Raqṣ sharqī*, like other forms of Egyptian art and entertainment at the turn of the century, emerged as a product of Egyptians actively defining and asserting their cultural and national identity while under the domination of a foreign occupying power. Consequently, this complex hybrid of Egyptian and non-Egyptian inspirations could be embraced by Egyptians as an authentic expression of their identity.

Chapter One establishes the foundation for the remainder of the book with an examination of the Egyptian arts and entertainment scene at the turn of the nineteenth and twentieth centuries. In this chapter, the role of "Western influence" on the development of Egyptian modes of entertainment such as theater, music, and dance is problematized and reassessed. The discussion demonstrates the intentional manner in which Egyptians adopted and adapted foreign ideas and technologies to create hybrid cultural expressions that would be embraced as authentically Egyptian. This discussion also reveals that Egyptians of all social classes participated in and contributed to this process. Further, this chapter examines how these turn-of-the-century developments in Egyptian arts and entertainment embodied the growing nationalist sentiment of the Egyptian populace. Finally, this chapter details how the establishment of formalized, dedicated spaces for the performance of arts and entertainment enabled the innovations of the late nineteenth and early twentieth centuries.

Chapter Two discusses the changing fortunes of Egypt's professional female entertainers, the *'awālim* and the *ghawāzī*. This chapter examines the circumstances that led many of these women to work in the newly-established entertainment halls described in Chapter One. This discussion reveals how a combination of governmental regulation and shifting performance opportunities set the stage for fundamental changes in the nature of Egyptian dance, culminating in the development of a new dance form that would come to be known as *raqṣ sharqī*.

Chapters Three, Four, Five, and Six detail the characteristics of this new dance form during the period of its origin and earliest development: from the 1890s through the 1920s. Chapters Three and Four reconstruct the technique and aesthetic, respectively, of *raqṣ sharqī* at the turn of the nineteenth and twentieth centuries. A consideration of primary source evidence, viewed in light of modern-day *'awālim* and *ghawāzī* dance, as well as footage of *raqṣ sharqī* performers from the mid-to-late 1930s, reveals the organic process by which the traditional dances of the *'awālim* and *ghawāzī* absorbed and integrated new and foreign elements to become a recognizably distinct dance form. Chapter Five explores the features of a *raqṣ sharqī* performance at the turn of the nineteenth and twentieth centuries, including the characteristics of the entertainment halls that presented dance, the organization of a typical show, and the nature and extent of interaction between audience and performers. Finally, Chapter Six examines the evolution of costuming for Egyptian *raqṣ sharqī*, revealing how the basic template of the *badlah*—the widely-recognized ensemble of bra, bare or barely covered navel, hip belt, and skirt—developed from the indigenous *'awālim/ghawāzī* costuming style, while absorbing foreign innovations. Taken as a whole, these chapters demonstrate that *raqṣ sharqī*, though a hybrid of indigenous and foreign elements, maintained an enduring connection to Egyptian tradition.

Chapter Seven explores how and why *raqṣ sharqī* became part of the cultural heritage of Egypt. Though born on the entertainment hall stages of Cairo and Alexandria, the popularity of the dance would extend far beyond the urban centers where it originated. Though its continuing connection to traditional Egyptian dance was key to allowing this urban concert dance genre to find national appeal, this chapter reveals that the advent of new technologies—film and television—was also a critical factor. The Egyptian films of the 1930s through the 1960s, brought to the wider Egyptian public through the new medium of television, would play a significant role in defining *raqṣ sharqī* as the accepted representation of Egyptian belly dance and as a recognized part of the Egyptian heritage. Meanwhile, the emergence of theatrical folk dance companies in the middle of the twentieth century, together with the nationalization and professionalization of the entertainment industry, would have a profound impact on *raqṣ sharqī* and its position in the public imagination.

I relied on a wide range of primary and secondary source materials in order to conduct this study. My research depended most heavily on primary sources from the nineteenth and early twentieth centuries, including both indigenous Egyptian source materials (e.g., newspaper and magazine articles, advertisements, and flyers) and foreign sources (e.g., textual descriptions of Egyptian dance derived from travelers' accounts and guide books, photographs, and picture postcards). Thanks to the digitization of a great deal of nineteenth and early twentieth century literature, I was able to access many works online through digital archives such as the Travelers in the Middle East Archive, the HathiTrust Digital Library, and the Internet Archive. I accessed digital versions of the Egyptian daily newspaper *al-Ahrām* through the paper's online archive. Many of the early photographs, postcards, prints, and ephemera that I used in my research were derived from my personal collection, although I was also able to access some of these works online through digital archives. I was able to access a great deal of relevant film footage through online archives such as the Library of Congress American Memory Collection and France's Institut National de l'Audiovisuel, as well as online video sharing platforms such as YouTube and Vimeo. I also relied on my personal collection of film and audio.

Accessing the primary sources proved easier than the arduous process of sifting through the complex and pervasive Orientalist biases present in the foreign source materials—biases which continue to insinuate themselves into present understandings of Egyptian dance. These materials were indispensable for this project; for, while film footage of *raqṣ sharqī* prior to the 1930s appears to be non-existent, and while indigenous Egyptian sources offer little regarding the actual "mechanics" of the dance, foreign sources provide descriptions and images of the dance, its associated costuming, and the venues in which it was performed. Yet, those descriptions and images are inevitably colored by their creators' perceptions of Egypt and Egyptians, which in many cases range from the benevolently paternalistic to the unabashedly disdainful.

Nineteenth and early twentieth century European and American observers approached Egyptian dance with a pre-existing set of attitudes and understandings about not only the dance, but Egypt, its people, and their cultures. These attitudes and understandings collectively embody the Orientalist framework through which Europeans and Americans have defined and navigated their relationship to the "Orient." As Edward Said has noted:

> In a sense Orientalism was a library or archive of information commonly and, in some of its aspects, unanimously held. What bound the archive together was a family of ideas and a unifying set of values proven in various ways to be effective. These ideas explained the behavior of Orientals; they supplied Orientals with a mentality, a genealogy, and atmosphere; most important, they allowed Europeans to deal with and even to see Orientals as a phenomenon possessing regular characteristics [Said 1979: 41–42].

This pre-existing "archive of information" about the Orient in general, and Egypt in particular, molded foreigners' expectations of what they would or should experience in Egypt, and when reality diverged from expectation, reality itself was dissected and reconstructed to fit belief. As Fahim notes:

> Europe's curiosity for the exotic Orient urged many travellers to visit Egypt to acquire a lively picture of medieval Cairo. Their travel accounts were meant to reconstruct the Oriental picture, and if reality was disappointing they patched it up from other places, such as Turkey, Persia or India [Fahim 1998: 9].

In spite of this, foreigners' accounts could not be dismissed or discarded as resources for this study, as they provide an accessible and comprehensive record of Egyptian dance and dancers in the nineteenth and early twentieth centuries. It therefore became necessary to tease apart the biases from whatever factual information could be gleaned from these materials. To accomplish this, I approached the foreign source materials in three ways.

First, I considered the unique circumstances and motivations behind each source. As an illustration of this process, consider the writings of Hector Dinning (1920), a captain of the Australian Army, Douglas Sladen (1911), a widely-traveled British author, and Sydney Moseley (1917), an outspoken British journalist. The accounts of each of these men provide valuable and interesting information about Egyptian entertainment venues at the dawn of the twentieth century. However, it is critical to consider their varying perspectives, which color their accounts in unique ways. Dinning's memoir of his service in the Middle East is largely a paean to the nobility of the Australian Light Horse, and his account is intended to paint a vivid picture of the lived experiences of these soldiers. Thus, his descriptions of visits to cafés and theaters in Cairo are incredibly vivid and detailed, while at the same time expressing his personal disdain toward the Egyptian people and the entertainment that they enjoyed. Dinning's account makes it clear that he had only minimal interest in associating with Egyptians, let alone in expressing their perspectives. Sladen's overview of Cairo is intended to pique readers' interest in the "Oriental"—i.e., non-Europeanized—aspects of the city through amusing anecdotes of his own experiences. Although his writing expresses a degree of the condescension toward Egyptians that is present in Dinning's work, Sladen demonstrates camaraderie with individual Egyptians and Arabs, at times truly capturing and expressing their humanity. His account of a visit to a native theater with two friends—a Syrian and an Egyptian—offers not only details about the venue and the performance, but about the differing opinions of his friends regarding the evening's entertainment. In contrast to both of these works, Moseley's account is a sharp and unflinching look at the British administration of Egypt. While his book does not provide the descriptive detail of Egyptian entertainment venues present in the other two works, his account offers vital information regarding governmental regulation of these venues in the early twentieth century. Additionally, his work tempers that of Dinning by detailing some of the negative behavior of Europeans in Egypt.

Second, I examined a wide range of foreign sources in order to counterbalance the limitations posed by individual sources. In other words, the collective value of the foreign source material was often able to overcome the problematic nature of individual sources. This process is also well-illustrated by the examples just described. The works of Dinning, Sladen, and Moseley are each limited in some way, though each work provides some valuable detail regarding Egyptian entertainment; it was when these works were considered together that their biases could be overcome to build a comprehensive and informative portrait of Egyptian entertainment venues at the dawn of the twentieth century. Fraser (2015), in her investigations into Egyptian female entertainers prior to 1870, relied heavily on the individual accounts of foreign visitors to Egypt. Taking a similar approach to her source material, she states: "...in the center of all these disparate gazes more and more clearly a real dance took shape for me. In sum, any weaknesses in the travel literature turned out to be primarily individual, while the collective impact of the data had enormous value" (Fraser 2015: 12–13). Yet, in engaging in this strategy, I was wary of falling into the trap of generating an Orientalist "translation" of this material, which would inadvertently reify the biased themes shared by these works (see Said 1979: 166)—for example, the assumption of European cultural superiority that is shared by the three sources just discussed.

Therefore, beyond the two tactics just described, I found it absolutely critical to engage the available documentation of Egyptian dance in the present day in order to "read" back into the foreign source materials. A comparison of footage and observations of modern-day *'awālim* and *ghawāzī* with text descriptions of these dancers in the nineteenth century reveals a remarkable degree of continuity in technique, including fundamental dance movements, the incorporation of features such as acrobatic feats and balancing acts, and styles of musical accompaniment. However, such a comparison also reveals a substantial disconnect between the meanings ascribed to *'awālim/ghawāzī* dances by nineteenth-century foreign observers and the perspectives of Egyptian dancers and their audiences in the modern day. Though *'awālim/ghawāzī* dances have by no means remained "frozen in aspic" from the nineteenth century until the present day, the fact that these dances continue to be part of Egyptian social celebrations such as weddings, and that they are still built upon the same fundamental technique of more than a century ago, indicates not only the possibility, but also the necessity, of reassessing nineteenth-century foreigners' accounts of these dances in light of the perspectives of modern-day Egyptians. Therefore, in attempting to reconstruct the emergence of *raqṣ sharqī* from the dances of the *'awālim* and *ghawāzī* at the turn of the nineteenth and twentieth centuries, it was necessary to leverage knowledge about *'awālim/ghawāzī* dances and *raqṣ sharqī* in the present day in order to clarify and balance the perspectives provided by foreign sources at the turn of the last century.

As noted earlier, the foreign primary source materials, in spite of their biases, provided a necessary complement to the indigenous Egyptian sources, which, though offering a wealth of detail in terms of the names of performers, the names and locations of venues, the price of admission, etc., often revealed little regarding specifics of the dance itself. The indigenous sources posed an additional challenge that had to be addressed. At the turn of the nineteenth and twentieth centuries, only a fraction of the Egyptian population was literate (4.8 percent in 1897, increasing to 11.8 percent in 1927) (Fahmy 2011: 33).[3] Literacy was limited to Egyptians of the upper and middle classes; lower-class Egyptians were largely illiterate. Arabic-language newspapers and magazines—such as those relied on for this study—were generally produced by middle-class urbanites. As Kholoussy notes: "Egypt's Arabic-language press (as opposed to its upper-class French-language press) was a middle class forum in which the founders, editors, and writers of the various newspapers and periodicals wrote in the language of the urban middle class" (Kholoussy 2010: 2). The low literacy rate, together with the middle-class orientation of the Arabic-language press, would seem to suggest that late nineteenth and early twentieth century Arabic-language newspapers, magazines, advertisements, and flyers had a very restricted readership and communicated the interests of a very limited subset of Egyptian society—namely, the urban middle class.

Yet, as both Fahmy and Kholoussy note, neither literacy rates nor the subscription and circulation rates of Egypt's various newspapers and periodicals reflect their actual reach among the Egyptian public (Fahmy 2011: 32–36, Kholoussy 2010: 14). Circulation and subscription rates do not account for the widespread practice of sharing newspapers and magazines; besides being borrowed and exchanged among readers, copies were often available in public settings like coffee shops and barber shops (Fahmy 2011: 33). More importantly, in spite of low literacy rates, many lower-class Egyptians who were unable to read were nevertheless exposed to the content of newspapers and periodicals through public readings conducted in popular gathering places (Fahmy 2011: 34–36).

Thus, though articles and advertisements regarding entertainment acts including acting, singing, and dancing appeared in newspapers and magazines produced and consumed by the urban middle class, this should not lead to the conclusion that entertainment events were never patronized by members of Egypt's lower class. On the contrary, Egyptians of all social classes patronized entertainment venues in Cairo and Alexandria. Here, again, the foreign primary source materials prove their usefulness, as foreigner's accounts of their visits to Egyptian entertainment establishments provide a great deal of insight into audience demographics and demonstrate that lower-class Egyptians did frequent at least some of Egypt's turn-of-the-century entertainment halls.

In short, though both the indigenous and the foreign primary sources posed challenges to my research, they provided a bounty of information that made it possible to develop a coherent and detailed portrait of *raqṣ sharqī* in its earliest years. Careful analysis of these sources, viewed in consideration of current understandings of Egyptian dance, has revealed a dance form firmly rooted in the earlier Egyptian dance traditions of the *'awālim* and *ghawāzī*. The new dance absorbed and integrated foreign techniques and innovations, without sacrificing its fundamental Egyptian authenticity.

I do not view this book to be the final word on the history of *raqṣ sharqī*. On the contrary, I hope that this study will encourage others to conduct their own empirically-based research that will build upon the foundation provided here, for there is still a great deal more to be learned about the early years of *raqṣ sharqī*. I particularly hope that this book will awaken an interest in further exploring the Arabic-language source material from the late nineteenth and early twentieth centuries. These sources offer a wealth of information about *raqṣ sharqī* in its earliest decades, and they easily dispel the shadows of myth and fantasy that have so long obscured the history of the dance. The unsourced narratives that continue to circulate among dancers and dance aficionados regarding the dance's origin and development have rendered Egyptians largely irrelevant to the process. Rather, Egyptians have been cast as passive reactors to powerful Western influences, and Egyptian dance has been framed as being static and unchanging until the innovations of the West are brought to bear on it. On the contrary, as the following chapters reveal, Egyptians actively adopted and adapted foreign ideas and technologies, but always on their own terms. In short, the development of *raqṣ sharqī* was driven by the interests and motivations of Egyptians. If this study inspires more attention to Arabic-language primary sources, and to Egyptian agency in the creation and development of *raqṣ sharqī*, I feel that my work has been a success.

One

Egyptian Arts and Entertainment at the Turn of the Nineteenth and Twentieth Centuries

An analysis of the origins and development of *raqṣ sharqī* must begin with an examination of the arts and entertainment milieu that both enabled it and shaped it. Egypt in the late nineteenth and early twentieth centuries experienced unprecedented growth in indigenous literature, music, and theater, as well as the birth of the Egyptian cinema. The first Egyptian novel, *Zaynab*, was published in 1914. In the early decades of the twentieth century, composers such as Muḥammad al-Qaṣabjī and Muḥammad 'Abd al-Wahāb explored the boundaries of traditional Egyptian music, incorporating foreign ideas and techniques to create innovative new song styles. In the 1870s and 1880s, the groundbreaking plays of Muḥammad 'Uthmān Jalāl and Ya'qūb Ṣannū' set in motion the growth and development of the Egyptian colloquial theater—a process that would culminate in the vastly popular comedies of Najīb al-Rīḥānī and 'Alī al-Kassār in the early decades of the twentieth century. The silent film *Layla*, considered by many to be the first truly Egyptian feature-length film (el-Charkawi 1963: 5), premiered at Cairo's Metropole Cinema in 1927.

During this period, Egypt also witnessed a proliferation of venues dedicated to the performing arts. By the dawn of the twentieth century, both of Egypt's major metropolitan centers, Cairo and Alexandria, were home to thriving arts and entertainment scenes (Danielson 1997: 42–51, Fahmy 2011). In Cairo, several areas of the city emerged as entertainment hubs, including the Azbakīyah district, located in the heart of the city, and 'Imād al-Dīn Street, situated just to the west of Azbakīyah (Figure 1).

Another, smaller, entertainment district, Rūḍ al-Faraj, was located to the northwest, along the east bank of the Nile. Muḥammad 'Alī Street, a long boulevard extending from Azbakīyah to the Citadel, was the commercial heartbeat of the budding entertainment industry; this street was home to many of Cairo's professional entertainers, as well as to a range of businesses connected to the entertainment industry, such as musical instrument manufacturers and—beginning in the early 1900s—record producers.

The district of Azbakīyah had been an important part of the landscape of Cairo since the fifteenth century (Hassan 1998, 1999; Sadgrove

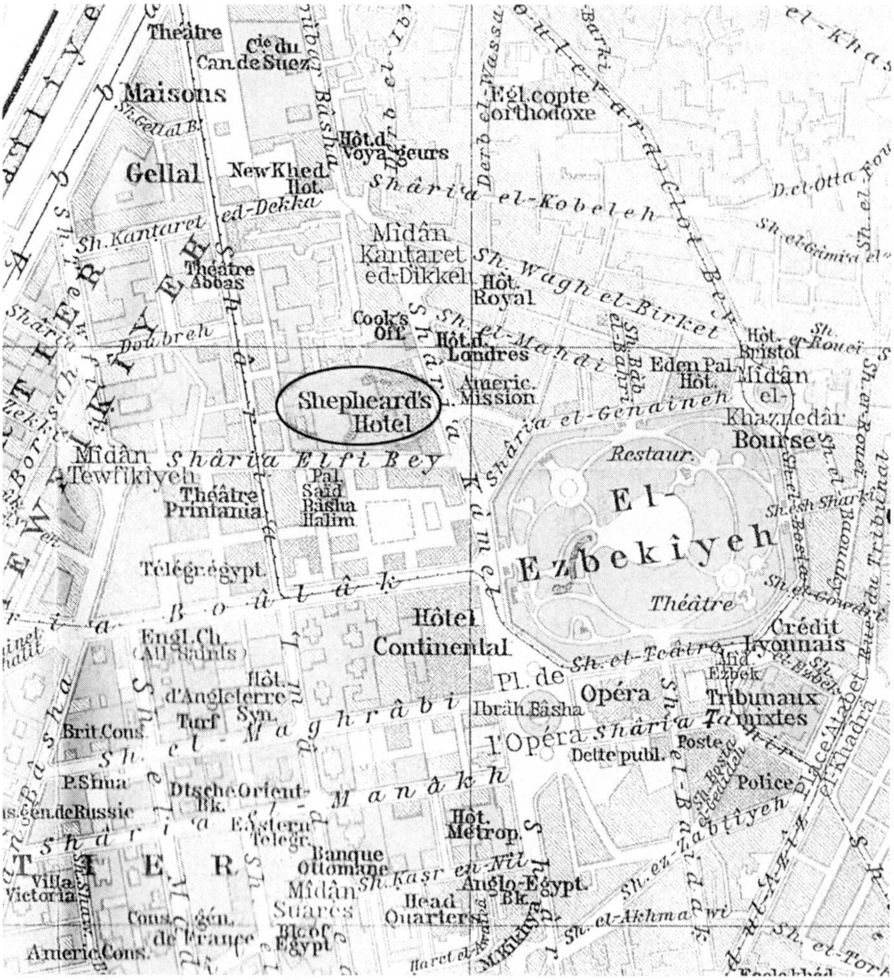

Figure 1. Map of Cairo entertainment districts (1911).

1996: 13–14). Originally the site of a lake that formed annually during the flooding of the Nile, the area had long been the location for important local celebrations incorporating traditional Egyptian entertainments. During the reign of Muḥammad 'Alī Bāshā (1805–1848), the lake was drained, and gardens were laid out on the site. Muḥammad 'Alī's grandson, Ismā'īl (1863–1879), continued the development of the gardens, employing a French landscape architect to create a lush setting styled after the public parks and pleasure gardens of Britain and France. The Azbakīyah Gardens became the focal point for the district's bustling entertainment scene, which by the end of the nineteenth century boasted not only the Khedivial Opera House, but also a range of smaller theaters and entertainment halls, including the Azbakīyah Garden Theater and the El Dorado entertainment hall.

At the dawn of the twentieth century, 'Imād al-Dīn Street began to rival neighboring Azbakīyah as a hub for arts and entertainment. Numerous entertainment halls were established on this street, as well as on its cross streets, such as Alfī Bik. In the 1910s, popular venues included the 'Abbās Theater, the Abbaye des Roses, the Casino de Paris, and the original Printania Theater. By the end of the 1920s, 'Imād al-Dīn Street was lined with entertainment venues, including Yūsif Wahbī's Ramses Theater, the Majestic Theater (which hosted the acting troupes of 'Alī al-Kassār and Amīn Ṣidqī), the new Printania Theater, and Ṣālah Badī'ah Maṣābnī, the first of Badī'ah's many entertainment establishments.

The entertainment halls of Cairo and Alexandria both enabled and nurtured the dramatic changes that were taking place in Egyptian arts and entertainment. These venues represented a fundamental break from traditional Egyptian modes of entertainment: as dedicated spaces where professional entertainment could be enjoyed for its own sake, these establishments disconnected entertainment from its traditional social contexts. In this new, formalized performance setting, Egyptian artists and entertainers created innovations in song, dance, comedy, drama, and more, by absorbing and adapting foreign ideas and technologies. Importantly, these developments took place in a climate of growing nationalist sentiment, as Egyptians struggled to define and assert their cultural and national identity in the omnipresent shadow of the British occupation. Consequently, the arts and entertainment generated on the stages of Egypt's entertainment halls would remain firmly rooted in traditional Egyptian aesthetics, interests, and values, and they would be embraced by Egyptians as authentically Egyptian cultural expressions, in spite of their hybrid nature. In essence, the entertainment hall served as a liminal space—at the intersection of indigenous and foreign, traditional and modern—in which Egyptians negotiated and contested their cultural and national identity in the face of Western colonial domination. It was in this dynamic environment that the Egyptian dance form known as *raqṣ sharqī* was born.

Repurposing the Foreign: Developments in Egyptian Arts and Entertainment

It is impossible to consider late nineteenth and early twentieth century developments in Egyptian arts and entertainment without acknowledging and addressing the expanding European presence in Egypt throughout the nineteenth century. The fact that indigenous Egyptian arts and entertainment were impacted by this foreign presence cannot be denied. Yet, it is patently inaccurate and overly simplistic to ascribe all of the developments in indigenous Egyptian theater, song, music, dance, and literature to the irresistible force of "Western influence." As noted at the outset of this study, to reduce the Egyptian role in this process to a response or reaction to the West is to reiterate the Orientalist paradigm that has pervaded European and American thinking about the Arab world since at least the eighteenth century. Within the Orientalist framework, Westerners have positioned themselves as the prime movers of Egyptian history, diminishing or even eliminating Egyptian agency in the process. At the turn of the century, such thinking led to dismissive assessments of Egyptian arts and entertainment such as the following:

> Even to-day there is no Arabic drama; there is only a drama in the Arabic language; for all plays that have appeared in the language of Muhammad during the last fifty years are nothing but translations, or, at best, imitations, of European works; and, before this period, all that was written and played in the form of dialogue can hardly be called drama in the real meaning of the word; it was simply a rudimentary form of it [Prüfer 1908: 872].

In the present day, such thinking persists in popular narratives regarding the emergence of *raqṣ sharqī*, such as the widely-accepted assertion that Egyptians created the dance to satisfy Western audiences, as well as upper-class Egyptian audiences with Western tastes.

Contrary to Orientalist discourse that treats "Western influence" on Egypt as total and unstoppable, and that views Egyptian arts and entertainment as poor imitations of Western ideals, the following discussion reveals the complex and intentional ways that Egyptians repurposed foreign influences toward their own interests and agendas. I demonstrate that Egyptians very deliberately adopted and adapted foreign ideas and technologies to create hybrid cultural expressions that were embraced as authentically Egyptian. Additionally, I demonstrate that these cultural expressions, rather than being targeted toward Western or elite Egyptian audiences, were frequently geared toward the Egyptian lower and middle classes.

From the late eighteenth century onward, Europeans were an established and influential population in Egypt's urban centers. Communities of southern Europeans, particularly Greeks, prospered in Egypt throughout the nineteenth century, with new waves of immigration from Greece, Italy, and Malta occurring at the dawn of the twentieth century (Fahmy 2011: 28, Lane 2005 [1836]: 33). During Napoleon's occupation of Egypt from 1798 to 1801, the French added another significant foreign presence. In the wake of Napoleon's defeat at Waterloo in 1815, many French military officials returned to Egypt and found employment in the army of Muḥammad 'Alī Bāsha (Marsot 1985: 56). Later in the nineteenth century, due to governmental missteps that left the Egyptian government indebted to European powers, the British became an intrusive and unavoidable force in Egypt, culminating in the "Veiled Protectorate" of 1882 to 1914 and the formal protectorate of 1914 to 1922 (Marsot 1985: 68–75, 79). At the turn of the nineteenth and twentieth centuries, the British were perhaps the most obvious—and resented—foreign population in Egypt, particularly as the British stationed thousands of soldiers in Egypt during World War I.

Besides hosting a resident European population, Egypt was regularly flooded with European and American travelers and tourists throughout the nineteenth century. This was the dawning era of the modern concept of leisure travel and its associated accoutrements, such as travel guidebooks and picture postcards. European and American visitors were attracted to Egypt not only by the monumental legacy of its ancient civilization, but also by the allure of its exoticism. However, many of the foreigners who came to Egypt in search of the timeless, primitive Orient of their daydreams and fantasies were disappointed by what they found. Guide books bemoaned the Europeanization of Alexandria and Cairo and steered travelers toward the areas of those cities that retained their Oriental character:

> Fortunately the 'Haussmannizing' of the Khedive Ismail's builders was mainly confined to the European quarter of [Cairo], and did not touch the region of the Bazaars, where it is still possible, when once the Mooski—no longer a purely orien-

> tal highway—is crossed, for the imaginative traveller to realise the dreams of the Arabian Nights of his childhood [Reynolds-Ball 1898a: viii].

Nevertheless, those same guide books were careful to list the range of European-style amenities and entertainments available to travelers (see, for example, Baedeker 1878: 17, 202–204, 229–233). Reynolds-Ball (1898a: 130) notes of Cairo in the 1890s:

> '[D]istractions' and social dissipations of all kinds, not to speak of the ordinary urban amusements in the form of concerts, theatres, and promenades, follow so unceasingly that there is some excuse for the neglect of the regulation sights and antiquities. When it is the case of a bicycle gymkhana, a polo match at the Turf Club ground, or a lawn-Tennis tournament at the Ghezireh Palace, or a visit to a gloomy old temple, it is perhaps only natural with young people that the ancient monuments should go to the wall.

After immersing themselves in the "undiluted Orient" (Sladen 1911: 44), foreign visitors were happy to leave it behind and retire to the familiar comforts provided by local hotels, restaurants, and entertainment venues. In this manner, foreigners experienced actual Egypt in much the same way that they experienced museum exhibits or world's fair exhibitions of an imagined Egypt (see Mitchell 1988).

A variety of theaters, music halls, and *cafés chantants* emerged in Cairo and Alexandria to satisfy the demand of both the resident foreign population as well as European and American tourists for European-style entertainment. In late nineteenth century Alexandria, popular destinations included the Politeama, Rossini, and Zizinia theaters for operas and operettas (Baedeker 1885: 206; Sadgrove 1996: 43–44, 69–70), and the Hotel and Casino San Stefano for concerts and gambling (Baedeker 1898: 18). In the same period in Cairo, audiences attended French and Italian operas at the Khedivial Opera House, and, in summer, Italian comedies at the Azbakīyah Garden Theater (Baedeker 1878: 231, 256). The El Dorado entertainment hall was also a favored destination for music, operettas, and other varied entertainments (Académie Royale des Sciences, des Lettres et des Beaux-Arts de Belgique 1870: 51; *al-Ahrām* 1 December 1888: 2; *The Queenslander* 27 February 1886: 336; Ward 2013a). In early twentieth century Cairo, the old Printania Theater on Alfī Bik Street hosted French acting troupes, the Abbaye des Roses next door offered European variety shows, and the nearby Kursaal Theater, at the corner of Alfī Bik and 'Imād al-Dīn, presented American and European variety shows, including the Bandman Comedy Company (Baedeker 1914: 41, Dinning 1920: 270, Wiltshire 1915–1916). Further north on 'Imād al-Dīn Street, the 'Abbās Theater was host to French and Italian operas, and just across the street, the Casino de Paris was a popular destination for variety theater (Baedeker 1914: 41, Lamplough 1907: 29–30). The new Printania, established in the mid–1920s on ʻImād al-Dīn Street, hosted European troupes like its predecessor (*L'Égypte Nouvelle* 5 April 1924: I).

Alongside the European-style entertainment just described, there existed a native Egyptian arts and entertainment scene that was fueled by indigenous demand and sensitive to indigenous tastes. In fact, many venues initially oriented toward European audiences, including those just mentioned, began offering indigenous entertainment in order to satisfy the emerging local demand. Egyptian actor and singer Shaykh Salāmah Ḥijāzī, a pioneer of Arabic musical theater, appeared at the Zizinia Theater, first as a member of the acting troupe of the Syrian Sulaymān al-Qardāḥī in the 1880s (Sadgrove 1996: 160), then with his own troupe in the 1890s (*al-Ahrām* 12 April 1890: 3). ʻAbduh al-Ḥāmūlī, one of the most influential Egyptian singers of the late nineteenth century, performed at San Stefano in the 1880s (*al-Ahrām* 31 May 1889: 3). Arab entertainers appeared at the Azbakīyah Garden Theater, the Printania Theater (both old and new), the Abbaye des Roses, and at the Casino de Paris throughout the early decades of the twentieth century. In the 1910s, the actor and playwright Najīb al-Rīḥānī developed his colloquial Egyptian character Kishkish Bik before the receptive audiences of the Abbaye Des Roses (Abou Saif 1973: 2–3, Worrell 1920: 135–136). At Cairo's El Dorado, the line-up at the turn of the century had shifted from European operettas to almost exclusively Egyptian-style entertainment, with Arab singers, dancers, and musicians performing for a primarily native audience (Loewenbach 1908: 218–220).

The native arts and entertainment scene was influenced by its European counterpart, just as the Egyptian government was influenced by European models of economics, governance, and urban planning. Indeed, over the course of the nineteenth century, Egyptians embraced many aspects of Western education, literature, music, politics, science, and technology. This process is frequently termed the *Nahḍah* (renaissance) and is often framed as the birth of "modern" Egypt. However, historian Peter Gran cautions against falling into traditional Orientalist constructs of the *Nahḍah* and nineteenth century Egypt, wherein Egypt is cast as a premodern cultural blank slate and "...all that is new or relevant to modernity is foreign. Internal adaptations and developments are scarcely worth mentioning. All that ever happens internally is a reaction to what is foreign and modern" (Gran 2005).

It would be a mistake to suggest that Egyptian artists and entertainers merely aped European or American models. Rather, foreign innovations were embraced, so long as they aligned with—or could be adapted to align with—native interests. Virginia Danielson, describing the early twentieth century arts and entertainment milieu in Egypt, writes:

> Audiences from all socioeconomic classes sought what was "modern" or *ḥadīth*—that is, new, useful, and, if necessary, imported—yet authentically Egyptian-Arab, or *aṣīl*. These attitudes informed patronage of arts. For some it was a matter of familiar practice and local pride. "I'm an Egyptian, noble of race," sang a character on Sayyid Darwīsh's stage at the time, touting his heritage. For some, support for Arabic art became an overt political statement [Danielson 1997: 40].

In this context, Egyptians artists and entertainers freely adopted and adapted foreign ideas and technologies toward Egyptian aesthetics and agendas, creating hybrid forms that found broad appeal with the Egyptian public. Importantly, Egyptians would embrace these hybrid cultural expressions as authentically Egyptian.

Danielson's discussions of early twentieth century Egyptian composers such as Muḥammad al-Qaṣabjī illustrate this phenomenon (e.g., Danielson 1997: 70–78). By the mid–1920s, al-Qaṣabjī was an established composer for many of the most famous singers in Cairo (Danielson 1997: 61). He was recognized as an innovator; as Danielson notes, he was the primary exponent of the monologue, a European-derived song style that emerged in the context of the Egyptian musical theater (Danielson 1997: 71). al-Qaṣabjī's compositions—described by Danielson as "syncretic"—incorporated a variety of new features, including harmony, instrumental introductions, melodic leaps, and triadic arpeggio-like passages. Nevertheless, many of al-Qaṣabjī's innovative works are now viewed by Egyptians as part of the *turāth*, or heritage, of Egyptian music (Danielson 1997: 78).

In similar fashion to the compositions of al-Qaṣabjī, the plays of famed Egyptian actor and playwright Najīb al-Rīḥānī demonstrate a deliberate repurposing of foreign means towards native ends. In crafting his earliest comedies, al-Rīḥānī merged the organizational, structural, and musical elements of French farce with the existing Egyptian comedic tradition, creating a new style christened "Franco-Arab" (Abou Saif 1973). Yet, al-Rīḥānī's stock characters were Egyptian and reflected contemporary Egyptian values and sensibilities, and his most famous creation, the character Kishkish Bik, was embraced by Egyptians of all ages and social classes (Abou Saif 1973, Fahmy 2011: 124). As these cases illustrate, the incorporation of foreign elements into native arts and entertainment did not diminish the "Egyptianness" of the latter in the minds of Egyptians themselves.

It would also be a critical error to assert that the developments in

Egyptian art and entertainment in the late nineteenth and early twentieth centuries were driven exclusively by educated and/or Europeanized elites. In reality, a great deal of late nineteenth and early twentieth century Egyptian music and theater catered to the Egyptian lower and middle classes, to the dismay of the religious and political elites, who criticized the themes of the productions and their use of the colloquial Egyptian dialect as "vulgar." The Egyptian playwright Amīn Ṣidqī, responding to such elite criticisms, wrote a scathing letter to the editor of *al-Ahrām* on June 10, 1915, in which he stated:

> Acting was not specially created for the likes of the honorable critic, who can't even express his own opinion. The theater was created for the masses and the majority who are illiterate or barely literate, and for this reason I never hesitated when I was asked by the director of the theater company to retranslate these plays in colloquial Egyptian [quoted in Fahmy 2011: 130].

In fact, as Ziad Fahmy's (2011) work has revealed, turn-of-the-century developments in mass media and popular entertainment were critical to the participation of non-elite Egyptians in nationalist discourse—an issue that will be explored in greater detail below.

The development of the Egyptian theater in the late nineteenth and early twentieth centuries provides a useful and clear-cut illustration of the dynamic repurposing of foreign concepts and technologies towards Egyptian interests, as well as the cross-class, indigenous appeal and impact of this new form of entertainment. European-style dramatic theater was introduced to Egypt around the beginning of the nineteenth century, though it is important to note that there was an existing indigenous tradition of folk drama and farce (Badawi 1988, Sadgrove 1996). For most of that century, theater in Egypt consisted primarily of French and Italian troupes performing European dramas, operas, and operettas, with little appeal to Egyptians beyond a very limited subset of the Egyptian ruling class. However, from the 1870s through the 1890s, Muḥammad 'Uthmān Jalāl translated a number of European comedies and dramas into colloquial Egyptian Arabic, making them accessible to a broader cross-section of the Egyptian public (Badawi 1988: 69–71, Fahmy 2011: 43–45, Sadgrove 1996: 100–105). Jalāl did not merely translate these works into Arabic—he transformed them into something Egyptian. As Ziad Fahmy notes:

> The uniqueness and importance of Jalal's work ... lay in the fact that many of his translations (mainly the comedies) were free adaptations of the European originals, reset completely in an Egyptian setting. Jalal's "translations" of Moliére's plays were entirely Egyptianized, from the Egyptian names and accents of the characters to the social and geographic milieus of the plays [Fahmy 2011: 44–45].

Contemporary with Jalāl, the Arab playwright Ya'qūb Ṣannū' began to create original theatrical productions geared specifically toward Egyptian interests and tastes (Badawi 1988: 31–42, Fahmy 2011: 45–47, Sadgrove 1996: 89–120). By the end of the century, the Egyptian theater had established itself as something distinct from its European counterpart, and there were a host of Egyptian and Syrian theatrical troupes performing colloquial works for native audiences, not only in the theaters and entertainment halls of Cairo and Alexandria, but also in the smaller towns of the Egyptian countryside (Fahmy 2011: 128).

To many Western observers, the Egyptian theater was a curiosity—a strange mingling of European and Arab artistic elements. Consider Hector Dinning's 1920 account of a visit to a popular theater—most likely the Egypsiana Theater, located on 'Imād al-Dīn Street in Cairo:

> There is a good deal of French influence in the performance, as there is now in all things Egyptian. A little of the music is pure French, and some of the Arab words are set to a French lilt. But there is a lot that is deliberately Arabic in the music; for the Arabs who attend the place and know no French must be catered for. But one thing is certain: there is nothing English about it. The French temperament is far nearer to the Oriental than the English ever could be. That is a good reason why the whole performance is intensely interesting to the English: it is so strange [Dinning 1920: 278–279].

At the time of Dinning's visit, the Egypsiana was managed by Najīb al-Rīḥānī, and it is quite possible that Dinning witnessed one of Rīḥānī's "Franco-Arab" comedies. Worrell's eyewitness account of one of al-Rīḥānī's plays notes the frequent, rhythmic repetition of humorous choruses in colloquial Egyptian, to the delight of the indigenous audience (Worrell 1920: 136–137).

Compare Douglas Sladen's 1911 description of an Arabic play that he attended—most likely at Salāmah Ḥijāzī's Dār al-Tamthīl al-'Arabī ("Arabic Playhouse"), located on a street just north of the Azbakīyah Gardens in Cairo:

> I believe it was quite a good play for those who knew enough Arabic to understand the dialogue. Unfortunately for the ordinary tourist, there was very little action or scenery—it was all talk. Some Arabic plays have almost as much singing in them as a comic opera, and the singing is generally excellent [Sladen 1911: 116].

Clearly, the performances described by these authors were not intended to please Western viewers, since the productions were presented in Arabic and targeted toward Arab tastes. As Badawi notes, aspects of modern Egyptian drama were "clearly the product of some deeply rooted attitudes and tendencies inherited from the past history of indigenous dramatic or semi-dramatic entertainment" (Badawi 1988: 7). Non-native elements were intentionally and thoughtfully absorbed and integrated into the indigenous dramatic tradition. An ad for Cairo's Casino de Paris on October 7, 1918, encapsulates the trends described here: the ad, appearing in the Arabic-language daily newspaper *al-Ahrām*, announces the play *Adī Illī Nāqiṣā*—a colloquial Egyptian expression meaning "That's what we're missing"—and proclaims "new style—Arabic and foreign" (*al-Ahrām* 7 October 1918: 2). From the perspective of Western observers, however, the Egyptian theater was a strange and disconcerting hybrid of Egyptian and non-Egyptian elements—"almost the same, but not quite" (to use Homi Bhabha's turn of phrase).

The developing indigenous Egyptian theater of the late nineteenth and early twentieth century was enjoyed by Egyptians from a range of social classes. In Dinning's description of the Egypsiana Theater, he notes:

> There is a simple division of the house: a row of boxes on the ground each side of the stalls; benches for the bourgeois behind the stalls; large and high rear gallery for the herd.... The herd is there, setting the pace in the clamour—with a large proportion of Bints. This is the only Egyptian theatre in which I have seen the yashmak [face veil] in force. The whole front row of the gallery is peopled by yashmaks and gleaming eyes. The fine, white, transparent yashmak of the aristocrat is scattered up and down the boxes; it is mostly the unveiled Syrians and Italians and French that sit with their men in the stalls—with their men and their families [Dinning 1920: 273–274].

Significantly, Dinning distinguishes the sheer white face veil of the aristocratic women in the boxes from the face veil worn by the women of the "herd" in the gallery. At the turn of the century, the sheer white *yashmak* was worn by upper class Egyptian women, while women of the middle and lower classes generally wore the black face veil known as the *burqu'* (see Baedeker 1914: 47 and Sladen 1911: 70–71)—though Dinning erroneously uses the term *yashmak* throughout his writing for both styles of face veil. Dinning's description suggests that the gallery was populated by members of the lower and middle classes, while a scattering of upper class Egyptians were seated in the boxes, and Syrians and resident Europeans sat in the stalls. Similarly, Worrell notes of his own visit to an Egyptian theater: "The audience consisted of all sorts of Egyptians and some Europeans, including many veiled women" (Worrell 1920: 136).

Compare Sladen's description of the Dār al-Tamthīl al-'Arabī:

> The theatre was not much more substantial or costly in its fittings than a Japanese theatre, which is little more than a shed in the shape of a circus-tent, with matchwood partitions between its boxes. Half the boxes here had harem-grills like Sicilian nuns' churches. There were hardly any women visible; only *tarbûshes* in front and turbans behind [Sladen 1911: 115].

Again, the description of dress styles is revealing. Here, the mention of "*tarbûshes* in front and turbans behind" indicates that middle or upper class Egyptian men (who typically wore the *ṭarbūsh*) were seated near the stage, and lower-middle or lower class Egyptians (who typically wore the traditional turban) were seated behind them (see Cunningham 1912: 21, Dinning 1920: 282, Murray 1888: 30–31, and Sladen 1911: 39–40 regarding the typical dress styles of Egyptian men at the turn of the nineteenth and twentieth centuries).

The previous discussion demonstrates that the developments in Egyptian arts and entertainment in the late nineteenth and early twentieth centuries can not be reduced to a simple reaction to Western influence, or an imitation of Western ideals. Rather, the evidence illustrates the intentional manner in which Egyptians adopted and adapted foreign ideas and technologies to create hybrid cultural expressions that would be embraced as authentically Egyptian. The evidence also shows that Egyptians of the lower and middle classes were important consumers of these uniquely Egyptian creations. In fact, rather than pandering to Western or elite Egyptian audiences, Egyptian arts and entertainment frequently gave voice to the nationalist sentiment that was growing among Egyptians of all classes throughout the late nineteenth and early twentieth centuries, culminating with the populist revolution of 1919. The following discussion reveals how turn-of-the-century developments in Egyptian arts and entertainment were firmly grounded in the growing nationalist sentiment of the Egyptian populace, and how arts and entertainment were important means by which Egyptians attempted to define and assert their cultural and national identity.

Popular Entertainment and Egyptian Nationalism

Egyptian nationalism had its beginnings in the late nineteenth century, after the establishment of the modern Egyptian state under Muḥammad 'Alī Bāshā and the elaboration of state institutions under his descendants. Jankowski notes that from the 1870s onward, there were two trends within Egyptian nationalism:

> One was a vivid sense of the historical as well as the contemporary uniqueness of the land and the people of Egypt. It was the territorial factor that received primary emphasis from early Egyptian nationalists: the historical, geographical, and political distinctiveness of the Nile Valley and its inhabitants. The other was the external loyalty to Egypt's formal sovereign, the Ottoman Empire. The centuries-old

> Ottoman link remained important on the symbolic level for many Egyptians even as its substance eroded over the course of the century. In addition, a continuing connection with the still independent Ottoman state came to be perceived as a useful instrument for resisting European imperialism as the latter first menaced and eventually engulfed Egypt [Jankowski 1991: 244].

The European imperial menace was the unifying factor that galvanized Egyptian nationalist sentiment and that allowed these two strands—territorial nationalism and Ottomanism—to coexist until the end of World War I. However, with the defeat and dismantling of the Ottoman Empire, Ottomanism was no longer a viable option for ending the British occupation, and territorial nationalism moved to the fore.

Until fairly recently, research into the development of modern Egyptian national identity has focused on the role of intellectuals and political leaders in shaping nationalist discourse. While it is true that Egyptian nationalism was initially formulated by Egyptian intellectuals and political activists, particularly individuals from the emergent urban middle class (the *afandīyah*), recent scholarship has drawn attention to the pivotal role played by the Egyptian masses in the negotiation and construction of Egyptian identity. For example, both Beinin and Lockman (1998) and Chalcraft (2005) have demonstrated how the interests of Egyptian artisans, craftsmen, and urban wage laborers intersected with those of bourgeois nationalists; indeed, labor activism at the dawn of the twentieth century was inextricably bound to nationalist concerns.

In a similar vein, the work of Ziad Fahmy (2011) has revealed how the development of new mass media, including the press, the theater, and the music industry, enabled the participation of non-elite Egyptians in nationalist discourse. These new media broadened the national conversation on Egyptian identity by utilizing the everyday colloquial Egyptian dialect of Arabic, rather than the formal *fuṣḥa*, or literary Arabic, employed in the writings of the intelligentsia. More importantly, at a time when the vast majority of Egyptians were illiterate, the development of popular performance media—such as the Egyptian theater—opened the forum of nationalist discourse to a broader cross-section of the Egyptian public. Popular entertainment thus became an important medium through which individuals from all levels of Egyptian society could participate in the national dialogue. As Fahmy states:

> Modern Egyptian mass culture—especially vaudeville and the music industry—transcended the bounds of literacy and gave room for (Cairene) colloquial Egyptian culture to develop a common, increasingly national forum for comprehensible, universally accessible, and socially relevant public discussions about political community, the state, and British imperialism.... These newly formed mass media were

> especially effective at mediating between the written Fusha discourses of the "bourgeois nationalists" and the colloquial expressions of the Egyptian urban masses, creating virtual Egyptian communities that were written, acted out, and sung on pages, stages, and phonograph records [Fahmy 2011: 167–168].

The important role of popular entertainment in the development of Egyptian cultural and national identity, as demonstrated by Fahmy's landmark 2011 work, is of tremendous relevance to the current study.

At the turn of the century, subtle assertions of Egyptian identity were embedded in the plays and songs that were performed in the entertainment halls of urban Cairo and Alexandria. Even as early as the 1870s, the plays of Ya'qūb Ṣannū' contained nationalistic references and social critique, as Ṣannū' grappled with the tensions between tradition and modernization in Egyptian society (Badawi 1988: 32–34, Fahmy 2011: 45–47, Sadgrove 1996: 112–116). His works bolstered the developing sense of Egyptian identity through their humorous and stereotypical characterizations of non-Egyptian personalities, in direct contrast to their favorable portrayal of the native Egyptian: the respectable, resourceful *ibn al-balad* (literally, "son of the country"). These characterizations, which were themselves grounded in earlier traditions of Egyptian farce, became a fixture in the Egyptian comedic theater at the dawn of the twentieth century and would persist in Egypt's developing film industry (see Shafik 2006). Fahmy states:

> [C]ontrasting the habits, demeanor, and, most important, the accent of the native Egyptian urbanites with those considered "foreign" was often dramatized in the latest jokes, in the cartoons and dialogues of the satirical press, and later in the theatrical sketches and plays of the developing comedic theater.... Many of these cultural productions emphasized the accented non-Egyptian pronunciations of Syrian, Sudanese, Greek, English, and other foreign residents and contrasted them with the fluency of a native Egyptian. In all these representations, fluent speakers of Cairene Egyptian Arabic were represented as de facto Egyptian and were automatically imbued with certain qualities, such as patience, goodness, resilience, perseverance, and intelligence. They were contrasted with the nonfluent, accented speakers, who were often characterized with opposing negative values, such as exploitative greed, laziness, disloyalty, and naïveté [Fahmy 2011: 28–29].

From the 1890s through the 1900s, a host of small Cairo-based acting troupes performed colloquial comedies embodying such assertions of Egyptianness, not only in Cairo and Alexandria, but around the Egyptian countryside. The widespread popularity of these troupes among the Egyptian masses ultimately led established dramatic troupes, such as that of the Syrian Sulaymān al-Qardāḥī, to incorporate colloquial comedy into their programs (Fahmy 2011: 68–69).

Overt expressions of Egyptian nationalism and resentment of the British occupation became more frequent in the years leading to the 1919 revolution. A precedent was set in the years immediately following the Dinshawāy Incident of 1906, when Egyptians used literature, music, and theater to vent their outrage at an event that was emblematic of the atrocities, injustices, and humiliations of the occupation (Fahmy 2011: 92–95).[1] While the subtle nationalistic wordplay that characterized earlier works continued to be present, the colloquial plays and songs of the 1910s were sometimes very direct in addressing nationalistic concerns. Fahmy notes that Najīb al-Rīḥānī's comedies often included explicitly nationalistic messages directed at the audience. For example, one of the songs featured in the play *Ish* (*Wow*) included a direct appeal for Egyptian national unity (Fahmy 2011: 127). al-Rīḥānī's *Qūlūluh* (*Tell Him*) dealt specifically with the events of the 1919 revolution and included nationalistic songs composed by Sayyid Darwīsh; many of these songs are still well-known among Egyptians (Fahmy 2011: 161).

The nationalistic import of these colloquial plays was not lost on contemporary foreign observers:

> With the lifting of the curtain on Egypt in 1919 we discover in Cairo a rude sort of musical comedy or operetta—though there is, in fact, no plot—in pure vernacular, sung throughout, with orchestral accompaniment, satirizing Cairo life. Although offered by the nationalist paper *Wadī-an-Nīl* and *al-Afkār* it has a nationalistic significance more profound than the demonstrations of agitators or the fulminations of Syrian editors. It is Egyptian in subject, language, presentation, and reception, without mentioning the flag-waving Fātima at the close [Worrell 1920: 135].

Nor was the nationalistic significance of popular entertainment lost on the Egyptian government. The British authorities, with the support of members of the Egyptian elite, frequently attempted to stifle such overt manifestations of Egyptian nationalism through censorship of the press and the entertainment industry. A press censorship law, previously enacted by the Egyptian government in 1881, was revived in 1909 (Fahmy 2011: 103–105). A host of repressive measures were added during the World War I years, including restrictions on public gatherings (Fahmy 2011: 117–119). Until 1919, the entertainment industry was faced with more limited censorship than that imposed on the Egyptian press. Still, entertainers whose performances were viewed as subversive risked censorship or suppression. Sladen mentions the existence of nationalistic theatrical performances that would cease if a European entered the room (Sladen 1911: 116–117). The famous singer Munīrah al-Mahdīyah frequently ran afoul of the British authorities; Nuzhat al-Nufūs, the coffee shop where she performed in the 1910s, was frequently closed by the British due to the nationalistic character of the performances (Danielson 1997: 46–47, al-Ḥifnī 2001: 87). With the advent of the revolution, this sort of repression intensified, and theatrical activities were suspended for roughly one month in spring 1919 (Fahmy 2011: 160). During this time, many entertainers actively participated in demonstrations.

The nationalist discourse that pervaded Egyptian popular entertainment in the late nineteenth and early twentieth century was not merely focused on Egyptian resistance to foreign domination, however. Colloquial plays and popular songs often challenged the contemporary social order in Egypt through subversive language and counterhegemonic role reversals. Fahmy notes how comic sketches at the turn of the century satirized and mocked both the Egyptian aristocracy and the religious elite; both groups were portrayed as inherently out of touch with the daily reality of ordinary Egyptian life (Fahmy 2011: 71). Lagrange details how the *taqtūqah* (plural *taqātīq*), a type of light song that was massively popular in the 1910s and 1920s, debated issues of gender and family structure in Egyptian society:

> *Taqātīq*, ostensibly 'light' entertainment, in fact addressed such serious themes as the reconstitution of family around the nuclear model, the dangers of polygamy, the right to get acquainted to the bride or the groom before marriage, the dangers of girls' autonomy for a family's wealth, the minimum age of marriage, the way spouses should deal with their husbands' misconduct, working women and women in the police and the army [Lagrange 2009: 229].

Rather than merely providing light entertainment, colloquial plays and popular songs were important vehicles through which ordinary Egyptians discussed and debated the realities of contemporary Egyptian society.

Though the turn-of-the-century Egyptian entertainment industry began as a largely urban phenomenon, its influence would extend well beyond Egypt's urban centers and would ensure the dominance of urban—particularly Cairene—conceptions of Egyptian identity in the coming decades. The introduction of new communication and transportation technologies, combined with state centralization, ensured that urban popular entertainment was able to penetrate rural Egypt. For example, the introduction of the phonograph enabled Cairo-based singers to be heard in villages and towns throughout rural Egypt, allowing some to become national celebrities (Danielson 1991: 304–305, Danielson 1997: 27–28, Fahmy 2011: 73–74). Similarly, the development of railroads in Egypt allowed Cairo-based theatrical troupes to travel and perform throughout the Egyptian countryside (Fahmy 2011: 26, 128).

Perhaps more importantly, rural audiences were able to embrace urban popular entertainment because of its clear connections to Egyptian tradition. The characters and dialogues of the late nineteenth and early twentieth century colloquial theater were firmly grounded in traditional forms of Egyptian comedy and farce, such as the *arājūz* (puppet theater, derived from the Turkish *karagöz*), the *faṣl muḍḥik* (a form of improvised comic skit), and the *khayāl al-ẓill* (shadow play) (Abou Saif 1973; Badawi 1988: 66–67; Fahmy 2011: 46, 68–69, 125–126; Troutt Powell 2001). The familiar Egyptian characters who dominated the landscape of early twentieth century comedy, such as Najīb al-Rīḥānī's village mayor (*'umdah*) and Alī al-Kassār's Nubian servant, had personalities and quirks that resonated with both urban and rural Egyptians (Abou Saif 1973, Troutt Powell 2001). As Fahmy writes:

> An important reason for the success of these new media [i.e., recorded music, variety theater, and the satirical press], aside from their use of a universally understood colloquial Egyptian language, was that they were "authentically" grounded in older forms of cultural expression. Egyptian vaudeville, recorded *taqatiq*, and the colloquial cartoons and dialogues of the satirical press drew liberally from traditional music, *azjal*, and street theater. To be sure, these older forms were completely transformed, "modernized," and reshaped to suit the new media; however, they retained enough of the culturally authentic and locally relevant elements to allow them to speak to most Egyptians effortlessly and familiarly [Fahmy 2011: 169].

In short, Egyptian song, music, dance, and theater remained firmly rooted in traditional Egyptian aesthetics, interests, and values, even as they incorporated the latest innovations, enabling them to be accepted by both rural and urban Egyptian audiences as authentically Egyptian cultural expressions.

One could argue that the entertainment industry had a more profound impact on Egyptian cultural and national identity formation than the literate discourses of Egypt's intellectual and political elite. Though many of the individuals at the forefront of Egypt's budding entertainment industry were literate and were influenced by the contemporary thinking of Egyptian intellectuals, their use of the colloquial dialect set them in opposition to many elite intellectuals, who rejected colloquial Egyptian as vulgar (Fahmy 2011: 17, 129). More importantly, their creations reflected the concerns and interests of the ordinary Egyptians who were the primary consumers of their work. As Egyptian entertainment became progressively more commercial, it catered increasingly to the tastes of the Egyptian masses. As Fahmy (2011: 132–133) notes: "The market-driven forces fueling the commercial production of theatrical and recording hits had revolutionary social implications, not only because they increased the level of homogeneity of national taste but also because they trumped the exclusivist Fusha cultural models pushed by the cultural elite and the Egyptian state."

The Egyptian Entertainment Hall: Incubator for Innovation

The complex and significant developments in Egyptian arts and entertainment described here were nurtured within the many entertainment halls that had emerged in Cairo and Alexandria in the latter decades of the nineteenth century and were widespread by the end of the 1920s. The designation "entertainment hall" is used for convenience, for in reality, a variety of Arabic terms were used for venues dedicated to professional entertainment, including *kāzīnū* ("casino"), *masraḥ* ("theater"), *ṣālah* ("hall"), and *tiyātrū* ("theater," from the Italian *teatro*). It is difficult to make strict comparisons to contemporary European venues. Structurally, some Egyptian entertainment halls were theaters in the contemporary European sense, with seating arranged in boxes and stalls, though several such theaters were roof-less, a point occasionally remarked on by foreign visitors (e.g., Dinning 1920: 273 and Worrell 1920: 136). Others were more akin to European music halls, where patrons sat around tables (e.g., El Dorado). The humbler of these venues were barely more than coffee houses (and went by the same name—*qahwah*, i.e., café), though they differed from the latter by scheduling professional entertainment and charging admission (see, for example, Steevens 1898: 39, *al-Zuhūr* November 1913: 359–362).

What most of these venues held in common was a "variety show" format wherein a single evening's program could include such diverse offerings as music, singing, dancing, theatrical performances, and more—in the style of European *cafés chantants* and music halls and American vaudeville theaters, but targeted toward an Egyptian clientele. The names of many turn-of-the-century Egyptian entertainment halls were adopted from those of their European and American models: Egyptian venues such as the Alhambra Theater, the Casino de Paris, and El Dorado all had famous namesakes in Europe (Christout 1998, Senelick 1998a). The scope of the entertainments offered certainly varied from venue to venue. Yet, even at the establishments primarily oriented toward the presentation of theatrical productions, a variety of other acts were presented before and/or after the central drama or comedy, and sometimes during the intermissions. For example, on February 4, 1911, the program at Salāmah Ḥijāzī's Dār al-Tamthīl al-'Arabī consisted of the play *Mary Tudor*, with musical performances during the intermission, and a comedy show afterwards (*al-Ahrām* 4 February 1911: 3). On September 2 and September 4, 1926, the program at the new Printania Theater consisted of two plays starring Munīrah al-Mahdīyah, along with dance, popular music, and a display by sword masters between the two shows (*al-Ahrām* 1 September 1926: 7).

Importantly, as formalized spaces dedicated to arts and entertainment, the entertainment halls of Cairo and Alexandria enabled fundamental changes in the nature of Egyptian entertainment and its role in Egyptian society. Prior to the establishment of these venues, professional performance of comedy, song, dance, and the like occurred in the context of traditional social occasions—especially weddings, circumcisions, public markets, and saint's day festivals—or at one of Egypt's many coffee houses. Professional entertainers frequented the many saints' day festivals, or *mawālid* (singular *mūlid*), public festivals held in honor of the birthday of an important religious figure, where they provided a range of amusements, including puppet shows, singing, dancing, and comic skits. Charmes provides a vivid description of the popular entertainments at Cairo's *Mūlid al-Nabī* (celebration of the birth of the prophet Mohammad) in the late 1870s:

> [T]he Boolak road is filled with booths, where the popular *almes*, the *carageux*, the mountebanks and Arabian orchestres give their representations. The sight of these booths is brilliant; a multitude of little traders are selling red or white sugar-plums, and thousands of articles in sugar, red or white, that represent all the animals in creation. Little flags are suspended from the shops, which the illumination of the night renders charmingly gay. All this fair, in the open air, is remarkably picturesque. In the Arabian cafés, story-tellers are reciting interminable adventures accompanying themselves with a sort of violin. Popular *almes* are dancing, or rather twisting themselves, with extraordinary agility. An odour of frying oil spreads everywhere. Every booth, lighted with candelabras filled with candles, is surrounded with a crowd of the curious, who are trying to penetrate there the mystery. Tarabooks, flutes, and tambourines fill the space with their noisy sounds. Great crowds in circles, fantastically lighted by *machallas*, surround the illustrious *carageux*, or rather Aly-Kaka; for the Turkish *carageux*, who is a simple marionette or Chinese spirit, is replaced in Egypt by a man in flesh and bone, who bears the more expressive name of Aly-Kaka [Charmes 1883: 179–180].

Entertainers such as storytellers, musicians, and dancers also gathered in Egyptian coffee houses, where they provided informal and spontaneous performances for the patrons (see Lane 1860: 333, 391 and Lane 2005 [1836]: 335, 386). These two settings in particular—the *mawālid* and coffee houses—were a primary source of entertainment for Egypt's lower class.

With the creation of the entertainment halls, arts and entertainment were no longer embedded in the traditional occasions and settings that had previously justified their performance; as Danielson states, they were "cut loose from the moorings of religious or celebratory occasions and removed from familial environments" (Danielson 1999: 118). Professional entertainments such as song, dance, and comedy could now be sought after and enjoyed for their own sake. Within this new performance environment, artists and entertainers developed and transformed indigenous Egyptian entertainment styles according to the contemporary Egyptian audience's interests and motivations. The entertainment hall created a kind of liminal space, where indigenous met foreign, and traditional met modern. In music, for example, traditional Egyptian song forms such as the *qaṣīdah* (plural *qasā'id*) came to be performed alongside new styles such as the European-derived monologue, which was developed specifically to suit the increasingly popular Egyptian musical theater (Danielson 1997: 45, 71). The *taqtūqah*, a commercialized evolution of a type of strophic song originally sung by *'awālim* in private, gender-segregated settings such as wedding celebrations, was performed in public, all-male or mixed-gender spaces—in spite of its sometimes coarse and sexually suggestive language (Lagrange 1994, 2009).

Clearly, many of the acts presented on the entertainment hall stages bore a strong connection to traditional Egyptian modes of performance and reflected the desire of Egyptian audiences for arts and entertainment with ties to indigenous Egyptian aesthetics and interests. Egyptian and other Middle Eastern and North African acts were in high demand at venues in both Cairo and Alexandria; as discussed earlier, even venues that were initially established to cater to foreigners eventually added indigenous entertainment to their programs. Singing and "Arabic dance" were on the bill at Alexandria's San Stefano on July 2, 1889 (*al-Ahrām* 2 July 1889: 3). In 1907, Egyptian singers, dancers, and musicians performed at Cairo's El Dorado entertainment hall for a primarily native Egyptian audience (Loewenbach 1908: 218–220). On April 28, 1910, Cairo's old Printania Theater presented an evening of Egyptian music featuring the famous Egyptian singer Shaykh Yūsif al-Manyalāwī (*al-Ahrām* 22 April 1910: 3). Also in the 1910s, Najīb al-Rīḥānī, as Kishkish Bik, amused Egyptian audiences at Abbaye Des Roses (Worrell 1920). On September 7, 1920, the Casino de Paris presented the play *al-Badawiya* ("The Bedouin Woman"), with a Middle Eastern orchestra performing "national" songs, in honor of the feast of Nayrūz, the start of the Coptic Christian year (*al-Ahrām* 7 September 1920: 2). On March 13, 1925, the grand Azbakīyah Garden Theater hosted a "beautiful Middle Eastern, Egyptian, and Sudanese *ḥaflat*—music, singing, dancing" centering on a play concerning "the great reformer" Muḥammad 'Alī Bāshā and a musical performance by a young Umm Kalthūm (*al-Ahrām* 10 March 1925: 2).

Yet, European and American-style acts often appeared alongside the Middle Eastern acts in the same program, or the Middle Eastern entertainment integrated foreign stylistic elements, demonstrating that Egyptian audiences were willing to embrace and absorb foreign ideas and innovations. As mentioned earlier, a play at the Casino de Paris on October 7, 1918 incorporated both Arabic and foreign stylistic elements (*al-Ahrām* 7 October 1918: 2). Similarly, on September 16, 1919, the Egypsiana Theater in Cairo presented an operetta described as both "foreign and Arabic" (a*l-Ahrām* 16 September 1919: 3). At the grand re-opening of Cairo's Kāzīnū al-Būsfūr on November 28, 1924, both Arabic and foreign dance were on the bill (a*l-Ahrām* 28 November 1924: 7). The variety show at the Bīrah al-Ahrām Theater in Giza on September 1, 1927 included a dazzling array of indigenous and foreign entertainment: a variety of Egyptian performers—including a singer, a monologist, and a comedian—dancers from across central Europe—Germany, Hungary, and Romania—and Turkish dancer Afrānza Hānim, interestingly, performing *raqṣ sharqī* (a*l-Ahrām* 1 September 1927: 6).

Entry fees were low enough to make many of these shows accessible to a broad cross-section of the Egyptian public. Fahmy observes that the price of admission for most plays in the 1910s was 5 piasters,[2] though some venues charged higher fees for first-class and second-class seating (Fahmy 2011: 122). Citing Najīb al-Riḥānī's diary, he indicates that al-Riḥānī's theater in 1917 (probably the Egypsiana) had a 10-piaster second-class section and a 15-piaster first-class section. Admission to a 1903 show at the al-Miṣrī Theater on Cairo's 'Abd al-'Azīz Street ranged from 4 piasters for third-class seating, to 70 piasters for the best seats in the house (Figure 2). The entry fee for the November 28, 1924 show at the Kāzīnū al-Būsfūr was 5 *ṣāgh* (another term for the *qirsh*/piaster coin) (a*l-Ahrām* 28 November 1924: 7). Regarding the evening of entertainment that he witnessed at Cairo's El Dorado in 1907, Loewenbach notes:

> The tickets are different prices, depending on how the client is dressed; the cashier judges us to be worth tickets at five piastres per person, but is content to give us a ticket for a single seat for the three of us.... In a large room the audience is almost entirely composed of natives, who do not seem to have paid an entry fee exceeding half a piaster; maybe they are let in for free [Loewenbach 1908: 218].

Programa del teatro Egipciano
Cairo Marzo 1° 1903
ليلة خصوصية خيرية
فى
التياترو المصري
الكائن باول شارع عبد العزيز
جوق مصر العربي بادارة حضرة اسكندر افندى فرح
يوم الاحد اي ليلة الاثنين
اول مارث سنة ١٩٠٣ الساعه ٩ افرنكى مساء
تمثل رواية
مغاير الجن
ذات ستة فصول
ولا بد ان تكون هذه الليلة من ابهى الليالى اصفاء واكملها هناء . تجتمع فيها العائلات الكريمة فتزيدها رونقاً وبهاء
ويشدو بها بلبل الافراح وزهرة الممثلين
الشيخ سلامه حجازي
وتختم هذه الليلة بتقديم فصل مضحك جدا. ولاتسل عما يوجب الاستغراب والاندهاش من مناظر
السنماتوغراف اى
الصور المتحركه
حيث سيقدم فى هذه الليلة جملة مناظر مستجدة منها منظر رواية علاء الدين الشهيره
اسعار الدخول
بنوار ٧٠
لوج ٥٠
كرسى خصوصى ١٥
فوتيل ١٠
ستال ٦
درجه ثالثه ٤

Figure 2. Flyer for the March 1, 1903, show at the al-Miṣrī Theater in Cairo.

Admission was free for the show at the Bīrah al-Ahrām Theater in Giza on September 1, 1927—and the show included free transportation from downtown Cairo—but patrons were encouraged to purchase a beer for 5 *ṣāgh* (al-*Ahrām* 1 September 1927: 6).

A cost of 5 piasters or less for an evening's entertainment was generally affordable for middle class Egyptians. In 1913, the average monthly salary for a middle-class government employee was 5 pounds (Kholoussy 2010: 18)—i.e., 500 piasters. Nor was this price out of the reach of some members of the urban working class; skilled laborers, such as those in the building trades (e.g., carpenters and masons), earned anywhere from 15–30 piasters per day (Beinin and Lockman 1998: 39)—an income comparable to that of a middle-class government official. A 1920 examination of the Egyptian cost of living details the average monthly expenditures of three categories of Egyptian heads of household ("clerks"—who would have been members of the middle class, "artisans"—who would have been from the highest ranks of the lower class, and other "laborers"—also members of the lower class); the study compares expenditures in the years immediately preceding World War I with those during the month of March 1920 (U.S. Department of Labor 1921: 62–63). Although entertainment expenses are not itemized in the study, two categories of expenditures—"cigarettes and petty expenses" and "other general expenses"—would presumably encompass the money spent on entertainment. The study suggests that prior to the war, middle-class clerks spent a monthly average of 55.3 piasters on "cigarettes and petty expenses" and 60.8 piasters on "other general expenses," while after the war, these expenditures rose to 110.2 and 121.2, respectively. By comparison, prior to the war, skilled artisans and certain other lower-class workers spent a monthly average of 31.2 piasters on "cigarettes and petty expenses" and 17.3 piasters on "other general expenses," and after the war, these expenditures increased to 62.7 and 34.4, respectively. The proportionally higher discretionary budget of the middle-class clerk suggests that entertainment would have been more affordable for him; however, even the lower-class artisan's budget could absorb the occasional cost of one or two 5-piaster tickets to an entertainment hall.

Many entertainment halls offered special shows for ladies only, as well as for families. A 1919 advertisement for the Egypsiana Theater indicates that ladies-only shows were offered on Tuesdays and Wednesdays, and shows for families were available on Thursdays, Fridays, and Sundays (*al-Ahrām* 16 September 1919: 3). Fahmy cites additional examples from 1917 (Fahmy 2011: 122, 207 n. 116). The Kāzīnū al-Būsfūr had special areas set aside for families (*al-Ahrām* 28 November 1924: 7). Badī'ah Maṣābnī, following established practice, eventually offered ladies-only shows at her establishments as well (e.g., *al-Ahrām* 1 October 1930: 6). Offering shows for women and families was an astute business move on the part of entertainment hall owner and managers, as it vastly expanded their potential revenue. More importantly, providing ladies-only and family-oriented shows made entertainment broadly available to Egyptians of both genders and all ages.

In short, Egypt's entertainment halls launched a new era in Egyptian arts and entertainment. Professional entertainments like song and dance were detached from their traditional social contexts, now enjoyed for their own sake in formal spaces dedicated to their production and consumption. Audiences from a range of social classes could take advantage of this new and innovative style of entertainment, as long as they could afford the cost of admission. Yet, the acts presented on the stages of Egypt's entertainment venues bore strong connections to traditional modes of performance. While Egyptian audiences embraced innovations, they continued to desire entertainment that maintained ties to indigenous aesthetics and values.

Summary

The late nineteenth and early twentieth centuries were a time of tremendous growth and innovation in Egyptian arts and entertainment. Egyptians absorbed and adapted foreign techniques and innovations to suit indigenous aesthetics and agendas, creating songs, dances, comedies, dramas, and more, all of which would be embraced by Egyptians themselves as authentically Egyptian cultural expressions, in spite of their hybrid nature. These developments were enabled and nurtured within the entertainment halls of Cairo and Alexandria. These venues broke from traditional Egyptian modes of entertainment by establishing dedicated spaces in which ordinary Egyptians could enjoy art and entertainment for their own sake. With their variety-show format, they brought together a diverse range of artists and entertainers—singers, dancers, composers, actors and actresses, etc. The result was "melting pot" of invention and innovation, where developments in each genre could impact all the others. The accessibility and popularity of these venues with a broad cross-section of Egyptians—both men and women, of all social classes—gave mass appeal to the entertainment created within their walls and supported the growing sense of national unity and pride among Egyptians. In the liminal space of the entertainment hall—at the interface of indigenous and foreign, traditional and modern—Egyptians produced and consumed hybrid arts and entertainment that were embraced as culturally authentic. It was in this context that the dances of Egypt's professional female entertainers, the *'awālim* and the *ghawāzī*, were transformed into the new Egyptian dance form known as *raqṣ sharqī*.

Two

The Rise of *Raqṣ Sharqī*

In eighteenth and early nineteenth century Egypt, the professional female entertainers known as *'awālim* and *ghawāzī* brought joy and levity to important social occasions such as weddings and festivals. For many Egyptians, no celebration would be complete without the singing and dancing that these women provided. Yet, in spite of their popularity, the *'awālim* and the *ghawāzī* faced a series of challenges from a variety of fronts: a capricious government, a public that was sometimes conflicted about their art, and an intrusive and exploitative foreign presence in Egypt.

By the end of the nineteenth century, a combination of increasingly systematic governmental regulation and shifting performance opportunities led the *'awālim* and the *ghawāzī* to pursue employment in the newly-established entertainment halls of Cairo and Alexandria. The entertainment hall provided a new, relatively stable place of employment for these women, who by this time were restricted in where they could perform in Cairo and Alexandria. More significantly, however, the transition from traditional performance contexts to the formalized performance setting of the entertainment hall enabled the transformation of the dances of the *'awālim* and the *ghawāzī* into the concert dance form that would come to be known as *raqṣ sharqī*. Further, it established the *rāqiṣah*—the dancer of the entertainment hall—as a different category of entertainer from her predecessors.

Female Professional Entertainers Before the 1830s

In the eighteenth and early nineteenth centuries, Egypt's professional female entertainers were known as the *'awālim* (singular *'ālmah*) and the *ghawāzī* (singular *ghāziyah*). At the dawn of the nineteenth century, the term *ʿālmah* carried a generally positive connotation. An *ʿālmah* was a "learned woman"—a female entertainer skilled in poetry, music, and dance, and frequently hired to entertain in upper-class Egyptian households on the occasion of an important event such as a wedding, a circumcision, or a *subūʿ* (party for a seven-day-old baby). Though favored by the Egyptian elite, the *ʿawālim* belonged to the "popular classes"—i.e., the lower strata—of Egyptian society (Chabrol 1822: 381). The *ʿawālim* were described by late eighteenth and early nineteenth century observers as gifted singers with the ability to improvise both verse and melody (Chabrol 1822: 381, Savary 1785: 149–150); in fact, some of the *ʿawālim* of the eighteenth and nineteenth centuries were exclusively singers, such as the famed *ʿawālim* Ālmaẓ and Sakīnah. However, it is clear from primary sources that many *ʿawālim* excelled at the native Egyptian dance (Lane-Poole 1846: 96, Savary 1785: 150–153, Villoteau 1809: 694–695).

Several authors of the period contrasted a lower class of *ʿawālim* who were termed the *ghawāzī* (Chabrol 1822: 418, Clot-Bey 1840b: 90–91, Jomard 1822: 733, Savary 1785: 155–156, Villoteau 1809: 694–695). Two important features distinguished the *ghawāzī* from the *ʿawālim*. First, while the *ʿawālim* generally performed for the elite, the *ghawāzī* provided entertainment to the Egyptian lower classes.[1] Second, whereas the *ʿawālim* normally performed in the privacy of the *ḥarīm*, or women's quarters, of the homes in which they were hired, the *ghawāzī* frequently danced and sang in public spaces for mixed-gender or male audiences. In essence, the *ghawāzī* were perceived as a lower class of female entertainers than the *ʿawālim*; they were the *ʿawālim* of the "masses."

It has also been suggested that the *ghawāzī* were of a distinct "race" or "tribe" (Lane 1860: 379–381, Lane 2005 [1836]: 373–376). Indeed, some modern-day *ghawāzī* self-identify with the various Dom Gypsy groups which reside in North Africa and the Middle East, suggesting that at least some of the *ghawāzī* are ethnically distinct from other Egyptians (Nearing 1993).[2] The three main groups of Dom Gypsies in Egypt are the Ghajar, the Ḥalab, and the Nawar (Marsh 2000, Thomas 2000).[3] These groups are well-documented by several nineteenth-century sources, including Lane (1860: 386–387, 2005 [1836]: 382–383), Newbold (1856), and Von Kremer (1864). In more recent times, the researcher Nabil Sobhi Hanna conducted fieldwork among a group of Ghajar east of Cairo (Hanna 1982). Lane makes no specific connection between the *ghawāzī* and Egyptian Gypsies, though he notes with interest that both groups occasionally claim descent from the Barāmikah (Lane 1860: 379–381, 387; Lane 2005 [1836]: 373–376, 382). By contrast, Von Kremer treats the *ghawāzī* as a Gypsy group (Von Kremer 1864: 264). Newbold makes no mention of the *ghawāzī* in his quite detailed overview of the Ghajar, the Ḥalab, and the Nawar, though he notes that many Ghajar women worked as rope dancers and musicians (Newbold 1856: 292).

Still, present-day sources make it quite clear that some *ghawāzī* are Gypsies. The Banāt Māzin, a family of *ghawāzī* performers from Luxor, identify as Nawar (Nearing 1993, 2004a, 2004b). Hanna, based on first-hand experience with the Ghajar, indicates that some families of Ghajar work as professional entertainers, with the women singing and dancing, and the men providing musical accompaniment (Hanna 1982: 31–33). Interestingly, Hanna states:

> [A]lthough financially well off, the people who practice this profession are despised by Ghagar and non-Ghagar alike. Some even pretend to have given up entertaining or say that they have forbidden their daughters and wives to sing and dance [Hanna 1982: 31–33].

> For the Ghagar who work as singers and dancers, there is a high frequency of marriages where both spouses have the same profession. The Ghagari girls who are dancers marry early because their work is considered an important source of income. Other Ghagar men who are not in this profession would not want a dancer for a wife [Hanna 1982: 41].

This would seem to indicate that even among Egyptian Gypsies, the *ghawāzī* have been marginalized.

In the early nineteenth century, the primary performance contexts of the *ghawāzī* were public festivals, particularly *mawālid*, and celebrations of birth or marriage among lower-class Egyptians. In addition to these settings, the *ghawāzī* could be found performing within or in front of Egyptian coffee houses (Fraser 2015: 76–78). These were not formal performances; rather, the *ghawāzī* seem to have lingered in or around coffee houses, occasionally providing spontaneous performances either as a way to earn a few piasters or as a means to advertise their availability for more lucrative engagements such as weddings (see, for example, Jollois 1822: 350). Egyptian musicians and storytellers similarly frequented the coffee houses, providing impromptu entertainment (Lane 1860: 333, 391; Lane 2005 [1836]: 335, 386). This practice—gathering in coffee houses awaiting employment or negotiating with customers—was standard among Egyptian entertainers of the lower and middle classes even into the latter decades of the twentieth century (see, for example, Van Nieuwkerk 1995: 67).

Unlike the *'awālim*, the *ghawāzī* were rarely invited to perform in the homes of the well-to-do. Further, Muslim families were far less likely to invite the *ghawāzī* into their homes than Europeans and non-Muslim Egyptians (Clot-Bey 1840b: 90–91). If the *ghawāzī* were engaged to entertain in the private home of a Muslim family, the performance took place in the *mandarah*, the sitting room in which the male members of the household received guests. The women of the home and the female guests observed the event from a window or balcony overlooking the *mandarah*. The *ghawāzī* might provide a separate performance for the women in the interior of the *ḥarīm*.

Interestingly, in the early nineteenth century, the *'awālim* and the *ghawāzī* were similarly attired for performance. Both classes of entertainers were richly dressed in the same style and quality of garments worn by well-to-do Egyptian women in the *ḥarīm*; only the poorest *ghawāzī* were attired less extravagantly (these garments will be described in detail in Chapter Six). However, in contrast to the *'awālim*, the *ghawāzī* would appear in public spaces wearing these "interior" garments. In this way, the *ghawāzī* reinforced their lower-class association, because only Egyptian women of the lower classes would appear in public with their faces unveiled; middle and upper class women always donned appropriate modesty garments while in public (Fraser 2015: 46–47, Lane 1860: 41–52, Lane 2005 [1836]: 49–59, Villoteau 1809: 699).

Both the *'awālim* and the *ghawāzī* were recognized and taxed by the Egyptian government, although at the turn of the eighteenth and nineteenth centuries, the government's regulation of their trades seems to have been minimal. Entertainers, like individuals in most other trades and occupations in Egypt's major cities and towns, were organized into guilds, which provided a convenient administrative mechanism for extracting taxes from the populace (Baer 1964: 43, 84–86; Clot-Bey 1840b: 300–301; Raymond 1957). At the dawn of the nineteenth century, the entertainers' guilds were controlled and taxed by a government-appointed official (Baer 1964: 43). According to St. John, the taxation of female entertainers was a lucrative source of revenue for the Egyptian government (St. John 1834b: 374).

In 1801, during Napoleon's occupation of Egypt, the French military compiled a list of the existing guilds in Cairo (Raymond 1957). On this list were three guilds of female entertainers: corporation 137 ("*chanteuses du Caire*"—female singers of Cairo), corporation 200 ("*danseuses qui sont au Caire dites Rakassin*"—female dancers of Cairo, called Rakassin), and corporation 192 ("*danseuses et musiciens qui les accompagnent qui sont au Caire*"—female dancers of Cairo and musicians who accompany them). The terms *'awālim* and *ghawāzī* are not mentioned in this list. However,

Kathleen Fraser makes the case that corporation 137 represented *'awālim* who were exclusively singers; corporation 200 represented *'awālim* who both sang and danced; and corporation 192 represented the *ghawāzī* (Fraser 2015: 38–42).

Part of Fraser's argument for identifying the *'awālim* with corporation 200 hinges on a reference to the use of the term *raqqāṣīn* (i.e., *rakassin* from the 1801 guild list) in the chronicles of the late eighteenth century Egyptian historian 'Abd al-Raḥmān al-Jabartī (Fraser 2015: 40). *Raqqāṣīn/ raqqāṣūn* are the plural forms of the word *raqqāṣ*, which signifies a male dancer.[4] The plural form can be used to refer to a group of male dancers, or to any collective of dancers, regardless of gender. Presumably, based on the French military's association of the term with *danseuses* (female and plural), the word was used with some frequency to refer to groups of female dancers. The specific mention that Fraser alludes to is in al-Jabartī's description of the upper-class wedding of the *amīr* Muḥammad Āghā al-Barūdī (al-Jabartī 1904, volume 2: 238). Referencing al-Jabartī, Fraser states that the term "existed in literary Arabic" and that "[al-Jabartī's] use of this term to describe a corporation of dancers associated with a wedding of the nobility of Egypt implies the raqqâsin had some social status" (2015: 40). Building on her assertion that the *raqqāṣīn*, i.e., the *'awālim*, were all high-status, she goes on to argue that only the *ghawāzī* were impacted by an 1830s ban on female entertainers and prostitutes (Fraser 2015: 65, 72).

Fraser's assertions are problematic, however. Although al-Jabartī was a scholar of the *'ulamā',* Egypt's educated religious elite, his writings were not written in pure *fuṣḥa*, or literary Arabic. Rather, his chronicles are pervaded with Egyptian colloquialisms, and the term *raqqāṣīn* appears in colloquial narrative. Moreover, other references to the *raqqāṣīn* in al-Jabartī's work suggest that at least some of these women had a poor reputation. The term appears in al-Jabartī's account of the inappropriate behavior of a group of Egyptian soldiers during Ramadan in 1814 (al-Jabartī 1904, volume 4: 227–228). Al-Jabartī laments that the soldiers, who were encamped just outside the city gates, not only brazenly broke the Ramadan fast by eating, drinking, and smoking, but engaged in a range of morally reprehensible activities, including carousing with prostitutes and smoking hashish. According to al-Jabartī, many women of "ill-repute" gathered around the soldiers' encampment; among those specifically listed were *baghāyā* (prostitutes), *ghawāzī*, and *raqqāṣūn* (al-Jabartī 1904, volume 4: 228). It is noteworthy that al-Jabartī also makes mention of the *ghawāzī* in his description of the activities surrounding the feast day in honor of *shaykh* 'Abd al-Wahāb (a minor local religious figure); the *ghawāzī* are again listed alongside prostitutes as an illustration of the moral depravity of the festivities (an unfortunate irony, for, as al-Jabartī points out, ʻAbd al-Wahāb was an ascetic) (al-Jabartī 1904, volume 1: 225).

Clearly, then, al-Jabartī's writings demonstrate that the *raqqāsin* could appear in both respectable settings, such as the upper-class wedding mentioned above, as well as in disreputable contexts. Yet, the *raqqāṣīn* were definitely a group distinct from the *ghawāzī*, since both groups are listed side-by-side in al-Jabartī's account. This lends some credence to Fraser's decision to align the *ʻawālim* with corporation 200. However, if the *raqqāsin* were *ʻawālim*, an incident such as the one that occurred in Ramadan 1814 would indicate that at least some of these women were engaging in the same sorts of questionable activities as *ghawāzī* and prostitutes; Van Nieuwkerk has argued that there was such an overlap between the *ʻawālim* and the *ghawāzī* in the early decades of the nineteenth century (Van Nieuwkerk 1995: 27–36). The Ramadan incident would also indicate that some of the *ʻawālim* were, in fact, vulnerable to the government pronouncement against "public women" in the early 1830s. Tellingly, in the French-Arabic dictionary compiled by Ellious Bochthor—a Coptic Egyptian who eventually became a professor of colloquial Egyptian Arabic in Paris—both *ʻālmah* and *ghāziyah* are listed under the entry for *danseuse* (*femme publique*)—female dancer (public woman) (Bocthor 1828: 231).

Financial pressures were likely a factor in why some *ʻawālim* resorted to performing in contexts that were previously the domain of the *ghawāzī*. These performance settings would have been less easily regulated and taxed than performances conducted in the homes of the urban elite—an advantage that would become critical in the face of the heavy taxation imposed by the government of Muḥammad ʻAlī Bāshā. Economic concerns may also have been the driving force that propelled both the *ʻawālim* and the *ghawāzī* to dance and sing for Europeans (Van Nieuwkerk 1995: 31). Indeed, in the early decades of the nineteenth century, female singers and dancers—as well as, notably, prostitutes—entertained Europeans with a frequency that alarmed both governmental and religious authorities.

The 1830s Ban and Its Impact

In the early decades of the nineteenth century, both the Egyptian populace and the Muslim elite of the *ʻulamā'* began to agitate for some sort of government action regarding female entertainers and prostitutes. The sources of agitation were threefold. First was the moral indignation, particularly among the *'ulamā'* and other pious Egyptians, regarding the government's receipt of revenue from the taxation of morally reprehensible occupations. Public outcry over the taxation of vice had led to the repeal of taxes on female entertainers several times throughout Egyptian history (Fraser 2015: 90, 158; see also Saleh 1979: 125–126, who mentions governmental restrictions on entertainers in the thirteenth century). Second, corruption and abuses in the application of the taxes on female entertainers and prostitutes generated significant public outrage. Tucker (1985: 151–152) documents the scandal that erupted when the tax farmer of prostitutes added several "honorable women" to his rolls in order to increase his revenues (as well as to enact personal retribution, as some of the women he registered as prostitutes were the wives and daughters of his personal enemies). Finally, as female entertainers and prostitutes increasingly plied their trade among foreigners, public indignation and resentment grew over this overt expression of foreign dominance in Egypt.

Ultimately, Muḥammad 'Alī was willing to sacrifice tax revenue in order to quell the growing discontent over "public women." In the early 1830s, he took the drastic action of banning public performances by the *'awālim* and the *ghawāzī* in Cairo and Alexandria (Clot-Bey 1840b: 90, Lane 1860: 377, Lane 2005 [1836]: 566). The same decree also banned prostitution in Egypt's urban centers. According to Lane (2005 [1836]: 566): "Women detected infringing this new law are to be punished with fifty stripes for the first offence, and for repeated offences are to be also condemned to hard labor for one or more years." Many entertainers fled the cities, while some were actually deported after they were found in violation of the law (see, for example, Didier 1860: 341). Although a few of the most prestigious *'awālim* managed to continue working in Cairo and Alexandria, as a result of the ban, the majority of *'awālim* and *ghawāzī* were forced to migrate to the smaller towns and villages of the Delta and Upper Egypt.

Life was more uncertain for entertainers in Egypt's rural areas. The *fallāḥīn*, the poor farmers who formed the majority of the rural population, could not afford to hire entertainers for their weddings, leaving the rural *mawālid* and performances for foreigners as the primary sources of income (Van Nieuwkerk 1995: 34). Further, security risks outside of the metropolitan centers of Alexandria and Cairo, combined with economic uncertainty, made some entertainers vulnerable to extortion by pimps, protectors, money lenders, and sometimes even the local police (Van Nieuwkerk 1995: 35–36). Thus, cross-purposes with the intent of the ban, the move to rural towns such as Isnā, Qinā, and Luxor actually propelled female entertainers further into performing for foreigners, as well as into prostitution. In the public eye, the distinction between the *ʿawālim* and *ghawāzī* gradually faded.

The 1830s ban and its profound effects on all classes of female entertainers initiated a transformation in the terminology for these women. Over the course of the next century, the term *ʿālmah* gradually lost its prestige. Though the term continued to be used for female singers even into the early twentieth century, by the 1930s, *muṭribah* became the preferred term for esteemed singers, as *ʿālmah* came to designate a common singer/dancer who performed for the lower and middle classes of urban Cairo and Alexandria (Lagrange 2009: 227–228). The term *ghāziyah* increasingly referred strictly to singer/dancers working in the rural villages and the *mawālid*. In essence, the terms *ʿawālim* and *ghawāzī* lost their class associations; rather, they began to convey a distinction between urban and rural singer/dancers, and neither group was highly esteemed in Egyptian society.

Ongoing Regulation and Shifting Performance Opportunities

While it has been frequently suggested that the ban was lifted during the reign of ʿAbbās Bāshā (1848–1854), Fraser's research has revealed that the ban continued to be enforced throughout his reign, and even later (Fraser 2015: 161–165). Taxation of both prostitutes and female entertainers resumed as early as 1866 (Duff Gordon 1875: 94–95), a manifestation of the substantial increase in taxation that took place under the administration of Khedive Ismāʿīl (Chalcraft 2005: 40–44). Yet, governmental restrictions on prostitution and public dance in Egypt's urban centers continued for the remainder of the century and into the next. Both Leland (1873: 130–131) and Warner (1900: 160) indicate that restrictions on public dance were in effect in Cairo in the 1870s. At the same time, dance could be seen at private events hosted by the wealthy (Leland 1873: 130–131) and within at least one *café chantant* near the Azbakīyah Gardens—certainly a public performance context (Linden 1884: 52, Warner 1900: 101–102). Adding to the confusion, Charmes indicates that female dancers performed publicly at the celebration of the Mūlid al-Nabī in Cairo in the late 1870s (Charmes 1883: 179–181). These discrepancies suggest that governmental regulation of public dance by female entertainers in Cairo and Alexandria in the latter half of the nineteenth century was somewhat arbitrary and inconsistent. In contrast to the situation in the urban centers, public performances by female dancers at rural *mawālid* continued to be commonplace (see, for example, Ebers 1887: 82 and Warner 1900: 46).

Restrictions on public dance in Egypt's urban centers continued after the commencement of the British occupation in 1882 (see, for example, Reynolds-Ball 1898b: 191–192). This is corroborated by an 1894 article in the Arabic-language arts and literature magazine *al-Hilāl*. The article commends the Egyptian government for implementing a ban on dance in "public cafés" (*al-Hilāl* 1 August 1894: 729).[5] It is quite possible that this move was in direct response to popular outcries about public dance; in 1891, *al-Ahrām* newspaper published a complaint from residents of Cairo's Muḥarram Bik neighborhood (in Rūḍ al-Faraj, a district with a heavy concentration of entertainment venues), who were concerned with "disreputable" dancers gathering and performing at cafés in their neighborhood (*al-Ahrām* 10 April 1891: 3). Yet, multiple sources indicate that Egyptian dancers were performing in Egyptian entertainment halls after the 1890s ban was put into effect (Baedeker 1898: 24, Penfield 1899: 30, Reynolds-Ball 1898a: 12). A more detailed examination of the Egyptian government's approach toward entertainment and entertainment venues at the turn of the century is necessary to resolve this contradiction.

Legal restrictions on public dance at the turn of the century coincided with broader and more systematic government regulation of public establishments such as bars, cafés, hotels, and theaters. Under the British occupation, the Egyptian government's bureaucratic and administrative functions became increasingly systematized, and governmental regulation of these establishments became intrusive and methodical. In 1889, 1891, and 1904, a series of ordinances were passed to regulate public establishments, including those presenting entertainment (Brunyate 1906: 64–65, Fonder 2013: 61–72, Scott 1908: 278). The 1889 legislation enabled the policing of public establishments, while the legislation of 1891 created licensing requirements. Laws Number One and Thirteen of 1904 amended and supplemented the earlier laws, further detailing the licensing requirements for public establishments, including those presenting music, song, and dance (Brunyate 1906: 64–65) (Figure 3).

Journalist Sydney Moseley describes the legislation that was in effect during his time in Egypt in the 1910s. Though not explicitly stated in his text, it is likely that he is referencing Laws Number One and Thirteen of 1904:

> One result of public agitation was the enactment of a drastic law curtailing the privileges of these night cafés, cabarets, music halls, and such places of ren-

> dezvous.... The new law divides public establishments into two categories. The first includes cafés, restaurants, cabarets, concert halls, sporting establishments, places of entertainment, clubs, and other similar places open to the public. The second comprises hotels, pensions, furnished apartment houses, and other similar establishments offering lodging to the public. In addition to the new law, theatres, etc., will be subject to the Theatre Law of 1912 [Moseley 1917: 207–208].[6]

Moseley goes on to detail how the "new law" established zoning regulations, licensing requirements for the sale of alcoholic beverages, and restrictions on hours of operation. Importantly, the new law also stipulated the following:

> No immoral entertainment or meeting can be held in these establishments, and no music, dances, or songs can be performed without a special permit, renewable yearly. No game of hazard can be played nor hashish be permitted on the premises [Moseley 1917: 209].

By the end of the 1920s, the government's systematic and direct regulation of entertainment in public establishments had extended beyond the urban centers of Cairo and Alexandria to the towns and villages of the Egyptian countryside. Figure 3 shows an entertainment license from December 22, 1927. This license was issued for an establishment in Aswan; the license permits singing, but not dancing, for a one-month period

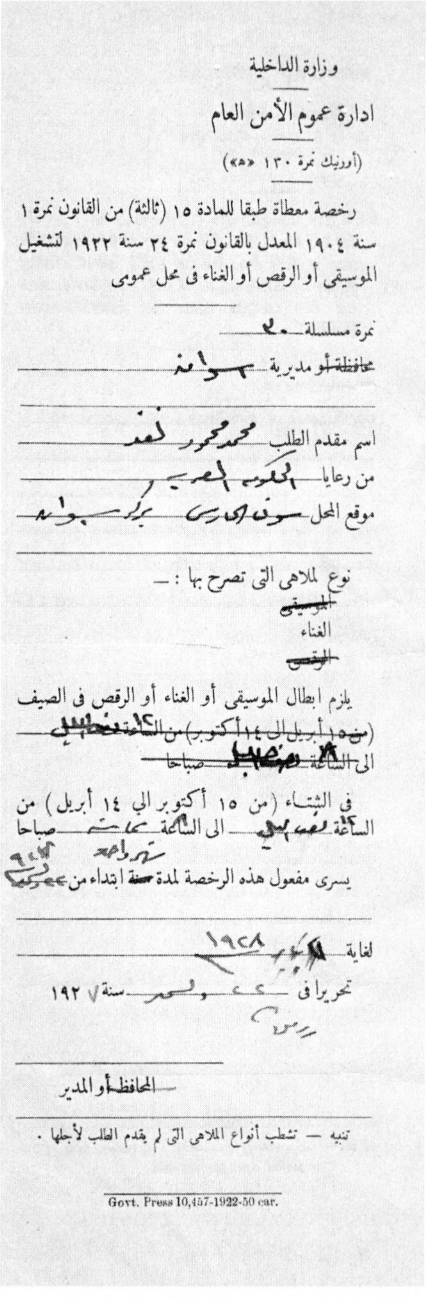
وزارة الداخلية
ادارة عموم الأمن العام
(أورنيك نمرة ١٣٠ «ه»)
رخصة معطاة طبقا للمادة ١٥ (ثالثة) من القانون نمرة ١
سنة ١٩٠٤ المعدل بالقانون نمرة ٢٤ سنة ١٩٢٢ لتشغيل
الموسيقى أو الرقص أو الغناء فى محل عمومى
نمرة مسلسلة
محافظة أو مديرية
اسم مقدم الطلب
من رعايا
موقع المحل
نوع الملاهى التى تصرح بها : —
الموسيقى
الغناء
الرقص
يلزم ابطال الموسيقى أو الغناء أو الرقص فى الصيف
(من ١٥ أبريل الى ١٤ أكتوبر) من الساعة
الى الساعة صباحا
فى الشتاء (من ١٥ أكتوبر الى ١٤ أبريل) من
الساعة الى الساعة صباحا
يسرى مفعول هذه الرخصة لمدة سنة ابتداء من
لغاية
تحريرا فى سنة ١٩٢
المحافظ أو المدير
تنبيه — تشطب أنواع الملاهى التى لم يقدم الطلب لأجلها .
Govt. Press 10,457-1922-50 car.

Figure 3. Entertainment license dated December 22, 1927.

commencing December 22, 1927 and ending January 21, 1928. The text of the license indicates that this license was "issued under Article 15 (third) of Law Number 1 of 1904, amended by Law Number 24 of 1922, pertaining to music, dance, and song in public establishments."

In its efforts to regulate entertainment and entertainment venues, the Egyptian government repeatedly found its hands tied by the Capitulations. Established under the Ottoman Empire, the Capitulations granted extraterritorial rights to certain European powers (Marsot 1985: 70–71). In essence, Europeans residing and doing business in Egypt were largely subject to the jurisdiction of their nation's consulate, rather than Egyptian law. Thus, though the Egyptian government passed numerous regulations pertaining to entertainment and entertainment venues, it sometimes found itself challenged to enforce them in cases involving Europeans. Brunyate, describing the legislation pertaining to public establishments that was passed in 1904, states:

> It is of a somewhat rudimentary character, owing to the fact that effective legislation as to such establishments would inevitably come into conflict with rights consecrated by the Capitulations, but it represents some advance towards effective control [Brunyate 1906: 65].

As mentioned above, numerous sources indicate that Egyptian dancers were a common sight in the entertainment halls of Egypt's metropolitan centers beginning in the 1890s, in spite of contemporary restrictions on public dance. Guide books mention the "native dancing girls" of El Dorado beginning in the 1890s (see, for example, Baedeker 1898: 24, Reynolds-Ball 1898a: 12). An American diplomat stationed in Cairo in the 1890s, Frederic Penfield, suggests the widespread presence of female dancers in Cairo's entertainment halls by the end of the century: "Another widely described institution, satisfying most spectators with a single view, is the dancing of the Ghawâzi girls, to be witnessed at a dozen Cairo theaters and cafes" (Penfield 1899: 30).

Given the previous discussion, it is noteworthy that many of the venues that presented Egyptian dance in the 1890s and 1900s, including El Dorado, were owned and/or managed by foreigners—particularly Greeks (Poffandi 1904: 90–92, 131, 281–282, 320). A 1913 article in the Arabic-language magazine *al-Zuhūr* notes that in the latter years of the nineteenth century, numerous cafés and theaters focused on Egyptian dance were opened by Greek entrepreneurs in Cairo and Alexandria (*al-Zuhūr* November 1913: 359–360). The article indicates that the Egyptian government closed several of these venues (*al-Zuhūr* November 1913: 361). Although the author does not provide a specific date, the text suggests that the government took this action sometime between 1887 and 1897. It is possible that the government was enforcing the 1890s dance ban mentioned in *al-Hilāl* (*al-Hilāl* 1 August 1894: 729). In fact, I would posit that the 1890s action described in *al-Hilāl* may have been a crackdown on venues that were in violation of the licensing requirements established in 1891. Notably, the *al-Zuhūr* article states that the café and theater owners took their case to the courts and were able to re-open. It is probable that these Greek entertainment hall owners were able to overcome governmental restrictions on public dance due to the privileges afforded to them under the Capitulations. The implication here is that at the turn of the century, foreign-owned entertainment halls may have held a particular attraction for Egyptian dancers, because they provided a means to evade contemporary restrictions on public dance.

What is clear is that as early as the 1890s, Egyptian dancers working in Cairo and Alexandria had begun the transition from traditional performance contexts to the decidedly non-traditional performance setting of the entertainment hall. Though restrictions on public dance remained in effect, the entertainment hall allowed dancers to continue working. Thus, while dancers were completely absent from events such as Cairo's Mūlid al-Nabī (Leeder 1913: 253, Sladen 1911: 225–234), they were nonetheless visible and accessible to the Egyptian public. The stage was set for a fundamental change in the nature of female professional dance in Egypt.

The Egyptian Entertainment Hall and the Emergence of Raqṣ Sharqī

The move from traditional performance settings such as weddings and *mawālid* to the stages of the entertainment halls initiated the transition of the traditional dances of the *'awālim* and the *ghawāzī* into the concert dance form that would come to be known as *raqṣ sharqī*. By definition, concert dance is entertainment for a non-participating audience, and two critical features that mark *raqṣ sharqī* as a concert dance and differentiate it from the dances of the *'awālim* and the *ghawāzī* are (1) Performance for the sake of performance, and (2) Performance for a primarily non-participating audience. These features were in place as early as the 1890s, indicating that the development of *raqṣ sharqī* was underway by the end of the nineteenth century.

On the entertainment hall stage, the dance was detached from the social contexts that had traditionally justified its performance. Previously, the *'awālim* and the *ghawāzī* were hired to perform if there was a special occasion to observe, such as a wedding or a *subū'*. In fact, in the early nineteenth century, it was considered in poor taste to hire entertainers without some specific social justification (Lane 1860: 188–189, 503; Lane 2005 [1836]: 191, 496). Dancers and other entertainers, such as musicians and story tellers, also performed in the context of public festivals, and they provided *ad hoc* entertainment in Egyptian coffee houses. Now, dancers were being hired to perform in venues which existed specifically for the display of performing arts like music, dance, and theater. The audience was composed entirely of paying customers who attended with the intent of seeing the show, as opposed to a *mūlid* or a wedding, where the entertainment was embedded in the occasion, rather than the *raison d'être* for the event. The dance was now sought after for its own sake.

Additionally, the formalized performance setting of the entertainment hall established a divide, both structural and social, between performers and audience that was not present in the traditional dances of the *'awālim* and the *ghawāzī*. While the *'awālim* and the *ghawāzī* were certainly performing for others, the boundary between the performers and the audience was not precise. Female entertainers were welcomed into private homes and treated with the same hospitality accorded to friends and family. Lagrange notes: "a standard *'âlma* was a woman respectable enough to be invited as a guest in an upper-class household and become a friend of the family" (Lagrange 2009: 227–228).

Western observers were often shocked by the casual association between female entertainers and their clients (Van Nieuwkerk 1995: 36–37). Consider Lady Duff Gordon's description of an experience with a dancer in Upper Egypt:

> I dined last night with Mustafa, who again had the dancing-girls for some Englishmen to see. Seleem Efendi got the doctor, who was of the party, to prescribe for him all about his ailments, as coolly as possible. He as usual sat by me on the divan, and during the pause in the dancing, called "El Maghribeeyeh," the best dancer, to come and talk to us. She kissed my hand, sat on her heels before us, and at once laid aside the professional gaillardise of manner, and talked very nicely in very good Arabic, and with perfect propriety, more like a man than a woman; she seemed very intelligent. What a thing we should think it, for a worshipful magistrate to call up a girl of that character to talk to a lady! [Duff Gordon 1865: 224–225].

Similarly, Isabella Romer describes the intimate association between a Cairene noblewoman and her favorite dancer:

> She was formerly one of the public ghawazee of Cairo, but her performance possessed so many charms for the Dey's daughter that she took her into her household, and has loaded her with jewels, and pays no visits without being accompanied by

> her. The nymph had on a splendid pearl necklace and diamond ear-rings presented to her by her mistress on the late occasion of the princess's marriage; and whenever she performs any particularly audacious feat in dancing she is rewarded by her with similar gifts.... The Dey's daughter spoke to no one but to this her especial favourite, whom she further honoured by allowing her to smoke out of her own *narghilé*; and the ghawazee never scrupled to snatch it from her mistress's lips whenever her fancy prompted her to pause in the dance and refresh herself with a puff [Romer 1846b: 127–128].

Also shocking to Westerners was the direct physical contact that sometimes occurred between female entertainers and audience members—particularly male audience members. Clot-Bey notes that dancers were sometimes observed embracing male audience members and sitting in their laps (Clot-Bey 1840b: 93–94), and both Clot-Bey and Lane describe men tipping *ghawāzī* by licking coins and applying them to the dancers' bodies (Clot-Bey 1840b: 94, Lane 1860: 501, Lane 2005 [1836]: 495).

As in other forms of Egyptian entertainment,[7] audience engagement and participation were intrinsic to dance performance, and this continued to be the case even within the formalized performance setting of the entertainment hall. In these venues, audiences showed their approval by applauding, exclaiming, or throwing small coins or bouquets of flowers, and Egyptian performers broke the "fourth wall" by engaging in verbal exchanges with audience members (e.g., Dinning 1920: 274–276, Giffin 1911: 39). One turn-of-the-century author describes the presence of a *muṭayyib*—an individual who would loudly and repeatedly proclaim the excellence of the performance:

> Throughout the song and throughout the dance an Arab of piratical mien walks to and fro among the audience yelling at the top of his voice. No one takes the slightest notice of his cries; no one asks that he may be ejected for disturbing the peace. This gentleman, indeed, is part of the show; he fulfills the important office of mutaib, the peripatetic claquer of the Arab "halls." That he earns his pay there can be no doubt. With a devotion worthy of some great and noble cause he calls on all there assembled to bear witness to the magnificence of the entertainment they are enjoying, to the skill of the musicians, the sweet voices of the singers and the proficiency of the beauteous maiden in the dance [*Hopkinsville Kentuckian* 30 May 1899: 7].

The profession of *muṭayyib* was rooted in traditional modes of Egyptian entertainment; Lagrange notes that the *muṭayyib* played an important role at private musical performances during the latter half of the nineteenth century (Lagrange 1994). The *muṭayyib* acted as an intermediary between the audience and the performers, not only by communicating the wishes and preferences of the audience, but also by receiving the host's payment and passing it on to the lead entertainer; in doing so, the *muṭayyib* spared the lead entertainer the indignity of receiving payment from an individual considered to be a friend.

In Egypt's turn-of-the-century entertainment halls, when dancers were offstage, their engagement with audience members seems to have been limited to two specific types of interactions. First, dancers sometimes moved through the audience to solicit tips (Loewenbach 1908: 220, *Star* 20 September 1902: 2). Loewenbach describes the process at Cairo's El Dorado:

> When [the dancer] is finished, she comes into the room to 'pass the hat' with a small saucer which she places successively on each table and which she leaves there for a few minutes, during which she stands aside discreetly. Most of the natives give a small coin. During this operation, she is tracked and monitored by a fine Egyptian with a great black mustache and a fierce expression, who does not lose sight of her for a moment, nor the money she collects, he is probably her impresario [Loewenbach 1908: 220, translated by the author, with assistance from Christine Ferhat].

Second, many dancers engaged in a practice known as *fatḥ* (literally, "opening," referring to opening bottles of alcohol), in which they sat with customers, drinking and socializing, in order to encourage spending. Van Nieuwkerk describes the abundance of this practice in the entertainment halls of the 1920s and 1930s (1995: 43–45), though *fatḥ* did occur in earlier decades (*Raqṣ Shafīqah* 1908, Ward 2013b, *al-Zuhūr* November 1913: 361).

The entertainment hall practices of tipping and *fatḥ* appear to have been formalized, structured evolutions of earlier traditional practices. Lane describes how the *ghawāzī* were plied with brandy and tipped with gold coins:

> In some parties where little decorum is observed, the guests dally and sport with these dancing-girls in a very licentious manner. I have before mentioned (in a former chapter) that on these occasions they are usually indulged with brandy or some other intoxicating liquor, which most of them drink to excess. It is a common custom for a man to wet with his tongue small gold coins and stick them upon the forehead, cheeks, chin, and lips of a Gházeeyeh [Lane 2005 [1836]: 494–495].

In *fatḥ*, the old custom of providing beer, brandy, or other spirits to female entertainers was turned to the financial advantage of the entertainment hall owner, as well as of the entertainers themselves, who received a portion of the profits from this activity. However, the sort of intimate physical contact between the entertainers and the audience described by Lane and other early nineteenth century sources is not evident in accounts from turn-of-the-century entertainment halls.[8]

Beyond establishing the fundamental features that distinguish *raqṣ sharqī* from traditional *'awālim/ghawāzī* dances—performance for the sake of performance, and performance for a primarily non-participating audience—the move to the entertainment hall enabled several factors that would eventually transform *raqṣ sharqī* into its recognizable modern-day form. First, it led to the mingling of Egyptian dancers with performers of other nationalities, creating the opportunity for Egyptian dance to absorb technical and aesthetic elements from non-Egyptian dance styles. Egyptian performers worked alongside entertainers from Europe, the Middle East, North Africa, and Turkey. In fact, among the earliest performers of *raqṣ sharqī* were Moroccans, Persians, Syrians, and Tunisians (*al-Zuhūr* November 1913: 359–361). Further, among the first *raqṣ sharqī* soloists to be mentioned by name in Arabic-language advertisements and flyers were Turkish performers, such as the in-demand dancer Afrānza Hānim, who appeared at a number of venues in Cairo and Alexandria from the late 1920s into the early 1930s.

Second, the entertainment hall milieu brought dancers and their accompanying musical ensembles into a setting where Egyptian music was being actively transformed through the deliberate adaptation of Western musical principles and technologies to the Egyptian musical tradition. The very nature of the performance space had a tremendous influence on Egyptian music: small ensembles composed of traditional musical instruments gave way to large orchestras incorporating Western instrumentation and capable of filling a large hall with sound. The transformations that took place in Egyptian music would eventually alter the nature of musical accompaniment for Egyptian *raqṣ sharqī*.

Finally, the entertainment hall environment brought Egyptian dancers into contact with various features of the contemporary Western music-hall, such as the use of choreography and chorus lines, as well as current trends in Western theatrical costuming. Choreography and chorus lines would eventually become a part of *raqṣ sharqī*—though improvisation would remain the preferred method of performance for soloists. Elements derived from Western theatrical fashion would be absorbed into the existing Egyptian dance costume.

Yet, even as it absorbed a range of foreign innovations, the new dance form maintained strong ties to it indigenous roots. From the 1890s through the 1920s, as *raqṣ sharqī* evolved into its recognizable modern-day incarnation, the dance's technique, aesthetic, and even costuming continued to display clear links to the traditional dance styles of the *'awālim* and the *ghawāzī*. The hybridization of tradition and innovation in the development of *raqṣ sharqī* will be explored in detail in the following chapters.

Naming the Dance

The term *raqṣ sharqī* did not become definitively tied to the emergent Egyptian concert dance style as defined and discussed in this study until the late 1920s or early 1930s. This raises some difficulty in interpreting certain Arabic-language sources from the late nineteenth and early twentieth centuries. Though mentions of dance and dancers had become fairly common in Arabic-language advertisements and flyers by the end of the 1920s, many of these sources use generic or ambiguous terms, making it difficult at times to conclude exactly what style of dance was being presented. For example, a July 2, 1889 advertisement for Alexandria's San Stefano announces an "Arabic dance" performance, but provides no details about precisely what type of Arabic dance (*al-Ahrām* 2 July 1889: 3). Similarly, a November 28, 1924 advertisement for Cairo's Kāzīnū al-Būsfūr announces a show with Arabic and foreign dance, but does not elaborate further (*al-Ahrām* 28 November 1924: 7). An ad from the following month, also for the Kāzīnū al-Būsfūr, announces a dance performance by an Arab performer named Fatḥīyah al-Maghribīyah, but offers no specifics about what style of dance she would be performing, though her surname suggests that she was Moroccan (*al-Ahrām* 19 December 1924: 7).

Compounding this difficulty, although the term *raqṣ sharqī* existed prior to the 1920s, its meaning was more generalized. The adjective *sharqī* ("eastern") was often used as a counterpoint to the adjective *afrankī/afranjī* ("Frankish," i.e., foreign) in order to draw a distinction between Middle Eastern ideas and practices and those of foreigners. Thus, *raqṣ sharqī* could be used generically to refer to any "eastern" dance form.

This is the usage that occurs in a 1901 letter to the editor published in *al-Hilāl* magazine, in which the term *raqṣ sharqī* is used to contrast the traditional dances of the Middle East with foreign dances imported from Europe—specifically, mixed-gender partner dances (*al-Hilāl* 10 April 1901: 412). This letter is of great interest, as it reveals the weight of the nationalistic sentiment behind the modifier *sharqī*. The author, a middle-class Egyptian woman, notes that women in her social circle were being pressured to dance in the *afranjī* way (with a man), rather than the indigenous *sharqī* way (solo). She rejects this mixed-gender way of dancing as a negative side effect of "modernization," and stresses that Middle Eastern people need not blindly copy foreigners. The fact that *sharqī* would become the defining descriptor of the dance form discussed in the current study is tremendously significant, as it indicates that the dance came to be firmly identified by Egyptians as indigenous, rather than *afrankī/afranjī*—Western.

A dance called *raqṣ sharqī* was part of the program on October 15, 1923 at the Azbakīyah Garden Theater (*al-Ahrām* 15 October 1923: 2). The featured entertainment that evening was a stage adaptation of one of the stories from the Arabian Nights, and the dance appears to have been part of the play. The advertisement reveals nothing about the nature of the dance performance. However, considering the theme of the play and its associated fantasy elements (the advertisement mentions "angels from the sky" and "djinn from the earth"), it is quite possible that the term *raqṣ sharqī* is here referring to a fantasy Middle Eastern dance created to be consistent with the style and feel of this particular play.

Nearly two years later, on January 23, 1925, *raqṣ sharqī* was again on the bill at the Azbakīyah Garden Theater (*al-Ahrām* 20 January 1925: 5), but evidence suggests that in this case, the dance may have been the specific dance form of interest in the current study. The advertisement for the show, which appeared in the January 20, 1925 issue of *al-Ahrām* newspaper, announces that the entertainment on January 23 would include acting, singing, and dancing. The advertisement indicates that several dance styles would be represented, including *baghdādī*, *'irāqī*, and *sharqī*. It is noteworthy that *raqṣ sharqī* is listed separately from other *sharqī*—i.e., Middle Eastern—genres; it suggests that *raqṣ sharqī* was understood to be a separate and distinct form of Middle Eastern dance.

Multiple mentions of *raqṣ sharqī* in the mid-to-late 1920s similarly suggest that the term was beginning to be associated with a unique dance style. The Turkish dancer Afrānza Hānim is mentioned in two advertisements for the Bīrah al-Ahrām Theater in Giza—one on June 1, 1927 and the other on September 1, 1927—(a*l-Ahrām* 1 June 1927: 6, a*l-Ahrām* 1 September 1927: 6). The June advertisement announces that Afrānza would be performing Turkish and European dances in that month's shows. The September advertisement announces that she would be dancing *raqṣ sharqī*. These ads indicate that *raqṣ sharqī* and Turkish dance—another "eastern" dance genre—were separate and distinct dances in Afrānza's repertoire, and that Afrānza's audiences recognized the difference.

By the mid–1930s, the term *raqṣ sharqī* had come to signify what Egyptians themselves recognized as a specific and distinctive dance form. This terminological development correlates well with what the evidence has revealed regarding the development of the dance. As discussed above, two defining elements of *raqṣ sharqī*—performance for the sake of performance, and performance for a primarily non-participating audience—were in place as early as the 1890s. However, other features that would come to shape the dance as it is known today, such as the inclusion of techniques from foreign dances, were absorbed into the dance over a thirty to forty year period—from the 1890s through the 1920s. Thus, although the emergence of *raqṣ sharqī* was underway as early as the 1890s, the various features that constitute the dance did not coalesce into a defined form until toward the end of the 1920s.

Naming the Dancers

A performer of *raqṣ sharqī* was described as a *rāqiṣah*, rather than an *ʿālmah* or a *ghāziyah*. *Rāqiṣah* is a general term for a female dancer, regardless of what style of dance she performs. This term was used for any female dancer performing in one of Egypt's late nineteenth and early twentieth century entertainment halls—whether a local Egyptian woman dancing *raqṣ sharqī*, or a European woman performing a foreign dance style.

There are actually two terms for female dancer in present-day Arabic: *rāqiṣah* and *raqqāṣah*.[9] These terms differ only slightly in spelling and pronunciation, and for most Arabic speakers, there is no distinction in meaning between them. However, in the Egyptian dialect of Arabic, these two terms carry different connotations: *raqqāṣah* is generally derogatory, while *rāqiṣah* is neutral or even positive—a distinction I verified with multiple native speakers of Egyptian Arabic, including ethnomusicologist George Dimitri Sawa (personal communication, February 20, 2016) and musician Sayyid Ḥankish (personal communication, February 7, 2016 and February 20, 2016). According to Sayyid Ḥankish, an accordion player from an established family of traditional entertainers from Cairo's Muḥammad ʿAlī Street, the term *rāqiṣah* is a more positive and respectful designation for a dancer, as it implies that she is an expert in her trade (Sayyid Ḥankish, personal communication, February 20, 2016).

I have found examples of the term *raqqāṣah* in turn-of-the-century sources. For instance, in the first edition of Joseph Habeiche's French-Arabic dictionary, published in 1890, the entry for *danseuse* (female dancer) lists *raqqāṣah* rather than *rāqiṣah* (Habeiche 1890: 136). The term *raqqāṣah* appears on two turn-of-the-century postcards depicting female dancers in Egypt (Figures 4 and 5); the style of these postcards indicates that they were printed after 1878, but no later than 1906.[10]

Yet, at roughly the same time as these examples, the term *rāqiṣah* was in use in the newspaper *al-Ahrām* (e.g., *al-Ahrām* 10 April 1891: 3). More significantly, the term *raqqāṣah* appears to have been entirely absent

Figure 4. Postcard reproduction of the 1864 painting *Danseuse au Harem* by Italian artist Giuseppe Bonnici. Though Bonnici's painting dates to the mid-1860s, the postcard itself was published between 1878 and 1906. The Arabic text (not original to the painting, but added to the postcard) states: "*raqqāṣāt fī Miṣr*" (female dancers in Egypt).

from Arabic-language advertisements for dance performances at theaters and entertainment halls. In these advertisements, which became widespread by the end of the 1920s, the preferred term for a female dancer was *rāqiṣah*. This is particularly interesting, given the nuance in meaning for this term, as described above.

Figure 5. This postcard was published between 1878 and 1906. The Arabic text states: "*raqqāṣāt fī Miṣr*" (female dancers, Egypt).

The terms *ʿālmah* and *ghāziyah* continued to be in common usage. In Joseph Habeiche's French-Arabic dictionary, the entry for *danseuse* (female dancer) lists both *raqqāṣah* and *ghāziyah* (Habeiche 1890: 136), and the entry for *cantatrice* (female singer) lists *ʿālmah* and *mughannīyah* (Habeiche 1890: 79). Similarly, Socrates Spiro's English-Arabic dictionary from 1897 lists *ghāziyah* for female dancer (Spiro 1897: 134) and *ʿālmah* for female singer (Spiro 1897: 441). However, I have found no instances of the terms *ʿālmah* and *ghāziyah* being used in late nineteenth/early twentieth century Arabic-language sources to refer to dancers performing in entertainment halls. The term *ʿālmah* appears periodically in reference to female singers. For example, an 1895 advertisement in *al-Ahrām* announces a musical performance by "*al-ʿālmah, al-muṭribah* [the singer], *al-sayyidah* [the lady]" al-Lāwandīyah (*al-Ahrām* 26 March 1895: 3).

By the 1930s, the terms *ʿālmah*, *ghāziyah*, and *rāqiṣah* had become strongly associated with particular performance contexts. As noted earlier, the term *ʿālmah* designated a common singer/dancer who performed at the weddings and other celebrations of the lower and middle classes of urban Cairo and Alexandria, while the term *ghāziyah* referred to singer/dancers working in the rural villages and the *mawālid*. The term *rāqiṣah* designated a dancer performing in an urban entertainment hall.

However, the emergence of this terminological distinction should not be interpreted to mean that the *rāqiṣāt* who performed *raqṣ sharqī* and the *ʿawālim/ghawāzī* were different women. Clearly, many of the early *rāqiṣāt* were *ʿawālim/ghawāzī* who found work in the entertainment halls of Cairo and Alexandria. Even in the modern day, there is some degree of overlap between the entertainers working in these disparate contexts. Though Van Nieuwkerk argues for a fairly clear-cut division between performers working the "nightclub circuit" and those working at *mawālid* and the traditional weddings of the lower classes (Van Nieuwkerk 1995: 18–19), even among her own informants, there are examples of women who straddled both worlds:

> Sayyida was in demand and worked at many towns outside Cairo. At sixteen, she worked for a few days in the *ṣâla* of Badîʿa Masabni, but the police prohibited it on account of her age. After reaching the required age of twenty-one, she occasionally worked in nightclubs.... She had roles as a dancer in seven films. The greater part of her work, however, was at weddings [Van Nieuwkerk 1995: 73].

Similarly, Sūsū, a retired dancer whom I interviewed in February 2016, worked throughout the 1970s and 1980s in both lower-class weddings and in the nightclubs of Haram Street (personal communication, February 3, 2016). The difference in the modern day is that the terms *ʿālmah* and *ghāziyah* have faded from common usage; present-day Egyptians generally use *rāqiṣah, raqqāṣah,* or *fanānah* (artist) to refer to any dancer, regardless of performance context. However, the connotations of *'ālmah* and *ghāziyah* noted above are still widely understood. The term *'ālmah,* for example, is still associated with the dancers who were based in and around Cairo's Muḥammad 'Alī Street, and who performed primarily at the weddings of Cairo's lower class.

Further, the use of the term *rāqiṣah* should not lead to the conclusion that early performers of *raqṣ sharqī* specialized exclusively in dance. Some of the dancers of the entertainment halls were well-rounded entertainers who not only danced, but sang (a clear connection to the traditional *'awālim/ghawāzī* mode of performance). Shafīqah al-Qibṭīyah was a turn-of-the-century entertainment hall performer who has often been linked to a specific dance act known as *raqṣat al-sham'adān* (i.e., the candelabrum dance, in which a candelabrum is balanced on the dancer's head) (Ward 2013b). However, it is clear that Shafīqah also sang. British author S.H. Leeder notes:

> [F]or years the most scandalous of the public singing women in Cairo bears a name which she has made so famous that I have never met an intelligent person anywhere in Lower Egypt who was not most familiar with it—*Shafika el Coptieh,* or Shafika the Copt [Leeder 1918: 107].

One of Shafīqah's singing and dancing performances is spoofed in a *circa* 1908 Odéon recording by the singer Bahiyah al-Maḥallāwīyah (*Raqṣ Shafīqah* 1908). Singing continued to be part of a *rāqiṣah*'s repertoire well into the twentieth century; dancers can be seen alternately singing then dancing in a variety of Egyptian films from the 1930s and beyond (see, for example, *Bint al-Bāshā al-Mudīr* 1938 and *Gilded Serpent Presents Badia Masabni* 2009 [ca. 1934]).

Summary

Throughout the nineteenth century, Egypt's female professional entertainers weathered the challenges posed by foreign occupation, a capricious government, and conflicting public opinion of their art. By the end of the century, a combination of increasingly systematic governmental regulation and shifting performance opportunities led these women, the *'awālim* and the *ghawāzī,* to seek employment in the newly-established entertainment halls of Cairo and Alexandria. The transition to the formalized performance setting of the entertainment hall enabled the transformation of the traditional dances of the *ʻawālim* and the *ghawāzī* into the concert dance form that would come to be known as *raqṣ sharqī*, and it established the *rāqiṣah*—the dancer of the entertainment hall—as a different category of entertainer from her predecessors. Over a period of roughly forty years—from the 1890s through the 1920s—*raqṣ sharqī* evolved into the dance form that is recognized today. The next four chapters examine specific aspects of the dance during this critical period.

THREE

Reconstructing the Technique of Early *Raqṣ Sharqī*

From the 1890s through the 1920s, *raqṣ sharqī* was emerging and becoming established as a new and distinct dance form. Motion pictures, introduced to Egypt in the 1890s, were growing in popularity during this same period. Yet, to date, no footage has come to light that could provide an incontrovertible visual record of the dance during these critical decades. Therefore, it is necessary to turn to other historical sources in order to reconstruct what *raqṣ sharqī* may have looked like as it developed on the entertainment hall stages of turn-of-the-century Egypt.

In fact, a number of lines of evidence allow for a fairly detailed reconstruction. Primary sources—those contemporary with the birth of *raqṣ sharqī*—include both foreign sources, such as the textual descriptions derived from travelers' accounts and travel guide books, photographs, and picture postcards, as well as indigenous Egyptian sources, such as Arabic-language advertisements and flyers targeted at the local Egyptian population. Secondary sources, including observations and film footage of Egyptian *'awālim* and *ghawāzī* from the 1930s through the present day, as well as film footage of *raqṣ sharqī* performers in the mid-to-late 1930s, supplement the primary evidence and allow some extrapolation. Taken together, these sources give a sense of the technique, aesthetic, performance format, and costuming of early *raqṣ sharqī*. The evidence reveals an organic process wherein, over a thirty to forty year period, the hybridization of the traditional dances of the *'awālim* and *ghawāzī* with new and foreign elements resulted in a recognizably distinct dance form—a process enabled by the move to the entertainment hall milieu. This chapter examines the technical elements of the dance. Aesthetic, performance format and costuming will be discussed separately in the following chapters.

Discussion of Sources

As detailed in the introduction, the accounts of foreign observers provide a vital, if problematic, resource for this study. Fraser (2015) also relied heavily on the observations of foreigners in her investigation of Egyptian dance prior to 1870. However, travelers' accounts from the late nineteenth and early twentieth centuries differ somewhat in nature and availability from those that formed the basis of Fraser's work. With the advent of mass commercial tourism to Egypt in the late nineteenth century, the personal travelogues, diaries, and letters that were commonplace early in the century declined in abundance. Further, with the increasing prevalence of Eastern-inspired dance acts in Western music halls, amusement parks, and circus sideshows in the wake of the various world's fairs (see Carlton 1994), Eastern exoticism became locally accessible to a curious public, and the detailed accounts of Egyptian dance that were typical of earlier periods were simply no longer of interest. While individual travelers' accounts from the late nineteenth and early twentieth centuries certainly exist, many of these narratives were not meant to serve strictly as travel diaries or memoirs, but rather as travel guide books in narrative form. Examples of this sort of travel diary *cum* guide book include Lothaire Loewenbach's *Promenade Autour de l'Afrique, 1907* (1908) and Douglas Sladen's often humorous *Oriental Cairo: The City of the "Arabian Nights"* (1911). Some travel memoirs in the more traditional sense are also available from this period, such as the diaries and letters of British and Australian servicemen stationed in Egypt during World War I; see, for example, Hector Dinning's *Nile to Aleppo, with the Light-horse in the Middle-East* (1920).

Travel guide books in the modern sense were first produced in the early nineteenth century; guide books focused on Egypt were widely available by the end of the century. These books provide valuable information regarding the entertainment venues in Egypt's metropolitan areas, as well as occasional mentions or descriptions of Egyptian dance. Examples include the guide books of Karl Baedeker, John Murray, and Eustace Reynolds-Ball.

Postcards and photographs provide an invaluable visual record of Egyptian dancers and entertainment venues during the critical period in which *raqṣ sharqī* was emerging. These resources corroborate and often supplement the helpful information mined from text sources, particularly descriptions of dancers' costuming. In addition to postcards, *cartes de visite*, small photo cards that were widely shared and collected in the 1860s (Staff 1979: 42–43), provide a valuable visual resource for this study. Though they predate the origin of *raqṣ sharqī* by several decades, their depictions of mid–nineteenth century Egyptian *'awālim* and *ghawāzī* are vital to reconstructing the origins and development of costuming for turn-of-the-century *raqṣ sharqī*. Since most of the postcards, photographs, and *cartes de visite* utilized for this study were produced by and for foreigners, these graphic sources required the same careful "sifting" for Orientalist bias as text sources.

Arabic-language sources from the late nineteenth and early twentieth centuries, particularly advertisements and flyers, reveal a great deal of information about certain aspects of early *raqṣ sharqī*. Many of these indigenous sources name not only the venues in which the dance was performed, but also some of its earliest performers. Further, they document what other types of entertainment were on the bill when *raqṣ sharqī* was performed, suggesting how the evolution of the dance was likely influenced by contemporary developments in Egyptian music and theater. However, as discussed in the prior chapter, terminological ambiguity in the Arabic sources creates difficulties with interpretation.

As previously mentioned, there seems to be no extant film footage of dancers performing in Egyptian entertainment halls during the critical late nineteenth to early twentieth century period when *raqṣ sharqī* arose. Footage of dancers in Egyptian-produced motion pictures prior to the 1930s appears to be lost to history, though dancers are purported to have appeared in some films, such as the silent film *Layla* (released in 1927).[1] The surviving film footage of dancers performing Middle Eastern or Middle Eastern-inspired dances at the nineteenth-to-twentieth century transition consists of a mere handful of films, many of them recorded by Thomas Edison in the United States. It is peculiar that these dance forms, which were such a fixation for European and American observers of the Middle East, would turn up so infrequently in the new medium of motion pictures. Among the Edison films are *Princess Ali* (1895), *Fatima's Coochee-Coochee Dance* from 1896 (Nugent n.d.; *Rare Glimpses: Dances from the Middle East, Volume I* 2007), and *Turkish Dance, Ella Lola* (1898). In addition to these films, there is footage by the Lumière brothers which provides a brief glimpse of dancers at the Exposition Universelle of Paris in 1900 (*L'Expo Universelle de 1900* 1983). Also, there is the American

Mutoscope and Biograph Company's footage of a performer known as Princess Rajah (*Princess Rajah Dance* 1904).

None of these films portrays dancing that is unequivocally Egyptian. Princess Ali's costuming, movements, and manipulation of scarves are all strongly evocative of Algerian dance. The dancers in the Lumière film are costumed as Egyptian dancers, and one of the two women is playing finger cymbals, as would be typical of an Egyptian performer of the time (as discussed later in this chapter). Yet, one of the women dances with scarves and executes movements that look more Algerian than Egyptian. This film will be revisited later in the chapter. The dances of Fatima, Ella Lola, and Princess Rajah all share some of the basic features of the dancing performed by Egyptian *ghawāzī* in the present day, such as stationary and traveling hip shimmies and shoulder shimmies; further, Fatima and Princess Rajah play finger cymbals during their performances—again, a significant feature of Egyptian dance at the time. Yet, both Ella Lola and Princess Rajah were American-born vaudeville performers; Rajah performed at various venues in and around New York City, including Huber's Museum and Hammerstein's (Senelick 1998b: 317). Fatima, whose ethnic origins are unclear, performed Algerian dances at Hammerstein's (Senelick 1998b: 317) and worked as a "cooch dancer" at Coney Island (Carlton 1994: 62). Although it is probable that Fatima, Ella Lola, and Princess Rajah learned some of their movements from native Egyptian dancers (whether directly or indirectly), their performances inform more regarding what was being performed on the American vaudeville circuit than what was being danced on the entertainment hall stages of Cairo and Alexandria. Thus, in the absence of verifiable film footage of turn-of-the-century *raqṣ sharqī* in Egypt, it is necessary to turn to later footage of Egyptian dancers in order to supplement the primary sources described above.

There is a great deal of film footage of *ghawāzī* and *'awālim* performing in the mid to late twentieth century. The most well-known and well-documented group of modern-day *ghawāzī* are the Banāt Māzin ("daughters of Māzin") of Luxor in Upper Egypt. They appear in at least two Egyptian films from the 1960s: *al-Zawjah al-Thāniyah* (*The Second Wife*) in 1967, and *Anā al-Duktūr* (*I'm the Doctor*) in 1968. Extensive footage of the Banāt Māzin is also available in Aisha Ali's documentaries *Dances of Egypt* (2006) and *Wedding in Luxor* (2014), both of which were based on her extensive field research in Egypt. The Banāt Māzin, their dance style, and costuming have also been described in detail in the writings of Edwina Nearing (Nearing 1993, 2004a, 2004b) and Magda Saleh (1979).[2] At the time of this writing, one of the Māzin sisters, Khayrīyah, still actively teaches lessons; I had the opportunity to take a lesson with her in 2013.

Footage of other, lesser known *ghawāzī* groups is also available. The documentary *The Romany Trail* (1992) includes footage and interviews with the Banāt Māzin, as well as brief footage of a group of *ghawāzī* performing outside of Cairo. The film *Latcho Drom* (1993) includes footage of a group of *ghawāzī* from Qinā in Upper Egypt. Footage of several *ghawāzī* performing at a wedding in Sūhāj, also in Upper Egypt, was recorded by Egyptian Muḥammad Ḥāfiẓ in 2005 and made available on his YouTube channel in 2011 (*Raqṣ al-Ghajariyāt* 2005). Footage of various other *ghawāzī* who currently perform at weddings and other celebrations in the vicinity of Qinā and Sūhāj can be found on YouTube.

Also noteworthy are two films of Egyptian dancers—most likely *ghawāzī*—performing in the late 1920s and early 1930s. The first is an extraordinarily brief appearance by a dancer in a British Pathé film from 1926 (*In Memory of Sayyid Ahmad al-Baidawi*). The film documents the *mūlid* of Shaykh Aḥmad al-Badawī in Ṭanṭā (in the Nile Delta) and shows a dancer in the crowd, but only from a distance. The second is a performance by a dancer, musicians, and singers in a film illustrating life in Upper Egypt *circa* 1930 (*Une Marché in Haute-Egypte*). There are aspects of this dancer's performance that are consistent with textual descriptions of Egyptian dance at the turn of the nineteenth and twentieth centuries, as well as with footage of *ghawāzī* in the late twentieth and early twenty-first centuries. Confusingly, however, there are other elements of her performance that are far more reminiscent of Maghrebi dances than anything Egyptian. This film will be revisited later in this chapter.

Footage of the modern-day *'awālim* of Cairo and Alexandria is available. A troupe of *'awālim* (one dancer accompanied by several *'awālim* playing drums) appears in the 1937 Egyptian film *al-'Izz Bahdalah* (*Too Much Money is a Nuisance*). The famous Muḥammad 'Alī Street *'ālmah* Nazlah al-'Ādil is featured in the 1991 German documentary *Die Königin der Mohammed-Ali-Strasse* (*The Queen of Muḥammad 'Alī Street*); the film includes three performances by Nazlah, as well as a performance by one of her protégés, a *ghāziyah* working in Manṣūra (in the Nile Delta). Additionally, Nazlah can be seen performing in the 1966 Egyptian film *Qaṣr al-Shūq* (*Palace of Desire*). Nazlah's dancing is also described by Magda Saleh (1979). Footage of the innumerable dancers who currently perform for Egypt's urban lower and middle classes is widely available via web sites such as YouTube and Vimeo.

To date, the earliest surviving film footage of *raqṣ sharqī* performers dates to the mid-to-late 1930s. The available footage includes performances by Badīʻah Maṣābnī and her troupe in the mid–1930s (*Gilded Serpent Presents Badia Masabni* 2009 [ca. 1934]), Taḥīyah Carioca in the 1936 film *Khafīr al-Darak* (*The Policeman*) and in the 1939 film *Layla Mumṭirah* (*Rainy Night*), Rūḥīyah Fawzī and another unnamed dancer in the 1937 film *al-ʻIzz Bahdalah* (*Too Much Money Is a Nuisance*), Bibā Ibrāhīm in the 1938 film *Shaī' Min Lā Shaī'* (*Something from Nothing*), and a dancer from the troupe of Naʻamat al-Miṣrīyah (possibly Naʻamat herself) in the 1938 film *Bint al-Bāshā al-Mudīr* (*Daughter of the Manager*). Taken together with the other lines of evidence already described, this footage reveals a great deal about the stylistic evolution of *raqṣ sharqī* from its initial transition to the entertainment hall stage to its widespread appearance on the silver screen in the 1930s.

An Overview of Early Raqṣ Sharqī *Technique*

Foreign accounts of *raqṣ sharqī* in Egypt's turn-of-the-century entertainment halls are consistent in their description of the dance:

> It was not what I would call dancing at all. She simply walked up and down the stage swaying her body about, the dancing being all from the hips up [*South Australian Chronicle* 17 June 1893: 16].

> [A] girl laden with jewels and ropes of pearls on her neck, and in every plait of her hair, twists and twirls about the stage with solemn slow iteration. She has on her hands rough castanets with which she beats the maddening time to a tune so hideous that the European nerves tremble at it. Her feet scarcely seem to move. But the expression comes from the centre of the body, which shakes like jelly. On and on she goes, round and round, perpetually twisting, wagging her body just as some people can wag their noses and their ears, until at last she sinks exhausted on a sofa [Scott 1894].

> The dance du ventre is not a dance in our acceptance of the term at all; it consists of tremblings, wrigglings and jerkings of the lower abdominal muscles, including those of the hips, loins, and back; the dancer in short steps, moves round and round the stage, sometimes back to the audience, in order that she may show, in detail, her movements in as great variety as possible [*Star* 20 September 1902: 2].

> A woman who resembles La Goulue rises, she is very young, but quite stout. She is dressed in pink, covered with gaudy trinkets, her belly is bare; she produces a variety of movements and tremors, it's called, as everyone knows, the belly dance. She accompanies herself with two pairs of small cymbals attached to fingers like castanets, and these contortions last a long time; however she pauses to empty a beer that is sent to her by an enthusiastic spectator [Loewenbach 1908: 219–220, translated by the author, with assistance from Christine Ferhat].

Accounts such as these, supplemented by descriptions and film footage of *'awālim* and *ghawāzī*, as well as film footage of *raqṣ sharqī* performers in the 1930s, suggest four fundamental technical elements of early *raqṣ sharqī*:

1. The dance was generally performed solo, though choreographed group dance and chorus lines began to appear sometime before the mid–1930s.
2. The primary movements of the dance were localized in the torso, with minimal footwork.
3. The dance was performed to the accompaniment of a *takht*, a traditional ensemble of singers and musicians; however, as early as the 1930s, the traditional *takht* began to give way to a larger and more elaborate *firqa*, with a mix of traditional and Western instrumentation.
4. The dancers frequently played finger cymbals during their performances.

The available evidence reveals the gradual adoption and integration of certain new, and often foreign, technical elements into the technique base of traditional *'awālim/ghawāzī* dance. The fundamental movements of early *raqṣ sharqī* were not drastically different from those of *'awālim/ghawāzī* dance. However, certain technical aspects of *raqṣ sharqī*, such as a more erect posture/alignment and the eventual incorporation of choreographed group dance, set it apart from the dances of the *'awālim* and *ghawāzī*.

Solo Performance

Among the *'awālim* and the *ghawāzī*, both historically and in the present day, both solo and pair/group performance occur (Arnold 1882: 92, Denon 1803: 119, Jomard 1822: 733, Knox 1879: 571, Taylor 1854: 134–137, Warner 1900: 380–381; see also footage of modern-day *'awālim* and *ghawāzī*). However, pair or small-group performance should not imply synchronization. Nineteenth-century text sources indicate that in some instances, pairs or groups of dancers coordinated their movements with one another (e.g., Warner 1900: 380–381). This coordination or synchronization is also evident among certain *'awālim* and *ghawāzī* performers in the modern day; for example, there is ample footage of the Banāt Māzin performing in well-synchronized pairs or groups (*Anā al-Duktūr* 1968, *Dances of Egypt* 2006, *al-Zawjah al-Thāniyah* 1967). Yet, nineteenth-century sources also describe pair or group performances wherein each dancer seems to move in her own distinct and individualistic manner (e.g., Taylor 1854: 136–137). In similar fashion, the *ghawāzī* filmed in Sūhāj in 2005 dance in pairs and as a group, but with little apparent coordination or synchronization with one another (*Raqṣ al-Ghajariyāt* 2005).

Solo performance seems to have been somewhat more common in early *raqṣ sharqī* than in the dances of the *'awālim* and *ghawāzī*. Postcards and photographs rarely depict multiple dancers performing at the same time, and travelers' accounts generally only allude to soloists. Arabic-language advertisements announcing *raqṣ sharqī* performances by featured soloists begin to appear in the 1920s. For example, an advertisement for shows on April 3, 4, and 5, 1927 at the Victoria Theater (located in Ramses Square in Cairo) announces: "During intermissions, *raqṣ sharqī* from the dancer Līnā" (*al-Ahrām* 3 April 1927: 5). Līnā was also featured in the May 15, 1927 line-up at the Azbakīyah Garden Theater (*al-Ahrām* 15 May 1927: 6).

At some point prior to the mid–1930s, *raqṣ sharqī* began to incorporate choreographed group dance and chorus lines, elements that would become commonplace in the Egyptian films of the 1940s and 1950s. Footage of Badī'ah Maṣābnī's troupe in the mid–1930s reveals a chorus line of choreographed dancers backing up Badī'ah as she sings, dances, and plays finger cymbals (*Gilded Serpent Presents Badia Masabni* 2009 [ca. 1934]). However, the currently available evidence does not reveal exactly when these features became a part of *raqṣ sharqī*. The concept of dance choreography as it exists in modern concert dance—a planned and set series of movements and steps executed in a consciously and deliberately structured performance space—is not indigenous to Egyptian dance (Fahmy 1987: 9). However, Egyptian dancers performing in the entertainment halls of Cairo and Alexandria were frequently exposed to choreographed European and American dance performances. The appearance of Egyptian dance performances with choreographed group dance and chorus lines marks one of the most significant adaptations of Western dance technique to *raqṣ sharqī*. The introduction of choreography into *raqṣ sharqī* also had implications for the dance's aesthetic; this issue will be addressed in the next chapter.

Fundamental Movements

Broad similarities exist between descriptive accounts of *'awālim* and *ghawāzī* from the early nineteenth century and those of entertainment hall performers from the late nineteenth/early twentieth centuries (such as those noted above), suggesting that the core torso-based movements of early *raqṣ sharqī* were present in the dances of Egypt's *'awālim* and *ghawāzī* much earlier in history. Consider Jomard's account from the early nineteenth century:

> The *a'lmeh* visit private homes, on the occasion of weddings and other circumstances; they dance to the sound of instruments and accompanied by song. The style of these dances is nothing like those which we know in Europe, if not in a part of Spain where the Moors have left their practices. It is known that the principal and even sole character of these dances consists of continual and more or less flexible movements of the waist: all these movements are able, and they follow the expression of the song. The dancer, the hands adorned with castanets, makes all sorts of amorous gestures; sometimes she sits down and performs the same movements with a flexibility and an ease that astonish [Jomard 1822: 733].

It seems that early *raqṣ sharqī* was also similar in technique to the dancing of rural *ghawāzī* in the latter half of the nineteenth century. Knox describes a performance by a group of *ghawāzī* at Qinā in Upper Egypt:

> The musicians struck up, and the girls—six in number—took their positions in a circle. At the sound of the music they began to move about the room with a sort of gliding motion, accompanied by a curious wriggle of the body at the hips, while all the rest of it remained still. It was a motion from side to side performed quite rapidly, and with due deference to the sound of the drums which were all the time kept in operation, and was quite unlike anything in the ballet as seen in Europe or America. There was none of the dancing of the kind for which Fanny Ellsler and Taglioni are famous, and from an occidental point of view it was rather disappointing as a dance [Knox 1879: 571].

Warner's account of a *ghawāzī* performance at the home of the American consular agent in Luxor is similar:

> At a turn in the music, the girl in red and the girl in yellow stand up; for an instant they raise their castanets till the time of the music is caught, and then start forward, with less of languor and a more skipping movement than we expected; and they are not ungraceful as they come rapidly down the hall, throwing the arms aloft and the feet forward, to the rattle of the castanets. These latter are small convex pieces of brass, held between the thumb and finger, which have a click like the rattle of the snake. In mid-advance they stop, face each other, *chassée*, retire, and again come further forward, stop, and the peculiar portion of the dance begins, which is not dancing at all, but a quivering, undulating motion given to the body, as the girl stands with feet planted wide apart. The feet are still, the head scarcely stirs, except with an almost imperceptible snake-like movement, but the muscles of the body to the hips quiver in time to the monotonous music, in muscular thrills, in waves running down, and at intervals extending below the waist. Sometimes one side of the body quivers while the other is perfectly still, and then the whole frame, for a second, shares in the ague. It is certainly an astonishing muscular perform-

> ance, but you could not call it either graceful or pleasing. Some people see in the intention of the dance a deep symbolic meaning, something about the Old Serpent of the Nile, with its gliding, quivering movement and its fatal fascination. Others see in it only the common old Snake that was in Eden. I suppose in fact that it is the old and universal Oriental dance, the chief attraction of which never was its modesty [Warner 1900: 380–381].

The technique described here is also observable among Egyptian *'awālim* and *ghawāzī* performers in the present day. Footage of the Banāt Māzin *ghawāzī* of Luxor, the Qinā *ghawāzī* featured in *Latcho Drom*, the Sūhāj *ghawāzī* recorded by Muḥammad Ḥāfiẓ, and the *'ālmah* in the film *al-'Izz Bahdalah* demonstrates the same focus on torso-based movements, particularly hip movements such as stationary and traveling hip shimmies, and the same lack of elaborate footwork. Head slides, which are alluded to by Warner, are also common among *'awālim* and *ghawāzī* in the present (see, for example, Nazlah al-'Ādil in *Die Königin der Mohammed-Ali-Strasse*), and they were performed by the *ghāziyah* in *Une Marché in Haute-Egypte* (1930).

Footage of *raqṣ sharqī* performers from the mid-to-late 1930s reveals broad similarities to the *'awālim* and *ghawāzī* movement vocabulary described above—in particular, a continued focus on torso-based movements, rather than on intricate footwork. It seems safe to conclude that hip movements, particularly stationary and traveling hip shimmies, were the central feature of the dance from the 1890s through the 1920s, just as they have been in the dances of the *'awālim* and *ghawāzī* throughout history. The universal presence of shoulder shimmies among present-day *'awālim* and *ghawāzī* as well as among performers of *raqṣ sharqī* in the 1930s strongly suggests that shoulder shimmies were also part of the movement repertoire of early *raqṣ sharqī*, even though they are not explicitly described by contemporary foreign observers. Similarly, head slides were probably among the typical movements of early *raqṣ sharqī*. Elaborate traveling steps were not part of the dance, nor were elaborate arm movements.

Importantly, the 1930s *raqṣ sharqī* footage reveals several movements in addition to this basic repertoire, though, it is unclear exactly when these movements were incorporated into the dance. A vertical "figure eight" of the hips—sometimes executed in place, sometimes performed while traveling—was a common movement in 1930s *raqṣ sharqī*. Certain arm and hand positions were common. In one position, the arms were partially raised, with the hands held together near the forehead; notably, the Sūhāj *ghawāzī* performed this action in 2005. In another, the arms were raised overhead, generally with the hands meeting. In both positions, elbows were usually bent. Arms and hands moved fluidly and gently from raised to lowered positions and back again. Hands were often softly turned or rotated at the wrists. Sometimes the dancer executed a rhythmic, two-handed finger snap, as seen in *al-'Izz Bahdalah* (1937) and in *Bint al-Bāshā al-Mudīr* (1938). This gesture, which is still performed by Egyptian dancers in the present day, is widespread in the Middle East, and probably of considerable antiquity (see Saleh 1979: 116–119).

Acrobatic feats have been commonplace in *'awālim* and *ghawāzī* dances throughout their history (*Die Königin der Mohammed-Ali-Strasse* 1991, Duff Gordon 1865: 160–161, Jomard 1822: 733). Examples include bending backward from a standing or kneeling position until the head touches the floor, descending to the floor in the splits, and other similar contortions. During these feats, dancers generally continued to execute torso-based movements. For example, in *Die Königin der Mohammed-Ali-Strasse* (1991), Nazlah al-'Ādil can be seen shimmying each of her buttocks while in the splits. Yet these exercises are rarely described by late nineteenth and early twentieth century observers of early *raqṣ sharqī*. In one of the dance performances in the 1938 film *Bint al-Bāshā al-Mudīr*, the dancer lowers herself partway to the floor in the splits, then descends completely to the floor on her knees and executes a full backbend. The presence of these sorts of feats in 1930s *raqṣ sharqī*, combined with their widespread prevalence among the *'awālim* and *ghawāzī*, suggests that they may have been a feature of early *raqṣ sharqī*.

Gymnastic feats remained an occasional part of *raqṣ sharqī* throughout the twentieth century. For example, Nabawīyah Muṣṭafa can be seen performing an extraordinary backbend while in the splits in the 1948 Egyptian film *Narjis*. However, these acts appear to have declined in prevalence as *raqṣ sharqī* continued to diverge from *'awālim/ghawāzī* dance. Tellingly, among present-day *raqṣ sharqī* performers, these sorts of acrobatic exercises are sometimes used to evoke early twentieth century *'awālim* dance and culture. See, for example, Fifi 'Abduh's *'ālmah*-style performance to the accompaniment of a Ḥasab Allāh brass band (widely popular in Cairo in the early twentieth century) in *Fifi Abdo: The Egyptian Star* (2005).

Dancing while balancing objects such as bottles, candelabra, and chairs has been common among the *'awālim* and *ghawāzī* from at least the mid–nineteenth century through the present day (Arnold 1882: 266–267, *Die Königin der Mohammed-Ali-Strasse* 1991, Klunzinger 1878: 190, Ninde 1886: 249–250, Vincent 1895: 185). Several travelers to Luxor in the 1880s and 1890s (Arnold 1882: 266–267, Ninde 1886: 249–250, Vincent 1895: 185) described dancers balancing a bottle, in the mouth of which was a lighted candle:

> After a brief pause one of the girls placed a bottle, full of water and containing a lighted candle, upon her head, and nicely poised it during a long dance of both slow and rapid movements, including lying down and turning over and over upon the floor [Vincent 1895: 185].

Descriptions and photographs abound of Egyptian dancers performing similar balancing acts at the various world's fairs that took place in the late nineteenth and early twentieth centuries. For example, an article in Spain's *Iris* magazine describes and illustrates dancers balancing objects as varied as cups, water pipes, and candelabra at the Exposition Universelle of Paris in 1900 (Mendoza 1900). Yet such acts are seldom described in contemporary accounts of performers in Egypt's entertainment halls.

One of the most distinctive balancing acts, *raqṣat al-sham'adān* (the candelabrum dance), has been performed by Egyptian dancers since the late nineteenth century. In *raqṣat al-sham'adān*, the performer balances a candelabrum on her head while performing acrobatic feats such as descending into the splits. Like other balancing acts, *raqṣat al-sham'adān* is well-documented among the Egyptian entertainers performing at the Exposition Universelle of Paris in 1900 (Mendoza 1900), and some version of this act was also performed at Chicago's Columbian Exposition in 1893 (Figure 6). Additionally, *raqṣat al-sham'adān* appears fairly frequently in Egyptian film beginning in the 1940s. Nevertheless, firsthand accounts of this dance being performed in turn-of-the-century Egyptian entertainment halls are few and far between. A rare account appears in Bruce Reynold's "pleasure guide" entitled *A Cocktail Continentale* (1926). Of a performer at a venue called "A Thousand Nights" (the Thousand and One Nights Theater, located near the Azbakīyah Gardens, and well-documented in other sources from the period), he writes:

> Next a Turkish Trophy, almost as fat, comes out, and does a real old-time Hootchy-cootchy. A candelabra on her head. And she wiggles and twists and tosses her body all over the place, still balancing the candelabra. All the Egyptian men in the audience shout their love to her [Reynolds 1926: 184–185].

This reference, combined with the widespread prevalence of balancing acts among the *'awālim* and *ghawāzī*, indicates that these acts were sometimes part of early *raqṣ sharqī*.

Western influences on dance posture and alignment become apparent in *raqṣ sharqī* in the 1930s. Emphasis on body lift and bodily extensions

Figure 6. This is a detail from a Charles Saalburg illustration that appeared in an 1893 issue of Chicago's *Inter Ocean* newspaper. The illustration depicts various scenes from the Midway Plaisance of the Columbian Exposition that was taking place that year in Chicago. At the center, detailed here, is a depiction of one of the Egyptian dancers who performed at the Exposition. It is unclear whether she is balancing an actual *sham'adān* or a tray of candles on top of a vase. Nevertheless, this illustration indicates that the precedent for something resembling *raqṣat al-sham'adān* was established as early as 1893 (courtesy of Cynthia Thornbury).

is central to Western dance forms such as ballet, but quite alien to many non-Western dance forms (Kealiinohomoku 2001: 38). Selma Jeanne Cohen, writing of the history of ballet, notes:

> Since the first ballet dancers were not professionals, but rather members of a monarch's court, they were expected to move with erect nobility of carriage as well

> as with precision. Soon, their technical dexterity, especially when it appeared effortless, was found attractive to audiences, so dancers were eager to develop it. They learned that rotating the legs outward from the hip gave them greater freedom of movement, and the *en dehors* position became a hallmark of ballet. As technical dexterity became increasingly important, the verticality of the body had to be controlled, so that the movement would appear effortless. A basic vocabulary of movements—steps, jumps, and turns—was established [Cohen 1998: 130].

Although the dance acts performed in European music halls and American vaudeville halls generally lacked the polish and refinement of the ballets performed on the grand European opera stages, they shared with the latter an aesthetic that valued an erectness or uprightness of bearing. The many popular dance manuals published at the turn of the century in Europe and the U.S. reiterate the importance of erectness in European and American dance:

> In the modern dances the dancer stands with lithe grace and ease, but very erect, and dances with her feet, not with her whole body. Her outstretched fingers rest against the palm of her partner's hand; her other hand rests on his arm, and there should be space between. Then the lady should hold herself erect, that this space may remain there. Flouncing elbows, pumping arms, fantastic dips, and whirlwind turns all detract not only from the grace of the dance, but from the charm of the dancer [Castle 1914: 136].

The value placed on erect posture in dance was firmly grounded in Euro-American cultural associations of upright carriage with honor, dignity, and proper etiquette (see Vigarello 1989).

A comparison of footage of *raqṣ sharqī* performers from the mid-to-late 1930s with footage of *'awālim* and *ghawāzī* performers from the twentieth century, as well as with photographs and postcards of performers at the turn of the century, suggests an adoption of Western posture and alignment sometime prior to the mid–1930s. The *raqṣ sharqī* performers of the 1930s exhibited a very erect posture, with the upper torso lifted and centered over the pelvis, in direct contrast to the posture of both the *'awālim/ghawāzī* and the earlier entertainment hall performers, in which the upper torso was relaxed and held slightly behind the center of gravity of the pelvis. Compare the posture of turn-of-the-century dancers onstage at Cairo's El Dorado entertainment hall with that of Taḥīyah Carioca in the 1939 film *Layla Mumṭirah* (Figures 8 and 9). These postural differences are also apparent in the 1937 film *al-'Izz Bahdalah* when one compares the two *raqṣ sharqī* performers with the *'ālmah* in the same film. The dancers of the 1930s also tended to perform with their legs closer together.

The postural changes in *raqṣ sharqī* have often been erroneously attributed to a shift from dancing barefoot to dancing in heeled shoes (see, for example, Buonaventura 1998: 150). However, as will be discussed in greater detail in Chapter Six, Egyptian dancers were performing in heeled shoes as early as the 1880s, long before the shift to a more erect posture took place. Rather than being attributable to a change in footwear, the postural changes described above likely reflect the deliberate incorporation of Western dance posture into *raqṣ sharqī* sometime between the 1910s and the 1930s.

There is little evidence that the adoption of Western posture and alignment was accompanied by a corresponding adoption of Euro-American attitudes associating upright bearing with honor, dignity, and good manners. *Raqṣ sharqī* performers were no more respected in Egyptian society than their *ʿawālim* and *ghawāzī* counterparts. In fact, because they performed in entertainment halls—where dance was detached from the traditional social occasions that had previously justified its performance, and where the practice of *fatḥ* was widespread—the performers of *raqṣ sharqī* were more prone to perceptions of impropriety than *ʿawālim* and *ghawāzī* (an issue that will be explored further in the next chapter). For these reasons, I treat the adoption of Western posture and alignment as a change in technique, rather than a change in aesthetic.

Other non-native elements that eventually became part of *raqṣ sharqī* include elaborate traveling steps and complex arm movements; these are generally considered to be derived from ballet and ballroom dance technique. However, these features are not immediately apparent in the footage of performers from the 1930s. In fact, the extent of the traveling executed by *raqṣ sharqī* performers of the 1930s were small steps—usually with accompanying hip movements—traveling forward, back, side-to-side, or in a small circle—not substantially different from the styles of the *ʿawālim* and *ghawāzī*. Dancers occasionally executed turns and spins, but again, these were not fundamentally different from the turns and spins sometimes performed by the *ʿawālim* and *ghawāzī*. The large, sweeping traveling steps and the elaborate turns and spins that have come to characterize the "Golden Age" of early-to-mid twentieth century *raqṣ sharqī* are not widely apparent until the Egyptian films of the 1940s and 1950s. As discussed earlier, typical arm and hand positions evident in the 1930s included one in which the arms were partially raised, with hands held together near the forehead, and another in which the arms were raised overhead. Arms and hands transitioned fluidly and gently from raised to lowered positions. Soft turns of the hands, as well as finger snaps, were commonplace.

Musical Accompaniment

At the turn of the nineteenth and twentieth centuries, *raqṣ sharqī* was generally performed to the accompaniment of a *takht*, a small ensemble of singers and musicians performing traditional music with traditional instruments. Textual descriptions, combined with photographs and postcards from the period, indicate that the early *takht* for *raqṣ sharqī* consisted of melody instruments such as the *'ūd* (fretless stringed instrument, ancestor of the lute), the *nay* (end-blown flute), and the *kāwālā* (another style of end-blown flute), and percussion instruments such as the *riq* (small frame drum with cymbals, similar to a tambourine) and the goblet-shaped drum known as the *ṭablah* or *darbūkah*. Other traditional Egyptian melody instruments such as the *mizmār*, the *arghūl*, and the *rabābah* were more typically associated with music and dance in Egypt's rural towns and villages, as they are to this day, and are rarely seen in photographs and postcards of dancers onstage in Egypt's urban entertainment halls. By contrast, the urban *qānūn*, an instrument often associated with "art" music, was frequently part of the *takht* for *raqṣ sharqī*. In the late nineteenth century, the violin was gradually incorporated into the Egyptian *takht*, and this Western instrument was a regular part of the *takht* for *raqṣ sharqī* as early as the 1920s.

Notably, it appears that the *'awālim* who continued to perform at the weddings and other celebrations of the urban lower and middle classes danced to the same accompanying instruments as contemporary *raqṣ sharqī* performers. Figure 7 shows the famous Cairo *'ālmah* Zūbah al-Klūbātīyah and another unknown *'ālmah* seated in front of a *takht* that included *'ūd*, *qānūn*, and percussion. At least in terms of the composition of the *takht*, there appears to have been no substantial difference between the musical accompaniment for *raqṣ sharqī* and that for contemporary urban *'awālim* dance.

The famed violinist Sāmī al-Shawwā recorded several dance tunes in the late 1920s and early 1930s. A number of these recordings are available in a compilation of al-Shawwā's works released by the Arab Music Archiving and Research Foundation in 2015 (*Sāmī al-Shawwā: Prince of the Violin* 2015). Four of the dance tunes included in this compilation, *Raqṣ al-Hawānim* (*Dance of the Ladies*), *Raqṣ al-Farfūrah* (*Dance of the Delicate/Spoiled*), *Raqṣ al-Ghandūrah* (*Dance of the Coquette*), and *Raqṣ Shiftishī* (*Revealing/Naughty Dance*), were recorded before 1927 and reveal what an early *raqṣ sharqī* performance may have sounded like (bearing in mind that these recordings were meant to showcase al-Shawwā's violin playing,

Figure 7. Cairo *'ālmah* Zūbah al-Klūbātīyah (right) and another unknown *'ālmah* seated in front of their accompanying *takht*. The *qānūn* player is Zūbah's second husband, Aḥmad 'Alī (courtesy of Sayyid Ḥankish).

so the violin is likely more prominent here than it would have been in a live dance performance).

These pieces are structured around binary rhythms, particularly common four-beat rhythmic patterns such as *maqsūm* and *waḥdah*. Notably, the music of the *ghawāzī* in the present day shares a similar binary rhythmic structure, with variations on the *maqsūm* being particularly common; see, for example, Aisha Ali's footage of the Banāt Māzin (*Dances of Egypt* 2006 and *Wedding in Luxor* 2014) and her music recordings (*Music of the Fellahin* 1997 and *Music of the Ghawazee* 2004). The accompaniment to al-Shawwā's violin is consistent with the urban *takht* described by contemporary observers and depicted in photographs and postcards. In *Raqṣ al-Hawānim,* al-Shawwā is accompanied by *'ūd* and *qānūn.* In *Raqṣ al-Farfūrah, Raqṣ al-Ghandūrah,* and *Raqṣ Shiftishī,* he is accompanied by *qānūn* and *ṭablah. Raqṣ al-Farfūrah* also incorporates a vocalist. Again, this instrumentation does not appear to differ in any substantive way from the *takht* of contemporary *'awālim.*

That the musical accompaniment for early *raqṣ sharqī* shared core features such as rhythmic structure and instrumentation with the music of the *ghawāzī* and the *'awālim* reveals a clear continuity between early *raqṣ sharqī* and the traditional Egyptian dances from which it originated. This point is further borne out by the fact that one of the tunes recorded by al-Shawwā, *Raqṣ al-Hawānim,* is traditional and pre-dates the development of *raqṣ sharqī.* Ethnomusicologist George Dimitri Sawa, citing the violinist Tawfīq al-Ṣabbāgh, notes that this piece was originally titled *Raqṣ al-'Awālim* and that it was performed by *'awālim* for women at weddings (personal communication, July 2, 2013). *Raqṣ al-Hawānim* has remained popular with *'awālim/ghawāzī* and *raqṣ sharqī* performers in the modern day; the *'ālmah* Nazlah al-'Ādil can be seen performing to it in *Die Königin der Mohammed-Ali-Strasse* (1991), and the *ghāziyah* Khayrīyah Māzin, together with researcher Aisha Ali, can be seen dancing to a rendition in *Wedding in Luxor* (2014).

The small traditional *takht,* performing the sort of dance music exemplified by Sāmī al-Shawwā's recordings, continued to accompany *raqṣ sharqī* performers well into the 1930s. Examples can be seen in the films *Khafīr al-Darak* (1936), *Bint al-Bāshā al-Mudīr* (1938), and *Layla Mumṭirah* (1939). However, from at least the 1930s onward, dancers were increasingly accompanied by larger and more varied musical ensembles. For example, refer to *Gilded Serpent Presents Badia Masabni* (2009 [ca. 1934]). This shift was in keeping with musical trends of the time, as the larger ensemble, or *firqa,* introduced and popularized in Egyptian musical theater gradually supplanted the smaller *takht* (Danielson1997: 45, 99; Racy 2003: 80–81, 93–94). Additionally, beginning as early as the 1930s, the accompaniment for *raqṣ sharqī* included a mix of traditional and Western instrumentation (beyond the violin, which, as previously noted, had already been incorporated into Egyptian ensembles in the late nineteenth century). Occasionally, dancers performed *raqṣ sharqī* to ensembles consisting entirely of Western instrumentation; an example of this can be seen in one of the performances in *al-'Izz Bahdalah* (1937). The shift from the traditional *takht* to the larger, more elaborate *firqa,* together with the incorporation of a variety of Western instruments, marks a significant divergence between *raqṣ sharqī* and the dances of the *'awālim* and *ghawāzī*.

Badī'ah Maṣābnī, in a 1966 television interview, states that she was the first to integrate Arabic and foreign music:

> I'm the one who mixed Arabic music with foreign music. It used to be that [*Arabic*] bands worked alone. Orchestras didn't work with bands. [*She means orchestras that played foreign music.*] I'm the one who mixed them both together and made them work together [*Badia Masabni in 1966 Television Interview* n.d.].

However, it is quite clear that this trend was well underway long before Badī'ah opened her first entertainment hall in 1926. For example, a performance at Cairo's Abbaye des Roses on February 9, 1917, included a mixed orchestra of Middle Eastern instruments and piano ('Abd al-Wahāb 2001: 47). It may be that Badī'ah meant that she was the first to integrate Arabic and foreign music as accompaniment for *raqṣ sharqī*, which is indeed possible, but not proven by the currently available evidence.

Finger Cymbals

Performers of *raqṣ sharqī* at the turn of the nineteenth and twentieth centuries routinely played finger cymbals during their performances. Photographs and postcards from the period frequently (though not universally) depict dancers wearing cymbals, and the accounts of contemporary observers indicate that cymbals were a regular part of dance performances in Egypt's entertainment halls. However, it is undeniable that dancers periodically performed without cymbals. For example, a postcard of Cairo's El Dorado entertainment hall shows two dancers wearing cymbals, while the third, instead of wearing cymbals, holds a small scarf in each hand (Figure 8). Similarly, while the *'awālim* and *ghawāzī* throughout history have generally played finger cymbals during their performances, there are abundant examples of these dancers performing without them. For example, the Sūhāj *ghawāzī* recorded by Muḥammad Ḥāfiẓ in 2005 did not play cymbals (*Raqṣ al-Ghajariyāt* 2005). In the documentary (*Die Königin der Mohammed-Ali-Strasse* 1991), the famous Muḥammad 'Alī Street *'ālmah* Nazlah al-'Ādil plays cymbals in only one of her three performances.

Finger cymbals continued to be played by *raqṣ sharqī* performers into the 1930s and beyond, but based on the limited available footage from the 1930s, it seems that performance without cymbals became more commonplace in that decade. While Badī'ah Maṣābnī can be seen playing

Figure 8. Dancers onstage at Cairo's El Dorado entertainment hall (Lichtenstern and Harari postcard, *circa* 1900).

cymbals in footage from the mid–1930s (*Gilded Serpent Presents Badia Masabni* 2009 [ca. 1934]), finger cymbals are absent from performances by Taḥīyah Carioca[3] in 1936 (*Khafīr al-Darak*) and 1939 (*Layla Mumṭirah*, Figure 9), Rūḥīyah Fawzī and an unnamed dancer in 1937 (*al-'Izz Bahdalah*), Bibā Ibrāhīm in 1938 (*Shaī' Min Lā Shaī'*), and a dancer from the troupe of Na'amat al-Miṣrīyah in 1938 (*Bint al-Bāshā al-Mudīr*).

The Question of Foreign Influence

What of foreign influences on the technique of early *raqṣ sharqī*? It is already clear from the previous discussion that *raqṣ sharqī* absorbed certain technical elements from European and American music and dance, and that these profoundly impacted the dance. By the mid–1930s, Egyptian *raqṣ sharqī* had incorporated the Western features of choreographed group dance and chorus lines. Further, sometime between the 1910s and the 1930s, Egyptian *raqṣ sharqī* performers adopted Western dance posture. Finally, following contemporary trends in Egyptian music, dancers from the 1930s onward were increasingly accompanied by a large musical ensemble that included a mix of indigenous and Western instrumentation.

Figure 9. Taḥīyah Carioca in the 1939 film *Layla Mumṭirah*.

In considering foreign influence, it is important to explore the impact of other Middle Eastern and North African dance styles on early *raqṣ sharqī*. As mentioned earlier, the *ghāziyah* in *Une Marché in Haute-Egypte* (1930) performs several seemingly non-Egyptian movements with significant implications for this discussion. Many aspects of this dancer's performance are fully consistent with textual descriptions of early *raqṣ sharqī*, as well as with footage of *ghawāzī* in the late twentieth and early twenty-first centuries. However, some elements of her performance are far more reminiscent of Maghrebi dances than anything Egyptian. At one point, she grasps two small scarves and performs a scarf dance that has no parallels in Egyptian *ghawāzī* dance, but does have analogues in Algerian dance (see Aisha Ali's *Aisha Dances Volume II* 2006) for an illustration of Algerian Ouled Naïl dance). Further, some of her pelvic movements (e.g., tucks or thrusts where the bottom of the pelvis is pulled forward) bear a strong resemblance to the dance of Algeria's Ouled Naïl performers. Notably, the postcard of Cairo's El Dorado entertainment hall referenced earlier shows a dancer holding a small scarf in each hand, in the same manner as the *ghāziyah* in the 1930 film (Figure 10). Was there an indigenous Egyptian scarf dance, now obsolete, that looked very similar to Maghrebi scarf dances? Alternatively, did Egyptian dancers somehow learn Maghrebi scarf dances and integrate them into their own repertoire?

There is compelling evidence for the second explanation. First, recall that in the Lumière footage of the 1900 Exposition Universelle of Paris, the two dancers are attired in Egyptian-style costuming, but one of the women dances with scarves and executes Algerian-style movements (*L'Expo Universelle de 1900* 1983). Dancers from all over the Middle East and North Africa performed at the world's fairs. The Lumière footage suggests the mingling of Egyptian and Maghrebi dance styles at the fair. Second, there is evidence of Maghrebi dancers living and working in

Figure 10. Detail of dancer onstage at Cairo's El Dorado entertainment hall (Lichtenstern and Harari postcard, *circa* 1900).

Egypt in the nineteenth and early twentieth centuries. For example, Lucy Duff Gordon, in one of her letters from the early 1860s, mentions a dancer named "El Maghribeeyeh" (the Moroccan) (Duff Gordon 1865: 224–225).

This evidence suggests that, given the opportunity, Egyptian dancers were willing to integrate features from other Middle Eastern and North African dances into their repertoire. Thus, it is tremendous significance that performers from all over the Middle East, North Africa, and Turkey appeared on the stages of Egypt's turn-of-the-century entertainment halls. An article from the November 1913 issue of *al-Zuhūr* magazine indicates that Egyptian dance—variously referred to as *al-raqṣ al-miṣrī* (Egyptian dance) or *al-raqṣ al-baladī* (native dance) by the author—was being performed not only by Egyptians, but by Moroccans, Persians, Syrians, and Tunisians in Cairo's cafés and theaters (*al-Zuhūr* November 1913: 359–361). A December 19, 1924 ad from *al-Ahram* newspaper announces a performance by a dancer named "Fatḥīyah al-Maghribīyah" (Fatḥīyah of Morocco) at Cairo's Kāzīnū al-Būsfūr (*al-Ahrām* 19 December 1924: 7). In the 1920s, Turkish dancers appeared as featured soloists at many popular venues. Blanche Hānim both acted and danced at Cairo's Ramses Theater on June 10, 1925 (*al-Ahrām* 6 June 1925: 6). Afrānza Hānim was a headliner at Badī'ah Maṣābnī's entertainment halls in Cairo and Alexandria in the late 1920s (*al-Ahrām* 10 March 1927: 6, *al-Ahrām* 16 June 1928: 6); she performed at other venues as well, such as Cairo's Kāzīnū al-Būsfūr (*al-Ahrām* 24 July 1930: 6) and the Bīrah al-Ahrām Theater in Giza (a*l-Ahrām* 1 September 1927: 6). Yet another Turkish dancer, Ḥikmat Hānim, was featured at the new Printania Theater in 1927 (*al-Ahrām* 15 January 1927: 5).

Interestingly, Badī'ah Maṣābnī herself claimed to have learned to dance in the Levant, not in Egypt (Adum 2015). In a casual interview recorded in a mid–1930s gossip column, she explains that she learned to dance in 1914 and that her first dance job was at a café in the Levant. She names two women as her primary teachers: Bahiyah Samakah and Muntaha al-Amrīkīyah (Muntaha "the American").

Dance styles from Turkey, North Africa, and throughout the Middle East were frequently part of the program in Egypt's entertainment halls. Turkish dance was performed by the numerous Turkish artists working in Egypt in the 1920s. Besides Turkish dance, there are examples of Levantine *dabkah* (performed at the Egypsiana Theater in 1918) ('Abd al-Wahāb 2001: 208), Iraqi dance (performed by Munīrah al-Mahdīyah at the new Printania in 1927) (*al-Ahrām* 12 January 1927: 7), Tunisian dance (performed by Badī'ah Maṣābnī at her own establishment in the 1930s) (*al-'Arūsah* 26 April 1933: 18), and others.

Badīʿah Maṣābnī, in the 1966 television interview cited earlier, states that she integrated elements of Latin, Turkish, and Persian dance into traditional Egyptian dance (*Badia Masabni in 1966 Television Interview* n.d.). Given the evidence presented here, it is unlikely that she was the first to do so. Badīʿah opened her first establishment, Ṣālah Badīʿah Maṣābnī on Cairo's ʿImād al-Dīn Street, in November 1926 (Adum n.d., *al-Ahrām* 4 November 1926: 3). However, dancers were not part of her programming until March 1927, when she began featuring Turkish dancer Afrānza Hānim (Adum n.d., *al-Ahrām* 10 March 1927: 6). Other Turkish dancers, such as Ḥikmat Hānim, were already performing at other venues in Cairo, suggesting that Badīʿah may have hired Afrānza Hānim in order to stay competitive with other establishments.

The critical implication of this discussion is that the divergence of *raqṣ sharqī* from the dances of the *ʿawālim* and *ghawāzī* may owe as much to the incorporation of elements of Turkish and other Middle Eastern/North African dance styles as to the assimilation of Western dance technique. For example, while it is generally assumed that the elaborate, graceful arm movements that came to typify *raqṣ sharqī* were derived from ballet and ballroom dance, it is worth considering to what degree these movements may be derived from non–Western dance forms such as Persian dance. Regarding Persian dance, Shay notes: "In Iranian dance, the performance of beautiful and intricate hand and arm gestures is highly prized and forms the major focus of interest in this dance tradition" (Shay 1998: 514, see also Friend 1996). As noted above, Persian dancers performed in Egypt's turn-of-the-century entertainment halls, and Badīʿah Maṣābnī specifically cited Persian dance as one of her creative influences. This suggests interesting and exciting possibilities for future research.

Summary

As this discussion has illustrated, the available evidence allows several conclusions regarding the technique of *raqṣ sharqī* as it was performed on the Egyptian entertainment hall stages of the 1890s through the 1920s. The dance was generally performed solo until the innovation of choreographed group dance and chorus lines sometime prior to the mid–1930s. As with the dances of the *ʿawālim* and *ghawāzī*, primary movements were localized in the torso, with minimal footwork. Early *raqṣ sharqī* was performed to the accompaniment of a small traditional *takht*, which gave way to a larger, more varied *firqa* beginning in the 1930s. Dancers frequently accompanied themselves with finger cymbals.

Egyptian dancers were (and are)[4] open to incorporating elements of non-Egyptian dance genres—both Western and non-Western—into their repertoires. This openness, when brought to bear within the culturally rich and diverse atmosphere of the Egyptian entertainment hall, effectively ensured that the dances of the *'awālim* and *ghawāzī* would be transformed into a new and distinct dance style. The evidence demonstrates that *raqṣ sharqī,* though a hybrid of indigenous and foreign elements, maintained an enduring connection to the dance technique of the *'awālim* and *ghawāzī.* The following chapter discusses what the same lines of evidence reveal regarding the aesthetic of early *raqṣ sharqī.*

Four

Reconstructing the Aesthetic of Early *Raqṣ Sharqī*

As the preceding chapter demonstrates, multiple lines of evidence provide a great deal of information regarding the technique of *raqṣ sharqī* as it emerged and evolved on Egypt's entertainment hall stages from the 1890s through the 1920s. The available sources reveal important technical features of the dance, and they demonstrate that early *raqṣ sharqī,* while absorbing innovations, retained many aspects of traditional *'awālim/ghawāzī* dance technique. What else can be concluded about the dance, beyond these straightforward technical elements? What do the available primary and secondary sources reveal regarding the dance's aesthetic—the characteristics that determined whether the dance was pleasing and beautiful to Egyptian audiences?

Unlike technique, which is concrete and observable, aesthetic is intangible and prone to the distortions of interpretation. The particular challenge in reconstructing the aesthetic of early *raqṣ sharqī* lies in untangling the bias present in the foreign primary source materials, for these sources provide the most abundant and detailed descriptions of actual dance performances prior to the 1930s. Europeans and Americans filtered their observations of Egyptian dance through their own aesthetic lenses, thus obscuring Egyptian attitudes and perceptions. A comparison of nineteenth-century foreign accounts of *'awālim/ghawāzī* dance with observations and footage of present-day *'awālim* and *ghawāzī* reveals a remarkable degree of similarity in technique, suggesting that foreigners were reasonably accurate in their descriptions of the technical elements of these dances. Yet, the same comparison exposes a substantial disconnect between the meanings attributed to these dances by nineteenth-century foreign observers and the perspectives of Egyptian dancers and their audiences in the modern day. While *'awālim/ghawāzī* dances have undoubtedly undergone some changes from the nineteenth century until today, the fact that these dances continue to play an important role in Egyptian social celebrations such as weddings, and that they are still built upon the same fundamental technique of more than a century ago, indicates the necessity of reassessing foreigners' descriptions of Egyptian dance aesthetic in light of the attitudes and perceptions of modern-day Egyptians. In attempting to reconstruct the aesthetic of *raqṣ sharqī* at the turn of the nineteenth and twentieth centuries, it is necessary to leverage modern-day Egyptians' perspectives on both *'awālim/ghawāzī* dances and *raqṣ sharqī* in order to clarify and balance the foreign sources.

When the foreign primary source materials are viewed in conjunction with present-day Egyptian perspectives, a coherent definition of early *raqṣ sharqī* aesthetic begins to emerge. The following discussion begins with a consideration of how both *raqṣ sharqī* and the dances of the *'awālim* and *ghawāzī* fit within the broader aesthetic context of Egyptian dance. This establishes certain general aesthetic characteristics shared by all Egyptian dances, before exploring several specific aesthetic features of early *raqṣ sharqī.*

The Aesthetic of Egyptian Dance

In a 1978 piece titled "Dance as an Expression of Islamic Culture," Lois Ibsen al-Faruqi identified five defining aesthetic characteristics of dances in the Muslim world (primarily North Africa and the Middle East): abstraction; improvisation; small, intricate movement; serial structure; and the unfolding of a series of mini-climaxes (al-Faruqi 1978). As Farida Fahmy has already pointed out, al-Faruqi's work tends toward oversimplification and arbitrary generalization (Fahmy 1987: 4–5). However, her five characteristics provide a useful framework for discussion.

The dances of Egypt are part of a larger artistic tradition that values abstraction over literal representation, and that prioritizes improvisation over programmatic or choreographed production (al-Faruqi 1978, Sellers-Young 2013: 5–6). The proclivity towards abstraction manifests in a variety of media; for example, it is apparent in the intricate calligraphic and geometric motifs that appear so frequently in Arabic art and architecture. Egyptian dances, in keeping with this affinity for abstraction, generally lack coherent narrative structure, though as Farida Fahmy points out, they do occasionally use pantomime (Fahmy 1987: 37–38). Rather than telling stories, the dances of Egypt frequently take the form of abstract improvisations to their accompanying music, with the execution varying according to the mood and interpretive choices of the performers in the moment.

Improvisation is a highly valued mode of performance in a range of Arabic art forms, including dance. As al-Faruqi states:

> Just as the musician, whether vocalist or instrumentalist, gives free reign to his improvisatory skill in a solo *layālī* or *taqāsīm*, just as the *qāri'* never chants a passage from the Holy Qur'ān exactly the way he has done it before, so solo dancers as well as dance groups are always involved in "on-the-spot" creations of beauty [al-Faruqi 1978: 8].

Given the great value accorded to improvisation in Arabic art, it is no surprise that the concept of dance choreography as it exists in modern concert dance—as noted in the last chapter, a planned and set series of movements and steps executed in a consciously and deliberately structured performance space—is not a feature of the traditional dances of Egypt, nor is it typical of dances elsewhere in North Africa and the Middle East (Fahmy 1987: 9, al-Faruqi 1978: 7–8).

al-Faruqi appears to have had the various forms of "belly dance" in mind when she listed small, intricate movement as the third characteristic of dance in the Muslim world. Small, intricate, torso-based movement is certainly an important technical feature of *raqṣ baladī, raqṣ sharqī,* and the dances of the *'awālim* and the *ghawāzī,* as discussed in the prior chapter. However, I would argue that this is not a central aesthetic characteristic of all of the dances of Egypt, let alone all of the dances of North Africa and the Middle East. For example, in *raqṣat al-'aṣāyah,* the Upper Egyptian stick dance, many of the fundamental movements are decidedly large and expansive, as the dance borrows many elements from the game of mock combat known as *taḥṭīb* (Fahmy 1987: 49, Saleh 1979: 240–266).

Rather than stating that all Egyptian dances are defined by their small, intricate movement, it is more accurate to say that Egyptian dances tend to emphasize torso-based movement over footwork (Fahmy 1987: 9). More importantly, the core movements of all Egyptian dances are closely linked to their accompanying music. In the words of al-Faruqi: "the most important thing is the intricate rhythmic interplay between movements of a particular portion of the body and the percussion or melodic accompaniment."

The close relationship of dance to music helps to explain why the dances of Egypt exhibit the final two aesthetic characteristics defined by al-Faruqi: serial structure and mini-climaxes. These elements are embodied in the structural organization of Egyptian (and Arab) musical performance, wherein the overall performance event is created over the course of several discrete, yet interconnected, performance segments. Consider Racy's description of a typical *jalsah*, an informal get-together of musicians and listeners:

> In its entirety, a jalsah event tends to embody a sequence of gradually unfolding and organically linked phases, an order of events that contributes significantly to the jalsah's transformative purpose [Racy 2003: 53].

In similar fashion, a typical Egyptian dance performance unfolds as a series of distinct, yet related, episodes. Each episode is internally coherent, following its own internal progression towards a climactic moment that marks the episode's completion. Yet each episode is integral to the overall progression of the dance performance as a whole. This format is evident in Saleh's description of a traditional *raqṣat al-ʿaṣāyah* performance, in which the entire event unfolds over the course of three distinct dance segments—the *juhaynah*, the *wāḥdah wa nuṣ*, and the *ʿarabī*—each marked by its own distinctive rhythmic accompaniment (Saleh 1979: 240–266). It is also illustrated in Bordelon's analysis of the progression of a modern-day *raqṣ sharqī* performance event, which generally consists of several dance segments, each defined by its particular style of musical accompaniment—an introduction piece, a light popular song, a folklore piece, and a classic love song (Bordelon 2013: 34–43). As both of these cases demonstrate, the format and progression of the dance performance are inextricably tied to the format and progression of the accompanying musical performance.

In short, four of al-Faruqi's five characteristics—abstraction; improvisation; serial structure; and the unfolding of a series of mini-climaxes—are largely applicable to the aesthetic of the dances of Egypt. However, it may be more useful to examine the final two features—serial structure and mini-climaxes—as manifestations of a more fundamental aesthetic element: the synergistic relationship between Egyptian dance and its accompanying music. These characteristics provide a helpful starting point for investigating the aesthetic of early *raqṣ sharqī*. However, in order to define the aesthetic of *raqṣ sharqī* in its earliest decades, it is necessary to examine the particular manner in which the broader Egyptian dance aesthetic is manifested in modern-day *raqṣ sharqī* and in the dances of the *ʿawālim* and the *ghawāzī*.

An Overview of Early Raqṣ Sharqī *Aesthetic*

Both present-day *raqṣ sharqī* and *ʿawālim/ghawāzī* dance fit within the larger aesthetic framework of Egyptian dance. However, these dances share several important and distinguishing characteristics:

1. Improvisation is critical, as it enables the expression and evocation of feeling.
2. The dancer's ability to improvise and to convey feeling hinges on her musical interpretation skills.
3. The dance may assume an erotic character, but the presence or absence of eroticism is dependent on the performer and the performance context.

Though these features emerge from the aesthetic matrix shared by all Egyptian dances, they form a unique and defining aesthetic that sets *raqṣ sharqī* and *ʿawālim/ghawāzī* dance apart from other Egyptian dance forms. The existence of these aesthetic elements in both present-day *raqṣ sharqī* and in the dances of the *ʿawālim* and the *ghawāzī* throughout their history suggests that *raqṣ sharqī* in the late nineteenth and early twentieth centuries shared these aspects as well.

Improvisation and Feeling

As has already been noted, the concept of dance choreography as it exists in modern concert dance is not indigenous to Egyptian dance (Fahmy 1987: 9). Rather, improvisation is a key attribute of traditional dance in Egypt, as it is elsewhere in the Arab world (Fahmy 1987: 9, al-Faruqi 1978: 7–8). Throughout history, the dances of the *ʿawālim* and *ghawāzī* have displayed this improvisational character. Clot Bey (1840b: 92), writing of the *ʿawālim* and *ghawāzī* in the first half of the nineteenth century, notes that "although they put a certain harmonic symmetry into their movements, one should not expect to see them forming figures and formal tableaux, such as those emerging from the theaters of our skilled choreographers." Similarly, Klunzinger (1878: 189), who observed *ghawāzī* performers in Upper Egypt in the 1860s and 1870s, states: "Their much-admired dances are, however, generally quite inartistic, having no regular figures, no keeping of time, no combined movements" (though other sources refute his assertion that the dances had "no keeping of time"). In the present day, Nearing (2004b) describes the dances of the Banāt Māzin *ghawāzī* as being "partially choreographed," in the sense that their dances employ a predictable pattern of movements and require some degree of synchronization among the performers. However, the dances of the Banāt Māzin are not choreographed in the sense that this term is understood in Western concert dances such as ballet.

Multiple authors have noted the improvisational nature of both *raqṣ baladī* and present-day *raqṣ sharqī* (Adra 2005: 31, Fahmy 1987: 64–67, Wood and Shay 1976: 23–24). Of *raqṣ sharqī,* Farida Fahmy (1987: 67) writes: "The manner in which the dance is executed, and how the movements are combined, depend largely on improvisatory skills, intuition, and mood of the dancer at the time of each performance." Yet, choreography *does* exist in modern-day *raqṣ sharqī,* raising the question of whether choreography was part of the dance when it first emerged.

Foreign accounts of *raqṣ sharqī* on the stages of Egypt's late nineteenth/early twentieth century entertainment halls offer no indication of choreography. Foreign observers describe dancers repeatedly executing the same repertoire of movements, with no apparent design or planning (Scott 1894, *South Australian Chronicle* 17 June 1893: 16, *Star* 20 September 1902: 2). The dancers moved about the stage, but not in the sort of deliberate and structured manner that would suggest choreography. Rather, the dancers simply traveled up and down the length of the stage, occasionally turning, thus ensuring that all of their movements were clearly visible to the entire audience (Scott 1894, *South Australian Chronicle* 17 June 1893: 16, *Star* 20 September 1902: 2).

Film footage reveals that as early as the mid–1930s, *raqṣ sharqī* began to incorporate choreography in the form of choreographed groups of dancers backing up a featured soloist (*Gilded Serpent Presents Badia Masabni* 2009 [ca. 1934]). Entertainment hall owners and managers hired professional choreographers to create dances for their chorus lines, as well as to train dancers on technique. For example, Badī'ah Maṣābnī hired Isaac Dickson to train and choreograph for her dancers (Adum n.d.); Dickson also coached soloists on their dance technique (*Samia Gamal Interview, Kawakeb Magazine, 1968* n.d.).

In spite of the adoption of choreography, however, it is evident from footage of *raqṣ sharqī* from the 1930s through the 1950s that Egyptians did not concern themselves with precision in their group choreographies. For example, in a wedding scene in the 1942 film *'Ala Masraḥ al-Ḥayāt* (*On the Stage of Life*), four dancers perform choreographed *raqṣ sharqī* around a singer. They vary tremendously in the timing and manner of execution of their movements, and each of them wears a slightly different costume. This rather loose approach to group choreography differs substantially from what was presented on contemporary stages in Europe and the U.S. and in European and American cinema. In fact, precision was so aesthetically pleasing to Western audiences that an entire genre of "precision dancing" emerged (Moulton 1998). Precise group choreography—with impeccably synchronized dancers and perfectly coordinated costumes—first appeared in Egyptian dance with the advent of two state-sponsored theatrical folk dance troupes in the late 1950s and early 1960s: Firqah Riḍā (the Riḍā Troupe) and Firqah al-Qawmīyah lil-Funūn al-Sha'bīyah (the National Troupe of Folk Arts) (Fahmy 1987, Shay 2002: 126–162). These troupes, crafted in the mold of the Soviet Moiseyev Dance Company, presented carefully choreographed and staged theatrical representations of Egyptian folklore. However, these troupes initially did not have a substantial impact on the aesthetic of *raqṣ sharqī.*

Until the 1950s, featured *raqṣ sharqī* soloists continued to improvise their performances. According to Ibrāhīm 'Ākif, his cousin, famous mid–twentieth century *raqṣ sharqī* performer Na'īmah 'Ākif, was the first soloist to incorporate choreography into her performances (Zamora Chamas 2009). In the second half of the twentieth century, it became commonplace for *raqṣ sharqī* soloists to choreograph (or to hire a choreographer for) at least a portion of their performance; in fact, Ibrāhīm 'Ākif was a choreographer to many dancers in the latter decades of the twentieth century. Importantly, it was in this regard that the Riḍā Troupe and the National Troupe of Folk Arts would begin to have an indirect yet substantial influence on the stylistic direction of *raqṣ sharqī*: beginning in the latter decades of the twentieth century, former members of these troupes would enter the world of *raqṣ sharqī* as solo performers and as trainers/choreographers, thus leaving an indelible mark on both the technique and aesthetic of *raqṣ sharqī* in the modern day.

Still, tremendous value continues to be placed on improvisation in present-day *raqṣ sharqī.* Randā Kāmal, a popular Egyptian dancer who teaches choreography to *raqṣ sharqī* students around the world (and herself a former member of the Riḍā Troupe), states:

> I never dance choreography on the stage.... I love choreography, to do [i.e., she loves creating choreography] ... but if I dance on the stage, I can't remember [choreography], so I love to be by my soul.... I listen, feel, do it. I love this more [*Randa Kamel Interview at Raqs of Course Festival 2014*].

Kāmal's statement hints at why Egyptian dancers will never abandon improvisation. In an improvised performance, the dance is created in the moment, as the dancer personally engages, interacts with, and responds to the music, the musicians, and the audience. The immediacy of the performance, combined with its interactive quality, creates a fertile atmosphere for the evocation and expression of feeling, which is often cited by Egyptians as a key element of a successful dance performance (Bordelon 2013).[1]

Accounts of the *'awālim* and the *ghawāzī* throughout their history reveal the important role of feeling in their dancing. Warner notes:

> Evidently the dance is nothing except with a master, with an actress who shall abandon herself to the tide of feeling which the music suggests and throw herself into the full passion of it; who knows how to tell a story by pantomime, and to depict the woes of love and despair [Warner 1900: 381].

Describing a performance he observed in Luxor in the early 1850s, Taylor remarks on the depth of emotion that a *ghāziyah* conveyed through her dance:

> The burden was: "I am alone; my family and my friends are all dead; the plague has destroyed them. Come, then, to me, and be my beloved, for I have no other to love me." Her gestures exhibited a singular mixture of the abandonment of grief, and the longing of love. While her body swayed to and fro with the wild, sad rhythm of the words, she raised both arms before her till the long sleeves fell back and covered her face: then opening them in wistful entreaty, sang the last line of the chorus, and bringing her hands to her forehead, relapsed into grief again. Apparently the prayer is answered, for the concluding movement expressed a delirious joy [Taylor 1854: 136–137].

Arnold (1882: 266) notes of one of the dancers he witnessed: "she seemed about to lose consciousness, so absorbed was the look in her eyes."

The performances not only expressed emotions; they also frequently elicited strong emotional responses from their Egyptian audiences:

> Old Achmet Gourgar, our Theban guide, however, was so enraptured that he several times ejaculated: "*taïb keteer*!" (very good indeed!) and Raïs Hassan's dark face beamed all over with delight. The circle of white turbaned heads in the rear looked on complacently, and our guard, who stood in the moonlight before the open door, almost forgot his duty in his enjoyment of the spectacle [Taylor 1854: 135–136].

Chabrol (1822: 463) describes young women "joining their voices with those of the singers and imitating the gestures of the *a'lmeh*" as they were swept up in the emotion of the performance.

Accounts of early *raqṣ sharqī* show a similar emphasis on feeling. Steevens, describing a performance in a small entertainment hall in the 1890s, writes:

> The music, to my ear, was one phrase over and over and over again; the dance, to my eye, a very slow methodical waggling of the belly, doubtless difficult to produce, but interesting mainly to the anatomist. But the yellow, and brown, and black faces

> went broad with grins, and their applause rose tumultuously above the screech of the smallest singer [Steevens 1898: 40].

Similarly, Giffin describes an audience swept away by their enjoyment of the performance (Giffin 1911: 39).

The great importance accorded to improvisation and feeling in *raqṣ sharqī*, as well as in the dances of the *'awālim* and the *ghawāzī*, has parallels in the Arabic musical tradition, and reaffirms the close ties between Egyptian dance and music. As Racy (2003: 4) notes, "Modern Arab musicians and musical connoisseurs stress that above all, Arab music must engage the listener emotionally." Importantly, Racy explains that improvisational genres are the primary musical means for transporting listeners to the pinnacle of emotional engagement, the state of *ṭarab*, or musically-induced ecstasy (Racy 2003: 93–96). In similar fashion, Egyptian dancers and dance aficionados assert that dance should engage the audience's emotions, and improvisation is the vehicle for this process. Skilled performers constantly read their audience's emotional state and adjust their performance accordingly; they guide the audience toward a transcendent emotional experience—culminating in some cases in a *ṭarab* state. Bordelon notes:

> Although it may be the music itself that generates *tarab*, the movement and various levels of interaction that unfold over the course of an Oriental dance performance create the potential for an enhanced, or at least, differently-felt, *tarab* experience [Bordelon 2013: 45].

The dancer's ability to improvise to Egyptian music, and to shepherd her audience through an emotional experience of the music, clearly depends on her understanding of the nuances of the music itself. Therefore, it should come as no surprise that the next aesthetic feature of *raqṣ sharqī* to be considered is the art and skill of musical interpretation.

The Critical Importance of Musical Interpretation

Present-day *raqṣ sharqī* is closely tied to the interpretation of Egyptian music. In the words of trainer and choreographer Ibrāhīm 'Ākif: "Just like a singer, where the voice interprets the notes of the composer, the dancer has to sing with her body" (*Cairo Unveiled* 1992). A skilled performer of *raqṣ sharqī* must be able to identify and embody important elements of the music, such as rhythmic structure, instrumentation, phrasing, and feeling. Dancers who do not understand or effectively interpret music are viewed as unskilled and inartistic. In a February 2016 interview with

Sūsū, a retired dancer, and Sayyid Ḥankish, her impresario, both complained about the overwhelming number of newer dancers in Egypt who lack this fundamental skill and who are thus contributing to a decline in the artistic level of the dance (personal communication, February 3, 2016).

Both historically and in the present day, the *'awālim* and *ghawāzī* have demonstrated a similar connection to the music. In the early nineteenth century, Clot Bey observed that dancers were unable to perform if their music was off-tempo (Clot-Bey 1840b: 91). Edwina Nearing, writing of the present-day *ghawāzī* of Upper Egypt, notes: "Each region has its favorite *mizmar* bands and its own style of rendering the music, to which good Ghawazi dancers are extremely sensitive" (Nearing 2004a).

Warner's account of the *ghawāzī* he observed in Luxor in the 1870s reveals how the close alliance between the dancers and their music manifested over the course of a single performance. From start to finish, the dynamic of the accompanying music shaped the ebb and flow of the dance performance. As the dancers sat waiting to perform, the music established the necessary mood:

> They are waiting a little wearily, and from time to time one of them throws out the note or two of a song, as if the music were beginning to work in her veins [Warner 1900: 379].

Shortly thereafter, a musical cue signaled the beginning of the performance, but the *ghawāzī* did not begin to dance until they "caught" the rhythm with their finger cymbals:

> At a turn in the music, the girl in red and the girl in yellow stand up; for an instant they raise their castanets till the time of the music is caught, and then start forward, with less of languor and a more skipping movement than we expected [Warner 1900: 380].

Over the course of the performance, as the music increased in speed and intensity, the dancers matched it with more rapid and "passionate" movements:

> After standing for a brief space, with the body throbbing and quivering, the castanets all the time held above the head in sympathetic throbs, the dancers start forward, face each other, pass, pirouette, and take some dancing steps, retire, advance and repeat the earthquake performance. This is kept up a long time, and with wonderful endurance, without change of figure; but sometimes the movements are more rapid, when the music hastens, and more passion is shown [Warner 1900: 381].

When not dancing, the *ghawāzī* sang songs. Over one hundred years later, the *ghawāzī* of Upper Egypt can be observed performing in a virtually identical manner: sitting near the musicians until the start of the music, rising to dance at a cue in the music, marking time with their finger cymbals, matching their movements to the speed and intensity of the music, and singing during the interludes between dance performances.

Contemporary accounts of early *raqṣ sharqī* offer no details regarding the relationship of the dance to its accompanying music. The available footage of *raqṣ sharqī* performers from the 1930s adds little additional information. Due to the manner in which the dance scenes were edited, dancers are generally not onscreen for the duration of their accompanying music. Rather, there are frequent cutaway shots that show audience members, musicians, etc. Without being able to observe the dancer over the course of her entire performance, it is difficult to draw conclusions regarding the relationship of the dance to the music. Nevertheless, the available footage does suggest that *raqṣ sharqī* performers in the 1930s were attuned to their music. For example, the dancer in *Bint al-Bāshā al-Mudīr* (1938) performs an interesting rhythmic sequence. First, in perfect time with the accompanying percussion, she repeatedly drops to one knee, simultaneously performing the two-handed finger snap. Then, she descends partway to the floor in the splits, and while in this position, taps one knee to the floor while rhythmically snapping her fingers. In light of footage like this, and given what is known about the importance of musical interpretation in both modern-day *raqṣ sharqī* and in *ʿawālim/ghawāzī* dance, it is probable that the earliest performers of *raqṣ sharqī* similarly aligned their performances to the nuances of their music.

In this consideration of musical interpretation in *raqṣ sharqī* and *ʿawālim/ghawāzī* dance, it is important to stress that in the present day, these dances involve abstract interpretation of rhythms, melodies, and moods, rather than literal representation of storylines with coherent narrative structure. Dancers do periodically mime words and phrases from their accompanying music. Describing the popular Egyptian dancer Fifi ʿAbduh in the mid–1990s, Lorius writes: "Skilled at expressing moods, musical motifs and words with consummate bodily movements and playful gestures, Abdou incorporates the latest manifestations of popular musical culture" (Lorius 1996: 286). However, neither modern-day *ʿawālim/ghawāzī* dance nor present-day *raqṣ sharqī* is a narrative dance with a structured storyline, nor is there evidence that early *raqṣ sharqī* was narrative in nature. Adra notes: "Traditional belly dance is above all lighthearted play. It is neither programmatic nor literal. Like traditional Arabic music, it has no storyline and no articulated goal other than to provide pleasure" (Adra 2005: 41).

Fraser argues that at least some nineteenth century *'awālim/ghawāzī* performances were both mimetic and narrative (Fraser 2015: 223–235). In fact, she identifies two specific narrative dance types: the "Love Duet" (Fraser's terminology) and the "Bee." She contrasts these with non-narrative dance, which she terms "Pure Dance."

According to Fraser, the Love Duet was a story of seduction and consummation usually (though not always) depicted by two dancers—one playing the role of a man, and the other playing the role of a woman. The "man" pursued the "woman," ultimately seducing her and "consummating" their relationship; occasionally, after the depiction of the sex act, there was a display of regret or shame. In the modern era, Egyptian dancers have been observed performing movements that mimic intercourse—an issue that will be addressed in greater detail below. Yet, the elaborate narrative leading up to the "consummation"—as well as the depiction of post-coital regret/shame—does not exist in modern-day *'awālim/ghawāzī* dance or in present-day *raqṣ sharqī*, raising questions regarding the historical reality of Fraser's Love Duet.

Numerous nineteenth-century accounts of *'awālim/ghawāzī* dance describe an escalation in the speed and intensity, or "passion," of the dancer's movements. The climax of this escalation was frequently followed by a pause or a lull, after which another dance sequence would begin. For example:

> [A]t first modestly coquettish, it became by degrees the excitement of wanton phrenzy, and at length died away in languor [Bartlett 1850: 114].

> At the commencement the dance was voluptuous: it soon after became lascivious, and expressed, in the grossest and most indecent way, the giddy transports of the passions [Denon 1803: 119].

> As the dancers became animated, their motions were more rapid and violent, and the measure was marked, not in pirouettes and flying bounds, as on the boards of Frank theatres, but by a most wonderful command over the muscles of the chest and limbs. Their frames vibrated with the music like the strings of the violin, and as the song grew wild and stormy towards its close, the movements, had they not accorded with it, would have resembled those of a person seized with some violent nervous spasm. After this had continued for an incredible length of time, and I expected to see the Almehs fall exhausted to the earth, the music ceased, and they stood before us calm and cold, with their breathing not perceptibly hurried. The dance had a second part, of very different character. Still with their lifted hands striking the little cymbals, they marked a circle of springing bounds, in which their figures occasionally reminded me of the dancing nymphs of Greek sculpture [Taylor 1854: 135].[2]

> Their movements were certainly graceful, if too suggestive, and as the music quickened they showed less reserve and threw more passion into their gyrations. After a brief pause one of the girls placed a bottle, full of water and containing a lighted

> candle, upon her head, and nicely poised it during a long dance of both slow and rapid movements, including lying down and turning over and over upon the floor [Vincent 1895: 185].

Certain accounts go a step further than these, assigning a literal—and sometimes quite detailed—seduction/consummation narrative to the dance's escalation (see, for example, St. John 1834a: 105–116). Accounts such as these appear to form the basis for Fraser's Love Duet.

As noted earlier, the format and progression of Egyptian dance performance are inextricably connected to the format and progression of the dance's musical accompaniment. Both historically and in the present day, *'awālim* and *ghawāzī* performers match their movements to their accompanying music, and as the music escalates in speed and intensity, so does the dance. This pattern is also apparent in the social dancing of ordinary Egyptians. Consider the following description of a man dancing at a coffee house:

> Excitement runs high when one of the men in the café steps forth and begins to dance.... These people all know their own native dances, and some of these are indeed, most curious. As the tom-tom beats faster, and the music from the other instruments gains in speed, so does the dance get more and more exciting, and as it progresses the audience sways with the music, and all clap their hands to it [*The Horsham Times* 12 November 1929: 4].

One wonders whether nineteenth-century foreign observers, after witnessing the sometimes sexually suggestive movements of Egyptian dancers, and taking into account that a great deal of Egyptian popular music revolved around themes of romantic love, took the creative liberty of ascribing a rather literal seduction/consummation narrative to what was in fact an abstract expression of the dynamics of the musical accompaniment. As Adra notes, Europeans and Americans "expect semantic intent in art," and when such intent is not apparent, they assign it (Adra 2005: 44). For example, consider the elaborate and fanciful temptation narrative that Leland ascribes to a dancer's acrobatic floor exercise:

> The girl at Girgeh performed a very pretty dance, which was quite a poem. Placing a cup, symbolic of temptation, on the ground, she danced around it in a style which was perfectly Spanish, turning the body and sinking low with great grace and exquisite art. The cup appeared to exercise a terrible fascination, but she was afraid to drain it. Five times, without aid from her arms, she almost lay on the ground with her thirsty lips just dallying with the edge, and then rising, swept in dance, and thrilled, and shivered, and turned, and sank again. The sixth time she had completed a circle, and no longer able to resist, she approached the cup with throbs and pauses, and then, without using her hand, lifted it from the ground with her lips alone, draining it as she rose, and the tragedy of temptation being over, merrily danced about the room in quick step, with her head thrown back, holding the cup all the time in her mouth [Leland 1873: 136].

As mentioned in the last chapter, acrobatic feats like the one Leland describes have been commonplace in both *'awālim/ghawāzī* dance and *raqṣ sharqī* throughout history. Observing such acts in the modern day, one finds little to suggest any symbolism. Yet, Fraser accepts Leland's narrative at face value and draws a connection that is tenuous, at best, between this dancer's cup dance and Arabic poetry:

> This choreography finds a close correlation in the Arabic poetic repertoire where various lines can involve wine and passing the cup. The lover begs his beloved to pass the cup, wine takes away all sorrows, the lover takes the cup and becomes intoxicated with the beloved's eyes, they lie under the jasmine for half the night, both enraptured. The erotic symbolism here is evident [Fraser 2015: 203].

Is erotic symbolism evident in the performance described above? Wine drinking and intoxication also figure in Ṣūfī poetry as metaphors for "mystical transformation" in the search for the Divine (Racy 2003: 149)—yet, neither Leland nor Fraser go so far as to suggest that the cup dance represents the dancer's quest towards a mystical union with God. To paraphrase a famous aphorism, sometimes a cup is just a cup.

In contrast to Fraser's Love Duet, the so-called "Bee" appears to be the one clear and indisputable example of a nineteenth century Egyptian dance with both mimetic and narrative qualities. The Bee was a pantomime in which the dancer, stung by an imaginary insect, gradually shed some or all of her clothing while in search of the insect. This dance is frequently described in European accounts from the early-to-mid–nineteenth century, but it disappears from the historical record by the end of the century. It remains unclear whether the "Bee Dance" was indigenous to Egypt. While Dinicu (2011: 99) dismisses The Bee as an invention created to titillate European tourists, Fraser (2015: 231–232) points to evidence of a similar dance in Iran, suggesting a Middle Eastern origin.

The Role of Eroticism

Adra rightly critiques the Western tendency to ascribe erotic meaning to belly dance: "When exposed to the quivering hips and shoulders of belly dance performance, they tend to assume intent, in this case, seduction" (Adra 2005: 44). Yet, it would be a mistake to suggest that eroticism and sexuality are never present. Both *raqṣ sharqī* and the dances of the *'awālim* and *ghawāzī* sometimes take on an erotic character—sometimes subtle, at other times explicit.

Foreign accounts provide numerous examples of nineteenth century *'awālim* and *ghawāzī* performing sexually suggestive movements, though, as noted above, their ascription of a literal narrative of seduction/consummation to these dance acts is questionable. Eroticism and sexuality could be present not only in the dance itself, but also in the performers' interactions with audience members; Clot-Bey notes how, during interludes in the dance, the performers would approach and embrace male audience members, sit on their laps, and "take liberties" with them (Clot-Bey 1840b: 93–94).

Throughout the nineteenth century, the *'awālim* and the *ghawāzī* could be seen performing with male buffoons, who accompanied them with sexually suggestive gestures and actions that left little to the imagination (Badawi 1988: 10–11). At rural *mawālid* and public markets, *ghawāzī* sometimes performed with the colorful character known as 'Alī Kākā (Figures 11 and 12), who was distinguished by the huge phallic tool which he wore dangling from his belt (Badawi 1988: 11).

Charmes describes an appearance by this comic character at Cairo's *Mūlid al-Nabī* in the late 1870s:

> The pen of Rabelais would be necessary to describe the scenes played by this personage, with the assistance of the spectators, among women and children, who laugh uproariously, and the gestures and witticisms of such grossness, that it is quite impossible to give the faintest idea of them. Aly-Kaka is a sort of circus clown, whom they belabour with blows and overwhelm with sarcasm and jokes; but then he takes his revenge in the exercise of his profession, in his own way. All that the imagination the most debased and polluted can conceive is nothing in comparison with the shameful spectacle, displayed in the rays of the sun, too, or by

Alikaka Dancers at the Arab Market, Zakazik, Egypt.
New York. London. Toronto Canada, Ottawa Kansas

Figure 11. *Ghawāzī* and musicians performing with 'Alī Kākā at a market in Zaqāzīq, in the Nile Delta (Underwood and Underwood stereograph, 1896).

the light of the *machallas*, in presence of an amazed crowd [Charmes 1883: 180–181].

The *ʿawālim*, too, were sometimes accompanied by a male buffoon; this individual was known as Khalbūṣ (Lane 1860: 501, Lane 2005 [1836]: 495).

Fraser describes the overt eroticism of some nineteenth century Egyptian dance performances, but states: "Explicit expressions can hardly be found today, as, in both East and West, belly dance performances clearly avoid extremes of this earlier meaning, implying it is deemed inappropriate to a modern aesthetic" (Fraser 2015: 249). On the contrary, eroticism and sexuality remain alive and well in both *ʿawālim/ghawāzī* dance and in *raqṣ sharqī*. In modern-day *raqṣ sharqī*, eroticism manifests primarily in the form of sexual innuendo and sexually suggestive gestures. Lorius, again describing Fifi ʿAbduh, writes:

> Abdou mimes to the words of songs and engages in banter with the couple and their guests, using improvised repartee that is thick with double meaning and innuendo [Lorius 1996: 287].

> Fifi Abdou uses music with a persistent driving tempo, expressing the rhythm, words and mood through her movements and gestures. From current popular songs she chooses those about love and sex, which explore themes such as desire, seduction, polygamy, infidelity, and jealousy, and the lyrics are often changed or elaborated to give her own gloss—one that usually renders them more explicit [Lorius 1996: 291].

Figure 12. *Ghawāzī* and musicians performing with ʿAlī Kākā at a market in Zaqāzīq, in the Nile Delta (Underwood and Underwood stereograph, 1896).

The dancer Saḥar Ḥamdī was infamous for her sometimes brazen sexuality. In fact, Saḥar's bawdy duet with singer Sāmī 'Alī, *Illy Sharṭit 'Aīnuh Bitjannin*, was explicit enough to be banned by the Egyptian government (Lorius 1996: 287). Interestingly, this song is still frequently performed—with varying degrees of suggestiveness—at the street weddings of the urban lower class.

The performances of modern-day *'awālim* and *ghawāzī* can be much more graphic than the wordplay and suggestive gesturing just described. For example, dancers sometimes embrace or kiss one another during performance. Aisha Ali witnessed this during her research with the Banāt Māzin, when one of the *ghawāzī* surprised her by kissing her on the mouth during a dance (Aisha Ali, personal communication, January 13, 2016; Wood and Shay 1976: 25). In an even more sexually charged act, a dancer may sit on the lap of—or even straddle—the bride and/or the groom and mimic the pelvic thrusts of intercourse. The 1991 German documentary *Die Königin der Mohammed-Ali-Strasse* includes footage of a *ghāziyah* in Manṣūra performing this action, to the amusement of the mixed-gender, mixed-age audience. Notably, these episodes show no evidence of the elaborate seduction/consummation narrative that Fraser has attributed to early nineteenth century *'awālim* and *ghawāzī* performances.

It would be misguided to attribute an erotic character to *all* performances of *raqṣ sharqī* and *'awālim/ghawāzī* dances. Yet, many nineteenth and early twentieth century foreign observers did precisely this, reflecting what Said termed "a remarkably persistent motif in Western attitudes about the Orient" (Said 1979: 188)—the association of the Orient (and the Oriental woman) with unbridled sexuality. Still, the occasional presence of eroticism and sexuality in both *raqṣ sharqī* and the dances of the *'awālim* and *ghawāzī* is undeniable and requires further consideration.

The presence or absence of eroticism depends in large measure on the unique personality of the individual performer, combined with the choices that she makes in the midst of her performance. For example, the famed *ghāziyah* Ṣafīyah of Isnā was requested to temper the more sensual aspects of her dancing during a performance for Englishwoman Isabella Romer in the 1840s; Romer notes: "She had been warned to restrain herself, and she did, for there was no absolute violation of decorum in her performance" (Romer 1846a: 276–277). On the other hand, the unnamed *ghāziyah* that Romer witnessed at the home of the Belgian Consul-General showed no such restraint: "...by the audacious licentiousness of her exhibition, [she] completely disgusted me" (Romer 1846b: 127).

The significance of the performer's personality and her personal choices in determining the eroticism—or lack thereof—of her performance is evident among Egyptian dancers in the modern day. Compare, for example, the vastly different stage personas of two contemporary *raqṣ sharqī* performers from the 1980s, Suhaīr Zakī and Saḥar Ḥamdī. While the former maintained a reputation of politeness and modesty throughout her career, the latter was notorious for her sexually-charged performances (Lorius 1996: 287, Sullivan 2002).

Beyond the personality and choices of the individual performer, however, performance context is key—not only in determining the presence or absence of eroticism, but also in defining its appropriateness. For example, eroticism and sexuality appear to be sanctioned in the context of wedding celebrations, where the sexuality of the dancer references and celebrates the sexual union of the newly married couple. In these settings, children are often present and witness these acts. As noted above, the raunchy performance of the *ghāziyah* in *Die Königin der Mohammed-Ali-Strasse* amused and delighted the women and children in the audience. However, when the dance is taken out of traditional contexts, the erotic and sexual elements become problematic:

> Whereas people characterize nightclubs as scenes of excitement, dishonesty, and drunkenness, they see weddings primarily as expressions of happiness connected to family occasions. Because of this, people view the same behavior of performers differently in the two contexts.... At weddings, for instance, a dancer occasionally performs in front of the couple and puts their hands on her belly and breasts while she rolls her belly and moves her breasts. I expected this to be considered outrageous behavior. Yet several people explained that it was innocent merriment and fun (*farfasha*). A nightclub dancer who exhibited the same behavior, lacking the context of a happy occasion and working in an atmosphere of sexual excitement, would be considered prostituting herself to earn money [Van Nieuwkerk 1995: 128–129].

As Van Nieuwkerk's work indicates, modern-day Egyptians have developed particularly ambivalent opinions regarding dance in "nightclub" settings, where it is performed without the social justification provided by a festive occasion such as a wedding. These conflicted attitudes have been embodied in—and reinforced by—the innumerable and widely varying portrayals of these venues in Egyptian cinema—from depictions of entertainment venues as hotbeds of seduction and sexual impropriety, to stories in which these venues offer a path to success and fame for a virtuous young man or woman (Shafik 2006: 163–165). Van Nieuwkerk notes that one of the main reasons that many of her informants disapproved of nightclubs was their association with the practice of *fatḥ*—in which female entertainers sit, drink, and socialize with customers (Van Nieuwkerk 1995: 122–123).

There are important implications here for early *raqṣ sharqī*. As Chapter Two has revealed, it was the move from traditional performance settings such as weddings and *mawālid* to the stages of the entertainment halls that initiated the transformation of *ʿawālim/ghawāzī* dance into *raqṣ sharqī*. Yet, by detaching the dance from traditional social contexts, the move to the entertainment hall ensured that the dance—and the dancers who performed it—would be placed in a precarious position with regards to social propriety. There is no concrete evidence to suggest that early *raqṣ sharqī* exhibited the sort of overt eroticism that can be found in *ʿawālim/ghawāzī* dance both historically and in the present day. On the other hand, from the end of the nineteenth century throughout much of the twentieth, the practice of *fatḥ* was commonplace in the entertainment venues that presented *raqṣ sharqī*. In the minds of many Egyptians, *fatḥ* is equivalent to prostitution—even though the women who practiced it did not, in most cases, engage in sex with their customers. Thus, even though early *raqṣ sharqī* seems to have lacked the explicit eroticism sometimes present in *ʿawālim/ghawāzī* dance, it appears that the widespread practice of *fatḥ* cast a pall of sexual impropriety over the entertainment halls where it was practiced, as well as over the dancers who worked there. The issue of *fatḥ* will be revisited in the next chapter.

The Question of Foreign Influence

The preceding discussion reveals that *raqṣ sharqī* is firmly situated within the larger aesthetic framework of Egyptian dance. Moreover, this discussion demonstrates a close aesthetic relationship between *raqṣ sharqī* and the dances of the *ʿawālim* and the *ghawāzī*. The one clear and incontrovertible example of the assimilation of European/American dance aesthetic noted in this chapter was the introduction of choreography into the dance sometime prior to the mid–1930s. Yet, until the middle of the twentieth century, choreography was limited to the chorus lines supporting featured soloists, and even after soloists began using choreography at mid-century, improvisation would continue to be the preferred mode of performance. Moreover, the imprecise—even haphazard—group choreographies that appeared in Egyptian films from the 1930s through the 1950s were a far cry from their contemporary American and European counterparts. For these reasons, it is safe to conclude that the aesthetic impact of Western choreographic approaches on early *raqṣ sharqī* was somewhat limited. What else can be concluded regarding foreign influences on the aesthetic of the dance?

There is little to suggest that performers of *raqṣ sharqī* were tailoring their dancing toward the aesthetic sensibilities of European or American viewers. In fact, it is apparent from their own accounts that Western observers' aesthetic experience of Egyptian music and dance differed profoundly from that of native Egyptians watching the same performances. Westerners were aware of the substantial disconnect between their own taste and that of the indigenous Egyptian population. Consider Arnold's account:

> After this fashion all the eight girls danced before us by pairs, and then joining, the musicians in the background gave us songs and choruses. Judged by Western taste the effect was more like prolonged and dismal yells than aught melodious; and yet there cannot be lacking in these immemorial songs and accompanying music a real indigenous charm—or how would it so fascinate its native hearers as it appears to do? Chorus and instruments certainly keep most admirable time; and, though the tune sounds uncouth to the European ear, its execution on their curious *darabūkas* (tambourines) and *rababs* (violins) is wonderfully precise, and the technic of the latter must be especially difficult to acquire. It is Paganini's great feat on one string perpetually repeated. The same criticism applies to their odd, but exquisitely supple, mode of dancing; and though to our ideas the exhibition is more a feat of muscle than art, to the Arab it conveys the highest sense of graceful movement, and must certainly be quite as hard to learn and successfully display as any *pas seul* that is practised by the *ballerinas* of Paris or London [Arnold 1882: 92].

This same disconnect is reflected in Steevens' observation (noted earlier) of an Egyptian audience's enthusiastic reaction to what he perceived to be a rather boring and repetitive performance in an 1890s entertainment hall (Steevens 1898: 40).

Arnold's remark that the dance is "more a feat of muscle than art" was a fairly common Western assessment of *'awālim/ghawāzī* dance and early *raqṣ sharqī*. Europeans and Americans generally found it difficult to accept that these dances, with their focus on torso-based movement rather than footwork, were, in fact, dances:

> A performance wherein the feet are seldom lifted from the floor can be termed "dancing" only by courtesy; but as an illustration of what the muscles of the body may be trained to do, the *danse du ventre* is in a way remarkable [Penfield 1899: 30–33].

Further, once they grew accustomed to the strangeness of the technique, Western spectators found the dances to be rather monotonous. Warner, writing of *ghawāzī* dance, states that "five minutes of it is as good as an hour" (Warner 1900: 381). Sladen, referring to early *raqṣ sharqī*, calls it as an "intolerably tiresome performance" and states:

> The musicians tum-tum on native drums and drawl out a monotonous sing-song, and the women stand in front of the footlights and wriggle their bodies in the most

> ungainly attitudes. It is difficult to imagine how they prove alluring to any one [Sladen 1911: 109].

Similarly, Reynolds-Ball dismisses early *raqṣ sharqī* as Cairo's famous "unvariety show" (Reynolds-Ball 1898b: 192).

As discussed earlier, Westerners were quick to ascribe erotic meaning to these torso-oriented dances, and they were surprised and dismayed that such dancing would be performed in front of women and children (see, for example, Bartlett 1850: 112–115). Yet Europeans and Americans failed to grasp that eroticism, when present, did not automatically imply lewdness or lasciviousness to Egyptian viewers. Impropriety in dance performance was differently defined for Egyptian viewers than for their Western counterparts. For Egyptians, the fundamental movements of *raqṣ sharqī* and *'awālim/ghawāzī* dance were not intrinsically improper. Indeed, most ordinary Egyptians were (and are) comfortable performing *raqṣ baladī*, the social form of belly dance, in appropriate social settings. Roushdy states:

> *Baladi* dancing most typically takes place at wedding celebrations and other festivities commemorating rites of passage. It is admirable of a woman or even a man to dance well, but not well enough to be taken for a professional [Roushdy 2009: 12].

The technique of the mixed-gender partner dances imported from the West was much more shocking to Egyptian sensibilities. In Chapter Two, I described a 1901 letter to the editor of *al-Hilāl* magazine, in which a middle-class Egyptian woman complains that ladies in her social circle were being pressured to dance in the *afranjī* way (with a man), rather than the indigenous *sharqī* way (solo) (*al-Hilāl* 10 April 1901: 412). She adamantly rejects this mixed-gender way of dancing, describing it as a negative side effect of "modernization." A few weeks later, in another letter to the editor, an Egyptian physician offers his support of this woman's position, suggesting that Western dances posed a health risk due to the Western fashion of wearing corsets while performing (*al-Hilāl* 1 May 1901: 437–439).

For Egyptians, performance context played a much more significant role than dance technique in determining the propriety—or lack thereof—of the dance. Professional dancers, by performing in public for mixed-gender or sometimes male-only audiences, transgressed Egyptian norms of appropriate female behavior, yet their dancing was still accepted—even expected—in traditional social contexts. Van Nieuwkerk notes:

> Professional dancers performing at weddings, although they interpret and bring out people's happiness, transgress these limits. However, they are regarded as necessary to enliven the party [Van Nieuwkerk 1995: 131].

The transition of Egyptian dance from traditional performance settings such as weddings and *mawālid* to the decidedly non-traditional stages of the entertainment halls ensured that *raqṣ sharqī*, and the women who performed it, would be prone to perceptions of impropriety, a situation compounded by the widespread practice of *fatḥ* in Egyptian entertainment halls. Yet, in this new and uncharted frontier of dance performance, Egyptians would employ spatial and temporal strategies to adjust the entertainment hall setting to Egyptian social norms—for example, by establishing designated seating areas for families, and by scheduling special performances for female audiences. These strategies will be touched on in the next chapter.

Summary

As this discussion has illustrated, a careful examination of primary source materials, in conjunction with a consideration of present-day Egyptian perspectives, reveals several aesthetic features of early *raqṣ sharqī*. First, improvisation was the preferred mode of performance—even after the introduction of choreographed group dance at some point prior to the mid–1930s—because improvisation is conducive to the expression and evocation of feeling. Second, dance performance was closely tied to effective musical interpretation. Finally, the dance periodically assumed an erotic character, but the presence or absence of this quality was dependent on the performer and the performance context.

In general, these features are shared by both *raqṣ sharqī* and *'awālim/ghawāzī* dance, and they reinforce the continuity between *raqṣ sharqī* and its predecessors. It is quite clear that *raqṣ sharqī* was shaped by the aesthetic tastes of Egyptian, rather than European or American, audiences (and evidence presented in the next chapter will reaffirm that the audiences for *raqṣ sharqī* were predominantly Egyptian). It is also evident that the dance's detachment from traditional performance contexts, combined with the widespread practice of *fatḥ* in the entertainment halls where it was performed, impacted Egyptians' perceptions of the propriety—or lack thereof—of *raqṣ sharqī* and its performers.

Taken together, Chapters Three and Four have demonstrated that in spite of the absence of film footage of early *raqṣ sharqī*, an array of other lines of evidence reveals a great deal about this dance form as it emerged and evolved on Egypt's entertainment hall stages. From the 1890s through the 1920s, in the liminal setting provided by the entertainment halls, the traditional dances of the *'awālim* and *ghawāzī* absorbed and integrated new and foreign elements, thus transforming into a new and distinct dance form. Nevertheless, this emergent dance style continued to share core aesthetic and technical elements with *'awālim/ghawāzī* dances, reaffirming its cultural authenticity in spite of its hybrid nature. With the basic aesthetic and technical characteristics of *raqṣ sharqī* now established, the next chapter turns to a consideration of the format of a performance at the turn of the nineteenth and twentieth centuries.

Five

Raqṣ Sharqī Performance at the Turn of the Century

As detailed in Chapters One and Two, the entertainment halls of Cairo and Alexandria established formalized spaces dedicated to arts and entertainment, and within their walls, *raqṣ sharqī* emerged and developed as a new and distinct dance style hybridizing native and foreign elements. For the price of admission, Egyptians could experience and enjoy this dance form, in a setting where the indigenous intersected with the foreign, and where tradition interfaced with modernity. In Chapters Three and Four, a range of primary and secondary sources were examined in order to reconstruct the technical and aesthetic elements of *raqṣ sharqī* from the 1890s through the 1920s. In this chapter, further analysis of the relevant primary sources yields important information regarding a typical performance, including the characteristics of the entertainment halls that presented dance, the organization of the show, and the nature and extent of interaction between audience and performers.

The available primary sources include foreign sources—text descriptions from travelers' accounts and travel guide books, photographs, and picture postcards—and indigenous Egyptian sources—particularly Arabic-language advertisements and flyers. These sources offer tremendous insight into the characteristics of a typical Egyptian dance show at a turn-of-the-century Egyptian entertainment hall. However, both the foreign and the indigenous sources pose specific challenges to this examination, reflecting the differing interests and agendas of their creators and their target audiences.

As previously discussed, by the end of the 1920s, mentions of dance had become fairly common in Arabic-language advertisements and flyers for Egyptian entertainment venues. The primary intent of these ads and flyers was to announce (and sell) performances to informed local Egyptian consumers. Thus, although they offer a great deal of detail in terms of the names of performers, the names and locations of venues, the price of admission, etc., these sources generally shed very little light on details of the performance, such as length, audience interaction, and so on. Moreover, many of these sources from the 1890s through the 1920s use nonspecific terms such as *raqṣ* (dance) or *raqṣ 'arabī* (Arabic dance), making it difficult to determine exactly what style of dance was being presented in advertised performances. Compounding these challenges, the term *raqṣ sharqī* was not definitively tied to its current meaning until the late 1920s or early 1930s (see Chapter Two). This terminological ambiguity makes it necessary to include in this analysis any entertainment halls that were advertised to have included dance in their program, even if the advertisements and flyers do not specifically name *raqṣ sharqī*.

By the mid–1930s, *raqṣ sharqī* began to figure prominently in the many entertainment-focused magazines that had emerged in Egypt in the late 1920s and early 1930s, and in much the same fashion as the celebrity gossip magazines of today, performers and venues were regularly discussed, described, and dissected. Karin Van Nieuwkerk's examination of early twentieth century Egyptian entertainment venues is largely informed by these sources (see Van Nieuwkerk 1995: 40–49). In addition, *raqṣ sharqī* performances were commonly depicted in Egyptian films from the mid–1930s onward. Though these magazines and films were produced after the period of interest in this study, they reveal interesting continuities between the dance performances in the entertainment halls of the 1930s and those of earlier decades; they thus offer a useful complement to the indigenous source materials of the 1890s through 1920s.

Due to the challenges posed by the native Egyptian sources, it is necessary to supplement them with the accounts of European and American observers, and the latter present their own problems. In the late nineteenth and early twentieth centuries, foreign travelers and tourists in Egypt seem to have been less inclined to experience native entertainment than entertainment geared specifically toward European and American audiences, leading them to patronize venues that offered the latter. When foreigners did visit entertainment halls geared toward the indigenous Egyptian population, their accounts often reflect a mix of bemusement, confusion, and distaste (see, for example, Dinning 1920: 270–279, Lamplough 1907: 30, Sladen 1911: 115–117).

Still, some foreigners—particularly long-term residents—patronized and enjoyed Egyptian entertainment with some frequency. Dinning notes the presence of French and Italians at the show he attended at the

Egypsiana in Cairo (Dinning 1920: 273–274). *L'Égypte Nouvelle,* a French-language magazine targeted at European residents and the Francophone Egyptian elite, published a review of an Arabic-language play at Yūsif Wahbī's Ramses Theater (*L'Égypte Nouvelle* 27 December 1924: II). Nevertheless, the same publication's review of several European-style productions featuring the troupe of the Greek actress Marika Kotopouli at Cairo's new Printania Theater offers no hint that the same venue was also host to some of the most popular Egyptian entertainers of the period, such as the singer Munīrah al-Mahdīyah (*L'Égypte Nouvelle* 5 April 1924: I).

The El Dorado entertainment hall, where Egyptian dance was regularly presented as early as the 1890s, is one of the few native entertainment halls to be mentioned and described in significant detail in numerous foreign accounts. Yet, to date, I have encountered only one contemporary Arabic-language mention of the venue (*al-Ahrām* 1 December 1888: 2). Nevertheless, foreign accounts clearly indicate that at the turn of the century, El Dorado was primarily patronized by Egyptians and that the Egyptian-style entertainment on the bill there was of little appeal to the few European and American audience members (see Loewenbach 1908: 218–220). It is noteworthy that this venue disappears from travelers' accounts and guidebooks after the 1910s, precisely when the government was enacting more stringent regulations on entertainment (see Chapter Two). Although there is no concrete evidence that illicit activities were taking place at El Dorado, its location amidst the unregulated foreign brothels of Wagh al-Birkat Street—and just adjacent to the native "red light" district of the *Wāsa'a*[1]—is telling (Ward 2013a). Egyptians seeking more family-oriented venues would have turned to other areas, such as 'Imād al-Dīn Street, where a wide variety of new establishments became available in the 1910s and 1920s.

In short, there is a substantial disconnect between foreigners' accounts and native Egyptian sources from the period of interest in this study, and both pose challenges. Therefore, in order to create a detailed picture of how *raqṣ sharqī* figured into the programming of Egypt's entertainment halls from the 1890s through the 1920s, it is necessary to rely on—and attempt to reconcile—both of these disparate lines of evidence.

The discussion to follow focuses on venues that offered entertainment targeted toward a native Egyptian clientele. It was at these establishments that Egyptian dance was presented for the enjoyment of Egyptians. Indeed, the audiences for *raqṣ sharqī* were overwhelmingly native Egyptian. As detailed in Chapter Four, an analysis of the aesthetic of *raqṣ sharqī* demonstrates that the dance was targeted toward the tastes of Egyptian, rather than European or American, viewers. Beyond the aesthetic evidence, however, the firsthand accounts of foreign observers clearly indicate that the audiences for *raqṣ sharqī* were Egyptian (for example, Giffin 1911: 39, Loewenbach 1908: 218, Steevens 1898: 39–42). Moreover, the wealth of Arabic-language advertisements for Egyptian entertainment venues establishes beyond a shadow of a doubt that they presented programs that were intended specifically for Egyptian audiences.

One contemporary European author, writing of Cairo venues where Egyptian dance was the main attraction, asserts: "They are, however, altogether lacking in local colour, and are, in fact, run by enterprising Greeks and Levantines for European visitors" (Reynolds-Ball 1898b: 191). Reynolds-Ball's statement is accurate regarding the ownership of many of these venues; a cursory glance through the list of cafés, *cafés chantants*, and theaters listed in a 1904 French-language directory of businesses in Cairo and Alexandria reveals that many of these venues were owned or managed by foreigners (Poffandi 1904: 90–92, 131, 281–282, 320). Similarly, a 1913 article in the Arabic-language magazine *al-Zuhūr* notes that numerous Greek entrepreneurs opened entertainment halls focused on Egyptian dance in both Cairo and Alexandria in the latter years of the nineteenth century (*al-Zuhūr* November 1913: 359–360). For example, El Dorado was owned by one Antoine Christou, while the Thousand and One Nights Theater, located near the Azbakīyah Gardens, was owned by Manoli Ioannidis (spelled Emm. Jeannides in the French directory) (Poffandi 1904: 92, *al-Zuhūr* November 1913: 359).[2] However, Reynolds-Ball's suggestion that these venues and the dance performed on their stages were targeted toward Europeans is simply not borne out by the evidence. Again, the aesthetic of the dance, the firsthand accounts of foreign visitors, and the abundant Arabic-language advertisements targeted toward the local Egyptian population clearly indicate that *raqṣ sharqī* was intended for Egyptian audiences.

Inside an Entertainment Hall

The available evidence reveals a great deal regarding the Egyptian entertainment halls in which dance was presented, including the seating arrangements, the cost of admission, and the amenities available to patrons, such as snacks and beverages. Additionally, the evidence illustrates how

Egyptians used spatial and temporal strategies—such as the establishment of dedicated seating areas for families, and the scheduling of ladies-only and families-only shows—to adjust the entertainment hall setting to Egyptian social norms, thus allowing a broader cross-section of the Egyptian public to attend shows. In short, the foreign and indigenous primary source materials, taken together, paint a vivid picture of the scene inside a turn-of-the-century Egyptian entertainment hall.

The venues where dance was presented were structurally diverse. As mentioned in Chapter One, while some Egyptian entertainment halls resembled contemporary European theaters, with seating arranged in boxes and stalls, others were more similar to European music halls, with seating organized around tables. Some of the venues that featured dancers, such as El Dorado, were of the latter style, though theater-style venues, such as the Azbakīyah Garden Theater, also incorporated dance performances into their programming. Some Egyptian entertainment venues were open-air settings (Dinning 1920: 243, 273; Sladen 1911: 62, 119). Some of these were seasonal and only opened during the summer (e.g., Sladen 1911: 119), while others stayed open year-round; at the latter, a temporary roof of Egyptian tent fabric was installed in the winter months (e.g., Dinning 1920: 273).

The layout of the music-hall style venues appears to have been fairly standard. Several textual descriptions and picture postcards (Figure 13) depict the interior of El Dorado:

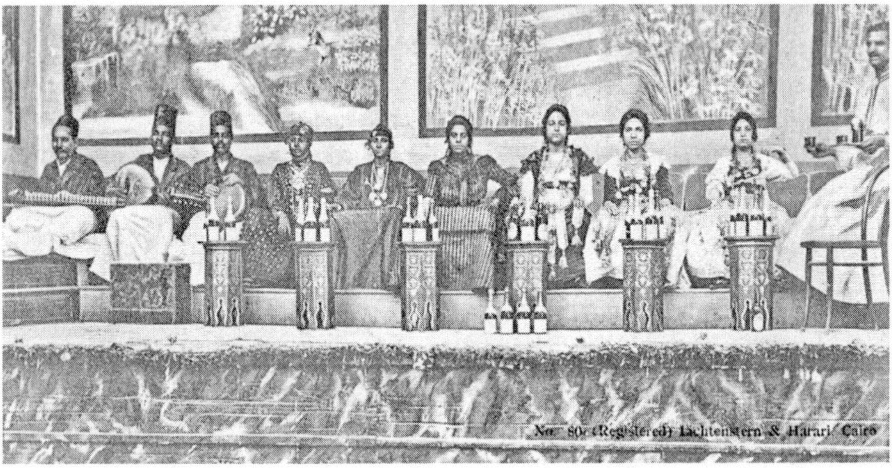

Figure 13. View inside the El Dorado entertainment hall (Lichtenstern and Harari postcard, *circa* 1900).

> An Arab café, or theatre, in Cairo, "the Eldorado," is filled with chairs, where drinks, cigarettes, and coffee are served to those of the audience wishing them [*Star* 20 September 1902: 2].

> At the end of the hall is a large stage, occupied by six men and as many women, seated in semi-circle facing the audience [Loewenbach 1908: 219, translated by the author, with assistance from Christine Ferhat].

A brief description of the Thousand and One Nights Theater suggests a similar venue:

> I saw also Towhida, the Raquel Meller of Egypt.... She sang in the Thousand and One Nights Theater in Cairo. She was painted according to the fashion of the Egyptian theater, wore many rings, bracelets and other jewelry and sat enthroned at the end of the theater with the audience below smoking and drinking coffee [*The Brooklyn Daily Eagle* 23 April 1927: 3].[3]

Foreign accounts of other, unnamed entertainment halls also describe a comparable set-up:

> Seated on divans on a stage at the end of the room are the performers, some ten in number—the orchestra and male singers on the right, the female singers in the center and the exponents of the eternal and monotonous dance on the left [*Hopkinsville Kentuckian* 30 May 1899: 7].

> The place was exactly like the Coffee Chantant in Florence, only not so vulgar. It was a large room, with a stage and tables and chairs all over the room at which you sit, and to which the moment you are seated up came the waiters to demand your order for drinks, just as in Europe [*South Australian Chronicle* 17 June 1893: 16].

> The whole show consists of a few wailing musicians sitting on a raised platform at one end of the café, accompanying the endless gyrations of a stout young woman of unprepossessing features ... [Reynolds-Ball 1898b: 191–192].

In short, these accounts describe a large hall with a raised stage at one end. Often, divans or chairs were arranged on the stage for the comfort of the entertainers. In some venues, the stage was bounded by a low railing (Steevens 1898: 39). Some of the simpler venues were barely a step above a coffee house:

> Really, it was only a double shop—blue and bluff plaster-walled, cigarette-stump floored, furnished with a coffee apparatus and benches. At one end were the performers, squatting on a divan-platform, raised about six feet; in front of it was a deal rail, with a row of candles stuck on to it by their own grease [Steevens 1898: 39].

These venues were frequently replicated at the various world's fairs that took place in the late nineteenth and early twentieth centuries. Photographs of the interiors of the world's fair venues align with the descriptions of the music-hall style Egyptian venues noted above (Figure 14).

Figure 14. Replica of a Cairo entertainment hall at the 1902 Exhibition of Commerce and Industry in Düsseldorf, Germany (F. Wolfrum postcard, 1902).

More recent incarnations of this sort of venue were widely portrayed in Egyptian films from the 1930s onward. These are the early twentieth century "nightclubs" described by Van Nieuwkerk (1995: 40–49). The nightclub scene in *al-'Izz Bahdalah* (1937) depicts a small venue with tables and chairs arranged facing a raised stage. Middle-class patrons—both male and female—sit around the tables sipping alcoholic beverages. A small band of Western instruments performs on the tiny stage, while the dance acts perform in the space just in front of the stage (two dance acts are shown in this scene: one a Latin partner dance, and the other *raqṣ sharqī*). A dance scene in the 1939 film *Layla Mumṭirah* depicts a virtually identical set-up—though here, the band is a traditional Egyptian *takht*.

At theater-style venues, a variety of seating options were available, including gallery and box seating. The grand Azbakīyah Garden Theater boasted orchestra stalls, two tiers of box seating, and a third-floor gallery (Figure 15). The seating at the Egypsiana Theater was simpler, but similar, with stalls, a row of boxes on either side of the stalls, and a high rear gallery (Dinning 1920: 273). The Kāzīnū al-Būsfūr advertised both covered and open seating (*al-Ahrām* 28 November 1924: 7). As with music-hall style venues, theater-style venues came to be frequently depicted in Egyptian film; examples include dance scenes in the 1946 film *Mā Aqdarsh* (*I Can't Do It*) and in the 1953 film *Anā Dhanbī Aīh* (*Is It My Fault*).

The price of admission for many of the entertainment halls that incorporated dance into their programming averaged around 5 to 10 piasters,

Figure 15. View inside the Azbakīyah Garden Theater (B. Arnaud postcard, *circa* 1910).

sometimes even less, and this pricing remained remarkably stable over a roughly forty year period. Interestingly, admission prices remained stable even through the periods of high inflation that plagued the Egyptian economy in the early decades of the twentieth century (e.g., 1907 and 1914–1918) (Kholoussy 2010: 25), indicating that over time, entertainments such as dance actually became more affordable, and therefore more accessible to a broader cross-section of the Egyptian public. Around 1890, first-class admission to a venue called The Louvre was 10 *ṣāgh* (10 piasters), while second-class cost just 5 *ṣāgh* (5 piasters) (*al-Zuhūr* November 1913: 359–360). Over thirty years later, the entry fee for the November 28, 1924 show at the Kāzīnū al-Būsfūr, which included "Arabic dance," was just 5 *ṣāgh* (*al-Ahrām* 28 November 1924: 7). Similarly, the admission fee for the November 24, 1931 show at Ṣālah Su'ād Maḥāssan was 5 *ṣāgh* (*al-Ahrām* 24 November 1931: 9). In May 1929, the door charge for the Sunday matinee at the Kit Kat Cabaret was 5 piasters, though admission for the dinner/show at the Kit Kat's restaurant was pricier, at 25 piasters (*al-Ahrām* 1 May 1929: 6). General admission to Badī'ah Maṣābnī's casino in Giza was 10 piasters (*al-Ahrām* 8 May 1930). Some establishments allowed free entry, but recovered their costs through drink purchases; examples include El Dorado and the Bīrah al-Ahrām Theater in Giza.

At many venues, admission was charged at the door. Some theater-style venues, such as the new Printania Theater and the Azbakīyah Garden Theater, encouraged patrons to purchase tickets in advance. These venues generally had a box office window where tickets could be purchased (e.g., *al-Ahrām* 1 September 1926: 7, *al-Ahrām* 15 May 1927: 6).

Contemporary sources suggest that drinks, and sometimes food, were available at most, if not all, the music-hall style venues (see, for example, Loewenbach 1908: 218–219, *South Australian Chronicle* 17 June 1893: 16, *Star* 20 September 1902: 2, Steevens 1898: 41–42, *The Brooklyn Daily Eagle* 23 April 1927: 3). Coffee was commonly served, but alcohol was available at many establishments as well. Snacks and beverages were also available at the theaters. Dinning describes the scene at the Egypsiana Theater:

> The hawkers are busy administering preliminary refreshment. Trays of coffee are hurried round; flagons of lemonade disappear at a draught. You will understand how a pint of lemonade goes at a gulp when you see what these people are eating—large slabs of cake with soft, poisonous-coloured icing; long chunks of nut toffee which whole families are noisily crunching. You will see mother and father and the two children each with a slab six inches long held in paper sold along with the toffee to protect the fingers. There is no more embarrassment in buying a blatant slab of toffee than there is shame in the noisy and abandoned mastication of it [Dinning 1920: 274].

Similarly, he comments on audience members avidly consuming snacks and drinks at a small theater in Rūḍ al-Faraj: "It seems to be the custom to come here for refreshment rather than entertainment" (Dinning 1920: 243).

Advertisements frequently include words such as *rāqīah* (classy or high-class) to indicate the luxury and refinement of the entertainment halls and their programs. However, the rather broad variation in the characteristics of the venues that were advertised with this sort of verbiage suggests that it is not an accurate indicator of the sort of clientele each venue attracted. For example, the Bīrah al-Ahrām Theater, which was advertised as "for high-class people," offered free admission and free transportation to the theater (though patrons were encouraged to purchase a beer while they watched the show) (a*l-Ahrām* 1 June 1927: 6, a*l-Ahrām* 1 September 1927: 6). Clearly, the performances at such a venue would have been accessible to Egyptians of all social classes. The Bīrah al-Ahrām Theater, like El Dorado, was geared toward a male clientele; an advertisement for the September 1927 program states that the show was for men only (a*l-Ahrām* 1 September 1927: 6). By contrast, Ṣālah Badī'ah Maṣābnī on

'Imād al-Dīn Street, which was advertised as "for high-class families," offered ladies-only shows (*al-Ahrām* 1 October 1930: 6).

In fact, many entertainment halls specifically marketed themselves as woman-friendly and/or family-friendly settings. The Kāzīnū al-Būsfūr had special seating areas reserved for families (*al-Ahrām* 28 November 1924: 7). Many venues advertised ladies-only or families-only shows (e.g., *al-Ahrām* 16 September 1919: 3, *al-Ahrām* 1 October 1930: 6; see also Fahmy 2011: 122, 207 n. 116). Dinning describes whole families attending and enjoying the show at the Egypsiana Theater (Dinning 1920: 273–274). These spatial and temporal adaptations—the designation of seating areas for families, and the scheduling of ladies-only and families-only shows—adjusted the entertainment hall setting to Egyptian social norms, thereby allowing a broader cross-section of Egyptians to patronize these establishments.

Still, it should not be assumed that male-dominated venues were necessarily sites of inappropriate behavior. Etta Josselyn Giffin, who visited Egypt in the course of her work for the American Association of Workers for the Blind, attended a performance at a Cairo entertainment hall and made the following observations:

> [S]everal of us visited a native music hall where Egyptian girls danced and sang to the accompaniment of native musicians. The audience of native men smoked cigarettes, seldom speaking, except when specially pleased, when they would raise both hands toward the stage and call "Allah!" "Allah!" sometimes tossing coins to the singer who was a beautiful girl,—who smiled and sang again and again. There were no words—only ah, or oh—or oo—but the tunes were full of suggestions and memories that charmed the initiated. To me they were sweetly clear, high notes with a peculiarly haunting, plaintive melody. There was no drinking and no boisterous behavior [Giffin 1911: 39].

The Structure of a Show

In addition to providing these fundamental details regarding the turn-of-the-century Egyptian entertainment halls that presented dance, the available evidence reveals a great deal regarding how the dance performances that took place on their stages were structured. Primary sources offer information regarding when and how dance was presented in the program, as well as the length of the dance performances. These sources indicate that some entertainment halls presented *raqṣ sharqī* as their main attraction, while others offered the dance as a secondary attraction in a variety show centered on a singer or a play. Indigenous sources sometimes identify certain *raqṣ sharqī* soloists by name, suggesting that these performers were famous enough to be box-office draws.

At some turn-of-the-century venues, *raqṣ sharqī* appears to have been the main attraction. The *al-Zuhūr* article noted above asserts that near the end of the nineteenth century, there were nineteen venues dedicated to Egyptian dance in Cairo (*al-Zuhūr* November 1913: 359–360). One such venue was El Dorado, though it is worth noting that prior to the 1890s, the program there was more varied (Académie Royale des Sciences, des Lettres et des Beaux-Arts de Belgique 1870: 51; *al-Ahrām* 1 December 1888: 2; *The Queenslander* 27 February 1886: 336; Ward 2013a). El Dorado was originally situated off Mīdān al-Khazindār, to the northeast of Azbakīyah Gardens, but sometime around 1880, it moved to a new location on Wagh al-Birkat Street; it seems that the shift in programming took place within ten to fifteen years of the move (Ward 2013a).

At other venues, either a singer or a play was the featured act. A dance performance (sometimes *raqṣ sharqī*, sometimes other styles) would occur before or after the main act, during intermissions, or sometimes embedded within a play. A 1927 observer of Egyptian plays remarked: "In Egypt muscle dances and native songs are presented between the acts" (*The Brooklyn Daily Eagle* 23 April 1927: 3). Dinning describes a child performer who sang and danced during the intermissions at the Egypsiana:

> There is a little girl of eight amongst them—the pet of the company. She takes her part in dancing and in solo work during a succession of solos. She is petted in the most obvious way at the height of the performance in an informal manner that is inconceivable on the English stage. She likes it, and responds to it with childlike abandon. Between the acts she is often sent before the curtain to sing. This she does with a mature rhythmical body-motion that brings down the house. Then the house pets her; and she responds to that [Dinning 1920: 276].

Dinning's description of the child's "mature" movements suggest that she may have been performing *raqṣ sharqī*. During the same production, men comically imitated women's dancing:

> When the men's ballet that impersonates Bints comes on, the real Bints on the stage can never resist it. And certainly there is something irresistibly comic in the spectacle of men, with men's gestures and guttural voices, wearing yashmaks and attempting a falsetto voice to accompany their belly-dance, which none but a Bint can do [Dinning 1920: 275–276].

At venues like El Dorado, where *raqṣ sharqī* was the main event, the typical dance show consisted of multiple performances by a single dancer, or else successive performances by a variety of soloists throughout the course of the evening. Each dance was generally from fifteen to thirty minutes in length. Between performances, the dancers would sit and rest on the stage, or else circulate through the audience to collect tips.

> [T]hese contortions last a long time; however [the dancer] pauses to empty a beer that is sent to her by an enthusiastic spectator.... When she is finished, she comes into the room to "pass the hat" with a small saucer which she places successively on each table and which she leaves there for a few minutes, during which she stands aside discreetly. Most of the natives give a small coin. During this operation, she is tracked and monitored by a fine Egyptian with a great black mustache and a fierce expression, who does not lose sight of her for a moment, nor the money she collects, he is probably her impresario.... The same show is repeated every half hour. It is followed by a cinematograph, and starting at one o'clock in the morning, the audience dances [Loewenbach 1908: 220, translated by the author, with assistance from Christine Ferhat].

> A dancer with an indescribable swagger leaves the divan and commences to posture on the platform. A hum of admiration rises from her many admirers, for she is a prime favorite with the habitués of the hall. For a solid quarter of an hour does this brown-faced nymph continue her hideous contortions—hideous, at all events, to persons of uncultivated tastes [*Hopkinsville Kentuckian* 30 May 1899: 7].

> Then her place is taken by another, equally ill-favoured and obese, who goes through the same interminable gyrations, to be relieved in her turn; and this goes on hour after hour. This strange "unvariety show" is, nevertheless, one of the established sights of Cairo, and is frequented in great numbers by tourists [Reynolds-Ball 1898b: 191–192].

> [E]ach Ghazeeyeh, after dancing, which occupies a tiresome twenty minutes or more, goes around among the audience, and solicits baksheesh (a present). Several of the Ghawazee sit in the background, awaiting their turn to dance [*Star* 20 September 1902: 2].

In advertisements for venues where dance was presented during intermissions or before/after the main act, the dancers are frequently identified by name, suggesting a higher level of fame or prestige for these performers. For example, an advertisement for the Victoria Theater announces that the dancer Līnā would be performing *raqṣ sharqī* during the intermissions on April 3, 4, and 5, 1927 (*al-Ahrām* 3 April 1927: 5). Līnā was also a featured soloist on May 15, 1927 at the Azbakīyah Garden Theater—she was billed as "the one and only" Līnā, suggesting some degree of notoriety (*al-Ahrām* 15 May 1927: 6). The Turkish dancer Blanche Hānim, who both acted and danced at Cairo's Ramses Theater on June 10, 1925, was billed as "the greatest and most famous dancer in Istanbul" (*al-Ahrām* 6 June 1925: 6). Similarly, the Turkish dancer Afrānza Hānim was billed as "the one renowned in Syria and Egypt" when she appeared at the Bīrah al-Ahrām Theater in June 1927 (a*l-Ahrām* 1 June 1927: 6). A December

19, 1924 advertisement announces a "marvelous" dance by Fatḥīyah al-Maghribīyah at Cairo's Kāzīnū al-Būsfūr, on the same night that the venue featured the up-and-coming young singer Umm Kalthūm (*al-Ahrām* 19 December 1924: 7).

The advertisement for Fatḥīyah 's performance is particularly interesting, as it was published nearly two full years before Badī'ah Maṣābnī opened her first establishment, Ṣālah Badī'ah Maṣābnī, in November 1926 (Adum n.d., *al-Ahrām* 4 November 1926: 3). Badī'ah did not include dancers in her programming until March 1927, when she began featuring Afrānza Hānim (Adum n.d., *al-Ahrām* 10 March 1927: 6). Līnā was performing *raqṣ sharqī* at the Victoria Theater at roughly the same time that Badī'ah began featuring Afrānza (*al-Ahrām* 3 April 1927: 5), and Ḥikmat Hānim was featured at the new Printania Theater several months earlier, in January 1927 (*al-Ahrām* 15 January 1927: 5). These references to featured dance performers in the mid-to-late 1920s indicate that Badī'ah was following a general trend when she decided to bill Afrānza Hānim as a featured soloist in the spring of 1927.

Interestingly, in some advertisements for venues where dance was part of a varied program, individual dance performances were given names or titles. For example, a January 4, 1925 production at the Azbakīyah Garden Theater portrayed the Biblical story of Samson and Delilah and included three dance performances with creative titles such as the "Dance of Freedom," "Dance of Love," and "Dance of the Shameless Women" (*al-Ahrām* 3 January 1925: 2). It is unclear from the advertisement what style of dance was being performed (though the advertisement bills the whole evening as a "*ḥaflat* of Middle Eastern and Egyptian music, acting, singing, and dancing); it is also unclear whether these dances were performed during the play or during the intermissions. Another advertisement for the Azbakīyah Garden Theater, this one for a March 6, 1926 program headlined by vocalist Umm Kalthūm, more explicitly notes that both Middle Eastern and foreign dance would be performed during intermissions (*al-Ahrām* 5 March 1926: 3). There were four titled dance performances: "Under the Light of the Moon," "The Dreams of the Lover," and "Happiness of the Married Couple."

Interaction Between Audience and Performers

As discussed in Chapter Two, the entertainment hall established a structural and social division between performers and their audiences.

The intimate and friendly association that characterized the relationship between *'awālim/ghawāzī* and their patrons was not apparent in the performance culture of the entertainment hall. Within these venues, interactions between dancers and audience members became more circumscribed. During performances, audiences expressed approval and admiration by applauding, exclaiming, or throwing small coins or bouquets of flowers (e.g., Dinning 1920: 274–276, Giffin 1911: 39). Additionally, as noted in Chapter Two, a *muṭayyib*—an individual whose role was to loudly and repeatedly proclaim the excellence of the performance—was sometimes present during dance performances (*Hopkinsville Kentuckian* 30 May 1899: 7).

The tendency of Egyptian entertainers to break the "fourth wall" during performances, and the informality of the audience and the performers calling out to each other during the program, came as a shock to some foreign observers. Dinning writes:

> Informality is of course the note of the performance when it does begin, as it is of the waiting audience. You will never have anything decorous in a Cairene native theatre. There is communication set up between the boxes and the stage at intervals—the performing ladies have their friends (and their fellow-artistes with "a night off") in boxes; they emit appraising remarks on their work to individual performers. The performers, in the course of their work, acknowledge them by retorts and grimaces. Small bouquets are shied as marks of appreciation: these missiles are being hurled all the evening. There are boys in the crowd who hawk nothing else. Hurled with vigour they are: the degree of vigour marks the degree of appreciation. I have seen a girl become a casualty on the stage through being hit in the eye with an admirer's bouquet. The ballet has to defend itself against these compact little bundles of flowers. Some of the girls are very adroit in catching them and saving their faces.... There is, of course, the informality between performers. They are interested in each other's work in a curiously detached way. They criticize each other; and they are often genuinely amused by each other [Dinning 1920: 274–275].

In spite of this informality, there seem to have been rules of etiquette that governed audience behavior in these settings, and these unspoken rules were periodically broken by foreigners. Moseley offers a scathing description of the liberties taken by British men at Egypt's entertainment halls:

> They would go to music-halls, sit in any seats they preferred, despite the remonstrances of the nervous attendant, interrupt the performance, throwing sallies of considerably heavy brilliance at the performers, and enter into indignant altercations with foreign members of the audience who resented this behaviour. Sometimes, I am afraid, our military men were the culprits, and one saw the spectacle of Tommy up in the "gods" looking down below where his trainers and commanders were making public nuisances of themselves [Moseley 1917: 204].

When dancers were offstage, two forms of audience-performer interaction are documented, and both were of a transactional nature that could benefit the dancer, the establishment, or both. First, there is evidence of dancers occasionally moving through the audience to collect tips. This practice is documented at El Dorado (e.g., Loewenbach 1908: 220, *Star* 20 September 1902: 2), and it likely took place at other venues as well (see *al-Zuhūr* November 1913: 359).

Second, there is abundant evidence of entertainers engaging in *fatḥ*, the practice of sitting and drinking with customers in order to encourage spending. Van Nieuwkerk demonstrates that *fatḥ* was widespread in the entertainment halls of the 1920s and 1930s (1995: 43–45). However, according to the aforementioned article appearing in *al-Zuhūr* magazine in 1913, the practice was already well-established by the end of the nineteenth century (*al-Zuhūr* November 1913: 361). In fact, *fatḥ* was so common at the turn of the century that it was referenced in popular music. In a *circa* 1908 Odéon recording, the singer Bahiyah al-Maḥallāwīyah mimics the style and mannerisms of the famous turn-of-the-century singer/dancer Shafīqah al-Qibṭīyah; she portrays a giggling flirt who is so inebriated after sitting and drinking with customers that she can barely sing and dance (*Raqṣ Shafīqah* 1908, Ward 2013b).

Not all dancers engaged in *fatḥ*. On the occasion that Loewenbach visited El Dorado, the dancer did not sit or interact directly with the customers at their tables; rather, the venue employed several women specifically for the purpose of *fatḥ*:

> [The native customers] do not buy drinks; but the institution recovers its expenses nonetheless, thanks to a few women, who go from one table to another and get paid to drink. A Sudanese, not pretty, but with an agreeable figure, sits down at our table. She judges Mr. Wertheim as the most generous of us and gets him to offer her two half-bottles of beer at 10 piastres, and thus we have completed our entry price [Loewenbach 1908: 218–219].

Also, the practice of *fatḥ* was not exclusive to the native Egyptian entertainers working in Egypt's entertainment halls. Foreign performers employed in these venues also sat, flirted, and drank with customers, both foreign and native. Various observers noted this activity at the Casino de Paris and the Abbaye des Roses, venues that were patronized by both foreign and indigenous clientele (e.g., Collett 1922: 47, Reynolds 1926: 185). Wiltshire, remarking on the young middle-class men of Cairo, states: "Despite their religion they can still indulge in dalliance with the daughters of the unbelievers I saw in the Abbaye de Rose" (Wiltshire 1915–1916: 53–55).

The practice of *fatḥ* by dancers should not lead to the conclusion that these women were prostitutes, although it is likely that some dancers did resort to prostitution if their financial circumstances demanded it. Nevertheless, in the eyes of many Egyptians, a female entertainer working in an entertainment hall was a woman of questionable morality—particularly if she sat with male customers and consumed alcohol. As Van Nieuwkerk notes:

> Female entertainers were paid to sit, drink, and dance or sing, not to sleep with customers. Yet they were generally regarded by the public as fallen women. Whether they were, strictly speaking, prostitutes or not did not really matter to the public [Van Nieuwkerk 1995: 45].

The Egyptian public's misgivings regarding the moral rectitude of female entertainers were frequently explored in Egyptian film beginning in the 1930s. For example, in *al-'Izz Bahdalah* (1937), the singer Zūzū (Zūzū Labīb) and dancer Rūḥīyah (Rūḥīyah Fawzī) seduce the main characters Shālūm and 'Abduh; both women charm the men during their performances, sit and drink alcohol with them while offstage, and later invite them to their boudoir. Still, it is important to note that dancers were not *universally* perceived to be immoral. For example, the author of a 1933 article in the Egyptian women's interest magazine *al-'Arūsah* defends Egyptian dancers against another writers' insinuations of their immorality; he suggests that if the other author really wished to understand dance, he should have interviewed a dancer of quality, such as Ḥikmat Fahmī (*al-'Arūsah* 8 February 1933: 6).

Summary

As this chapter has demonstrated, a careful examination of the available primary source materials provides valuable insights into the characteristics of a typical Egyptian dance show at a turn-of-the-century Egyptian entertainment hall. In spite of the particular challenges posed by both the foreign and the indigenous sources, they yield important information regarding a typical performance, including the characteristics of the entertainment halls that presented dance, the organization of the show, and the nature and extent of interaction between audience and performers. The establishments that presented dance ranged from modest music-hall style venues to grand theaters such as the Azbakīyah Garden Theater. Admission was affordable—and remarkably stable over a period of several decades—allowing Egyptians from a broad range of social backgrounds to patronize these venues. The availability of ladies-only and family-oriented shows enabled all Egyptians—men and women, young and old—to enjoy the performances. In some cases, *raqṣ sharqī* was the venue's main attraction, while in others, the dance was integrated into a larger program focused on a play or a musical performance. Dancers who performed during intermissions or before/after the main act were frequently identified by name in contemporary advertisements and flyers, suggesting that these women had achieved some degree of fame as solo performers. In the entertainment hall milieu, dancers were separated spatially and socially from their audiences. Yet, Egyptian entertainers continued to break the "fourth wall" during performance, harking back to traditional modes of entertainment, in which the relationship between entertainers and their patrons was more casual and friendly. Beyond this, however, contact between dancers and their audiences was limited to two types of interactions: tip collection and *fatḥ*. The practice of *fatḥ* contributed to the Egyptian public's conflicted perceptions of *raqṣ sharqī* performers.

Six

The *Raqṣ Sharqī* Costume in Historical Context

What were the earliest performers of *raqṣ sharqī* wearing when they took the stage? The *badlah* ("suit"), an ensemble consisting of a bra, a belt, and a skirt, usually with the midriff bare, is now widely recognized as the typical costuming for *raqṣ sharqī*. Yet, exactly when and how the *badlah* came to be the "uniform" for *raqṣ sharqī* is not well understood, and knowledge regarding the development of costuming for *raqṣ sharqī* has suffered from the same lack of empirical research as other aspects of the history of the dance.

The commonly accepted origin story for the *badlah* asserts that it was created in the West, a byproduct of Orientalist visions of an imagined East, and was then adopted by Egyptian dancers in response to Western influences and desires. An oft-cited example of this narrative is derived from Buonaventura's *Serpent of the Nile*:

> It will be recalled that dancers were formerly accustomed to perform in their everyday dress. Special costumes are the product of a highly developed theatrical tradition which did not obtain in the Arab world. In the 1920s a costume emerged which largely owed its inspiration to Hollywood, where female allure was associated with the vamp. The Western Oriental dance outfit, a combination of bra, low-slung gauzy skirt with side slits and bare midriff, was adopted by Arab dancers and became the cabaret uniform [Buonaventura 1998: 151–152].

In reality, although most early nineteenth century *'awālim* and *ghawāzī* wore essentially the same garments as middle- and upper-class women, by the 1860s, specific elements had begun to emerge that differentiated the professional dancer's costume from everyday dress. By the 1890s, these elements had developed into a distinct and recognizable dance uniform that was worn both by entertainment hall performers and by many of the *'awālim* and *ghawāzī* who continued to perform at *mawālid*, weddings, and other private celebrations. The early *badlah* shared several features with this turn-of-the-century costuming style.

As with other aspects of the origin and development of *raqṣ sharqī*, the history of costuming for the dance reveals foreign influence; however, the evidence indicates a deliberate integration of foreign elements into an existing indigenous costuming aesthetic, rather than Egyptians simply copying a pre-existing Western fantasy costume. An examination of primary source materials from the dawn of the nineteenth century until the end of the 1930s suggests that the basic template of the *badlah*—bra, bare or barely covered midriff, hip belt, and skirt—evolved from an indigenous (though Ottoman-influenced) costuming style, while absorbing foreign innovations, such as stockings, fashionable European shoes, and new fabric choices and design elements. This hybridization of costuming is consistent with the broader trend of adapting and integrating foreign ideas and influences into a native Egyptian aesthetic, as discussed in previous chapters.

Costuming Before the Mid–Nineteenth Century

In the early decades of the nineteenth century, the costuming of most *'awālim* and *ghawāzī* appears to have been an elaboration on the everyday garments worn by middle- or upper-class Egyptian women in the privacy of the *ḥarīm*, or women's quarters, of the home (Jomard 1822: 733; Lane 1860: 41–45, 377–382; Lane 2005 [1836]: 49–52, 372–377). However, as Clot-Bey wryly notes: "Their dress is almost the same as that worn by the elegant ladies of the country ... but it is tinged with this particular character that everywhere distinguishes the appearance of the courtesan from that of the honest lady" (Clot-Bey 1840b: 91–92). That "particular character" largely consisted of a flashiness or gaudiness not present in the attire of ordinary women:

> Their *toilette*, all tinsel, if it does not satisfy the taste, catches the eye with its shimmering effects; their long braided hair falls to the shoulders; they wear around their hips a rich belt tied loosely, serving to hold large pantaloons of cashmere, all tinged with vivid and brilliant colors [Voilquin 1866: 451–452].

In essence, dancers' attire was simply a showier and slightly more revealing variation on ordinary women's clothing.

The typical attire of middle- and upper-class women in Egypt was a variation on what was worn by well-to-do women elsewhere in the Ottoman Empire. The basic ensemble included a long chemise, a type of robe known as a *yelek* (or sometimes a shorter version of this garment, known as an *'antarī*), a pair of blousy trousers called *shintiyān*, a shawl tied loosely around the hips, and slippers with pointed toes (Lane 1860: 41–45, 377–382; Lane 2005 [1836]: 49–52, 372–377).[1] The chemise was made of fabrics such as linen, cotton, muslin, crepe, silk, and a striped silk/cotton blend (Lane 1860: 30, 41; Lane 2005 [1836]: 38, 49). This garment was ordinarily quite sheer, and frequently exposed the throat, the chest, and part of the bosom. At the turn of the eighteenth and nineteenth centuries, the chemise extended to the ankles, but by the mid–1830s, it extended only to the knees. The *yelek*, *'antarī*, and *shintiyān* were made of fabrics such as silk, striped silk/cotton blend, and muslin (Lane 1860: 41–43, Lane 2005 [1836]: 49). The *yelek* and the *'antarī* were long-sleeved garments, form-fitting down to the waist, and buttoned down the front; both were frequently cut in such a way that they left a substantial portion of the bosom covered only by the sheer chemise. While the *yelek* extended to the floor, the *'antarī* was cut just below the waist. Apparently, dancers either shortened the sleeves of the *yelek* or secured the sleeves above the elbow, for Clot-Bey notes that dancers' arms were frequently bare (Clot-Bey 1840b: 91–92). Indeed, Luigi Mayer's illustration from the Napoleonic period shows dancers with bare arms (Figure 16).

In addition to the garments just described, it is likely that some women periodically incorporated a short, sleeveless vest, known as a *ṣudayrī*, which would have been worn over a chemise, but under a *yelek*/*'antarī*. Although Lane makes no mention of this garment in his description of middle- and upper-class women's attire, he makes passing mention of it being worn by women of the lower classes (Lane 1860: 47). Lane goes into greater detail regarding the *ṣudayrī* worn by middle- and upper-class Egyptian *men*, indicating that this garment was worn during winter or cool weather (Lane 1860: 40). Didier notes that Gazal, a dancer whom he attempted to engage for a performance, wore a *ṣudayrī* under her *yelek* (Didier 1860: 339); tellingly, his encounter with Gazal took place in the middle of winter (Didier 1860: 332). The *ṣudayrī* begins to figure quite prominently in the costuming of dancers beginning *circa* the 1860s or 1870s.

Dancers typically wore a great deal of jewelry on their person, but again, they appear to have differed from ordinary women only in the quantity of the ornamentation. According to Lane: "The ornaments of the women of Egypt are so various that a description of them all would far exceed the limits which the nature of this work allows" (Lane 2005 [1836]: 549). Even so, he goes on to describe a dazzling array of headdresses, earrings,

Figure 16. Detail from *Egyptian Dancing Girls* by Luigi Mayer (aquatint, 1802).

necklaces, rings, bracelets, and anklets, as well as the hair ornaments known as *ṣafa*.[2] The *ṣafa* consisted of black silk cords which were braided into the hair, and from each cord dangled tiny ornaments and coins (Lane 1860: 566–567, Lane 2005 [1836]: 556–557). The *ṣafa* was generally worn by women of the middle and upper classes, but it was also adopted by some women of the lower classes. According to Lane, however, it was more typical for lower-class Egyptian women to divide their hair into two plaits, each of which was braided with red silk cords in a similar manner to the *ṣafa* (Lane 1860: 570, Lane 2005 [1836]: 560). Following the style of most Egyptian women, dancers styled their hair in numerous plaits adorned with the *ṣafa*.

Another common style of ornamentation among ordinary Egyptian women was the practice of wearing amulet cases, a custom also followed by dancers. According to Lane, amulet cases were "attached to a silk string or a chain, and generally hung on the right side above the girdle, the string or chain being passed over the left shoulder" (Lane 2005 [1836]: 558). Various authors from the first half of the nineteenth century describe female entertainers wearing amulet cases (e.g., Lane-Poole 1846: 104, Romer 1846a: 274). Isabella Romer, who observed a performance by the *ghāziyah* Ṣafīyah of Isnā in the 1840s, notes: "Three large silver amulet-cases, containing charms, were hung over the shawl girdle" (Romer 1846a: 274).

Several authors commented on the sumptuousness of female entertainers' attire. Sophia Lane-Poole, describing two *'awālim* who performed at the royal wedding of Zaynab Hānim, notes:

> They were tastefully attired, and a diamond crescent and star glittered on the right brow of each. One wore also a charm, contained in a little box very elegantly set with diamonds, and hung on a silk cord which passed over her left shoulder and under her right arm [Lane-Poole 1846: 104].

Isabella Romer was struck by the opulence of Ṣafīyah's garments and jewelry: "We computed that she carried about three hundred and fifty pounds on her person in coins alone, without including her other ornaments" (Romer 1846a: 275).

However, in spite of the richness of their dress and ornamentation, it is important to remember that female entertainers belonged to the lower strata of Egyptian society. One aspect of their physical appearance that reinforced this class association was the occasional presence of tattoos. As Lane notes, only women of the "lower orders" sported tattoos (Lane 1860: 39–41, Lane 2005 [1836]: 48–49). These tattoos, consisting of geometric shapes such as circles, stars, and lines, were placed on the forehead, the chin, between the breasts, on the backs of the hands and feet, and on the arms. The Luigi Mayer illustration noted earlier depicts dancers with a variety of tattoos (Figure 16).

Evidently, only the poorer *ghawāzī* costumed themselves in a manner different from that described above. These women wore the same sorts of garments worn by women of the Egyptian lower class, to wit, a chemise and *shintiyān*, covered by a loose-fitting *thawb* (similar to a loose robe) (Lane 1860: 47, 381; Lane 2005 [1836]: 55, 376).

Mid–Nineteenth Century Innovation

The mid–nineteenth century witnessed several changes in middle- and upper-class Egyptian women's dress. Dancers adopted some of these changes, but their costuming began to deviate from ordinary women's attire. Perhaps most importantly, dancers began incorporating a distinctive ribbon belt into their costuming; this belt has no parallels in the contemporary day-to-day dress of ordinary women and may mark the earliest divergence between a defined "professional" dance costume and ordinary female dress.

Middle- and upper-class women continued to wear the basic elements of chemise, *yelek*/*'antarī*, *shintiyān*, and shawl tied about the hips. However, photographs and *cartes de visite* reveal that by the 1860s, both the chemise and the *'antarī* had undergone significant changes (*Carte-de-Visite Album of Egypt and Egyptians* 1860; Jacobson 2007: 40, 139, 214).[3] The chemise was much shorter than in prior years, sometimes extending barely to the waist. If it was long enough, the chemise was tucked into the *shintiyān*. The *'antarī*, too, was significantly more abbreviated than in prior years; the mid–nineteenth century *'antarī* extended to just below the bust. The sleeves of the *'antarī* could be form-fitting or loose and blousy, but gathered at the wrists.

As the century progressed, Egyptian women, particularly those of the upper class, showed an increasing affinity toward Western dress and hairstyles. Upon entering the *ḥarīm* of Khedive Ismā'īl for the first time, Emmeline Lott, British governess to the Khedive's son Ibrahim, noted the "huge cases of fashionable Parisian boots, shoes, and slippers" (Lott 1867: 32). Less than ten years later, Ellen Chennells, British governess to the Khedive's daughter Zaynab, bemoaned the influence of European fashion on her charge: "I had often told my female friends how much prettier my pupil looked in her simple harem costume, with her beautiful hair bound back with a ribbon, than in an elaborate tight-fitting European dress, and a scaffolding on her head of curls, plaits, and diamonds" (Chennells 1893: 361). Still, some traditional aspects of middle- and upper-class female dress were retained through the mid–nineteenth century. Though Clot-Bey suggests that women of the middle and upper classes had begun to abandon the *ṣafa* as early as the 1840s (Clot-Bey 1840a: 326–327), the Viscountess Falkland describes a well-to-do woman wearing the *ṣafa* in the early 1850s

(Falkland 1857: 69). The practice of plaiting the hair with *ṣafa* persisted much longer among women of the lower classes and the Bedouin (see, for example, Cooper 1914: 157 and Klunzinger 1878: 51).

Dancers of the mid–nineteenth century had largely abandoned the *yelek*,[4] but they embraced the new, shorter *ʿantarī* (Figure 17). Interestingly, some dancers began to wear the sleeveless *ṣudayrī* in place of either the *ʿantarī* or the *yelek* (Figure 18). The practice of substituting the *ṣudayrī* for the *ʿantarī/yelek* would continue throughout the remainder of the century and into the next. In the latter half of the century, some dancers began to favor European-style skirts rather than *shintiyān* (Leland 1873: 134); this trend would be widespread by the beginning of the twentieth century. With the shift to skirts came the adoption of European stockings—often patterned or striped—and heeled European shoes. Dancers continued to ornament their hair with the *ṣafa* (Knox 1879: 570, Warner 1900: 380), and this practice would persist into the early twentieth century.

As noted above, many ordinary women continued to wrap shawls around their hips (Chennells 1893: 257; Falkland 1857: 69, 104). At mid-century, dancers wore shawls as well. Bayard Taylor observed dancers wearing shawls at their hips during a performance he witnessed in Luxor in the early 1850s (Taylor 1854: 135). Interestingly, Taylor notes that the dancers' shawls were ornamented with "jingling bits of metal."

Rather than tying a shawl around the hips, however, many dancers began wearing a distinctive ribbon belt (Figure 17). This unique accessory has no analogue in contemporary Egyptian women's dress. It was constructed from several lengths of ribbon—probably silk or satin—wound around a belt of unknown material. The ribbons were wound in such a way that the ends would hang from the front of the belt, but not the back. Each of the ribbons terminated in a fringed tassel. The ribbon belt appears to be the earliest clear divergence between dancers' costuming and ordinary Egyptian women's attire. By the end of the nineteenth century, the ribbon belt was a standard feature of the Egyptian dance costume; it is ubiquitous in photographs and illustrations of Egyptian dancers at the turn of the century.

Some authors in the latter half of the nineteenth century also describe dancers wearing a belt or girdle of amulet cases, seemingly in order to accentuate hip movements. Leland describes this girdle being worn by the dancers that he observed at Jirjā (in Upper Egypt) in the 1870s:

> Around the waist was a silver girdle with high bosses, and dependent from it in loops was a very curious and massive ornament or chain, made of eight or ten triangular silver boxes, and many large silver beads [Leland 1873: 134–135].

Figure 17. Unidentified Egyptian dancer (Désiré and Company photograph on Royer and Aufière *carte de visite, circa* 1860s).

Figure 18. Unidentified Egyptian dancer (*carte de visite, circa* 1860s).

Arnold details the same girdle, this time worn by a dancer in Luxor at the end of the 1870s:

> [A]nd on her ankles, wrists, and neck she wore a profusion of ornaments, the strangest of which was, perhaps, a girdle surrounding her waist, or more properly speaking, the region where her waist should have occurred according to European

> ideas. The waist proper of her gown was marked by a string of gold coins, drawn tight round her chest underneath the arms. The girdle beneath consisted of half-a-dozen triangular boxes of silver, threaded on two narrow cords, which, as she danced, jingled against each other and with the many silver coins and beads she wore [Arnold 1882: 91].

Warner's description of a *ghāziyah* in Luxor in the 1870s suggests a similar item: "...a mass of heavy twinkling silver ornaments hangs about her waist." (Warner 1900: 380). An 1863 watercolor by Dutch artist Willem de Famars Testas shows a dancer wearing the girdle; this illustration is reprinted in Fraser's 2015 work (Fraser 2015: 141). As noted earlier, female entertainers, following the fashion of ordinary women, were observed wearing amulet cases at the hip several decades prior to these accounts; the belt or girdle described by Arnold, Leland and others appears to be an evolution of the earlier practice.

Some dancers in the latter half of the nineteenth century performed in a dress or a *jalābīyah* rather than in the ensemble just described. Warner, describing the garments of a trio of Luxor *ghawāzī* in the 1870s, indicates that each dancer wore a sumptuous silk dress (he calls one a "costly Syrian dress"), but he states: "The dresses of all are plainly cut, and straight-waisted, like an ordinary calico gown of a milkmaid" (Warner 1900: 380). This description suggests an ordinary woman's *thawb* or *jalābīyah*. Knox states that the *ghawāzī* he observed at Qinā wore white dresses, over which they wore short embroidered jackets—probably the *'antarī* (Knox 1879: 570). The illustration accompanying Knox's description suggests these dancers wore *shintiyān* under their dresses (Knox 1879: 571). By contrast, the dancers observed by Warner wore stockings (Warner 1900: 380).

A photograph in Jacobson (2007: 263) shows a *circa* 1880s dancer wearing a light-colored dress cinched at the waist with European stockings and shoes. Similarly, stereographs from the 1890s show *ghawāzī* attired in a simple *jalābīyah*, stockings, and shoes as they perform with the comic character 'Alī Kākā at a Zaqāzīq market (Figures 11 and 12). In the early twentieth century, costuming in a dress or a *jalābīyah* would continue to exist alongside the more elaborate ensemble of chemise, *ṣudayrī*/*'antarī*, skirt/*shintiyan*, and ribbon belt.

In general, dancers' dress continued to display the opulence of earlier in the century. The richness of their dress and ornamentation set them apart from other Egyptian women of similar social station. William Cowper Prime, who encountered a pair of *ghawāzī* near Luxor in the 1850s, describes their dress as follows:

> Their taste in dress was far above the ordinary run of women in Egypt; for the natives of the lower classes, as I have already stated, wear but a single long, loose garment, while these girls were loaded with the usual full dress of the lady of the harem [Prime 1874: 401].

Kathleen Fraser has suggested the emergence, and rather rapid disappearance, of what she considers to be a unique costuming style around the middle of the nineteenth century:

> In artists' renditions of that period, one finds: a heavy waist belt as a major feature, with metal ornaments that swing with the movements; bareness of the top of the body; semi-bared breasts; the costume covering legs but not necessarily waist; a swinging skirt revealing parts of the legs; bare feet; a profusion of gold and silver ornaments, long hair, and well-defined eyes [Fraser 2015: 250].

Fraser attributes the development of this style—what she terms the "bare costume"—to the influence of the costuming style of contemporary male dancers (Fraser 2015: 187–193). In nineteenth-century Egypt, there were two categories of male dancer: the *khawal* (a native Egyptian dancing boy or man) and the *jink* (a foreign dancing boy or man—usually Armenian, Greek, Jewish, or Turkish) (Lane 1860: 381–382, Lane 2005 [1836]: 376–377). Lane describes male dancers as wearing "a tight vest, a girdle, and a kind of petticoat" (Lane 1860: 382, Lane 2005 [1836]: 377); Fraser's argument appears to be largely informed by this description. Among the particular features of female entertainers' dress that Fraser argues are derived from male dancers' costuming are short, tight vests; sheer, abdomen-baring chemises; and—later in the century—skirts. She also suggests that "bareness" as a feature of Egyptian dance costuming disappeared by the end of the nineteenth century.

There are a number of problems with Fraser's suggestion of this supposedly idiosyncratic costuming style. All of the features that she attributes to the influence of male dancers' costuming were present in contemporary Egyptian women's clothing. As noted earlier, the short, sleeveless vest known as the *ṣudayrī* was a garment that was worn over the chemise, but under the *'antarī* or the *yelek*, particularly during cold weather. Dancers began substituting the *ṣudayrī* for the *'antarī* and the *yelek* sometime around mid-century. Chemises—both those worn by ordinary women, and those worn by dancers—were invariably sheer, and the mid-nineteenth century chemise was very short, sometimes barely reaching the waist. Additionally, Egyptian women began adopting European-style skirts in the latter half of the nineteenth century, thus it is unsurprising that dancers are described and depicted wearing skirts during this period. Finally, the "bareness" that Fraser alludes to—the exposure of large areas of the dancer's torso due to the sheerness/shortness of the chemise—remained a feature of Egyptian dancers' costuming through the remainder of the nineteenth century and into the next. Perhaps most problematic of all, Fraser makes no mention of the ribbon belt, which was certainly being worn by many Egyptian dancers in the final decade of her study period.

The Turn-of-the-Century Professional Dance Costume

At the dawn of the twentieth century, women of Egypt's upper class continued to absorb Western fashion trends. Their affinity for the latest Parisian fashions was noted by numerous foreign observers (e.g., Cooper 1914: 129–130, Giffin 1911: 40, Leeder 1918: 21–22). Among the upper class, the only acquiescence to standards of traditional dress was to don public modesty garments such as the veil, and even these were discarded when not on Egyptian soil (Cooper 1914: 130–131, Sladen 1911: 71).

As women of the upper class continued to look westward, women of the middle class were more conservative. Cooper notes:

> The women of this great class dress, when outside of their homes, similarly to those in the highest social scale [in other words, they don modesty garments], but within the house they wear a galabeigh, a sort of glorified empire-gown hanging straight from the shoulder or gathered to a yoke, and having a long train behind. This garment is made of silk or satin, and often is elaborately trimmed. If custom restricts them to black while in the street, they exercise their individual taste in regard to colours within their apartments. I have seen a group of ladies with their pink, blue, and yellow galabeighs, looking like a flock of gaily plumaged birds [Cooper 1914: 134].

Meanwhile, dancers' costuming became completely distinct from ordinary day-to-day dress, and the attire worn by dancers during their performances was recognized by Egyptians as a professional dance costume (see *al-Zuhūr* November 1913: 359) (Figure 19). In performance, dancers continued wearing the old-style Ottoman chemise, *ṣudayrī*, and/or *'antarī* that were now obsolete among Egyptian women. As in prior decades, the chemise was quite sheer; a contemporary Arabic source describes it as being made of *shāsh* ("gauze") (*al-Zuhūr* November 1913: 359). The same source uses the term *ṣidrah* rather than *ṣudayrī* for the dancer's vest, describing it as a colorful silk garment that covered the breasts. In some cases, the *ṣudayrī*/*ṣidrah* and/or *'antarī* were covered with coins (*Concert Égyptien* 1889). In others, the *ṣudayrī*/*ṣidrah* and/or *'antarī* incorporated elements of Edwardian fashion, such as elaborate

Figure 19. Unidentified Egyptian dancer (B. Livadas and Coutsicos postcard, *circa* 1910).

Figure 20. Unidentified Egyptian dancer (R.G. Lombardi postcard, *circa* 1910).

ruffled-lace trim (Figure 20). In another nod to current fashion, dancers abandoned the *shintiyan* once and for all, opting for ankle-length skirts paired with European stockings and heeled shoes. Even as the costume began to incorporate foreign elements, the ribbon belt remained an integral part of the costume. The belt was sometimes elaborately decorated with sequins, and the ribbons occasionally terminated in multiple tassels (Figure 20).

This general style of costuming persisted through the 1910s in Egypt's entertainment halls, and much later in the Egyptian countryside. A variation on the ensemble was worn by the Banāt Māzin of Luxor as late as the 1970s. The Banāt Māzin can be seen wearing this costume in the Egyptian films *al-Zawjah al-Thāniyah* (1967) and *Anā al-Duktūr* (1968), in Aisha Ali's documentary *Dances of Egypt* (2006), and in the writings of Edwina Nearing (Nearing 2004a, 2004b) and Magda Saleh (1979: 143, 147). Differences between the Banāt Māzin costume and the traditional costume just described include a shorter skirt, decoration of the skirt with tiers of beaded fringe, and broader panels on the ribbon belt. In addition, the Banāt Māzin's ribbon belts were constructed differently than those of the late nineteenth and early twentieth century. Rather than winding long ribbons around a belt, the Banāt Māzin constructed several shorter ribbon panels that were then individually attached to a belt (Aisha Ali, personal communication, November 9, 2015; Habiba 2005). Regarding the Banāt Māzin's distinctive headpiece, although the Banāt Māzin have stated that they invented this headpiece, which they termed *tāj* ("crown"), to replace a simpler kerchief, or *mandīl* (Nearing 2004b), there is evidence of this sort of headpiece being worn by early twentieth century dancers (Figure 20).

As in the latter decades of the prior century, some dancers performed in a dress or a *jalābīyah* rather than in the elaborate ensemble just discussed. These dancers sometimes wore European shoes and stockings with the traditional *jalābīyah*. The *jalābīyah* itself sometimes incorporated European elements such as Edwardian-style lace trims. Interestingly, several of the dresses worn by the Sūhāj *ghawāzī* in *Raqṣ al-Ghajariyāt* (2005) bear lace trims around the bust, the sleeves, and the hip area.

The Beginnings of the Badlah

At this point, it is important to note the conspicuous absence of documentation of authentically Egyptian *raqṣ sharqī* costumes from the 1920s.

To date, I have not been able to locate authentic, sourced photographs or film footage of Egyptian entertainment hall dancers in costume from this decade. This is problematic, since the costumes of the 1930s diverge in several ways from the costumes of the 1910s. Without concrete evidence of what Egyptian dancers were wearing in the 1920s, it is impossible to conclude whether the stylistic changes of the 1930s represent an abrupt break from the past, or were a natural outgrowth of stylistic developments throughout the 1920s. Further investigations are necessary to resolve this issue.

The costumes of the 1930s were the first costumes worn by Egyptian dancers that could be accurately termed *badlah*. The core components of the costume were a bra-like top, a fitted sash or belt (usually constructed of the same fabric as the top), and a skirt (though it is not always apparent whether the skirt is separate from the sash/belt or attached to it). The heavy, opaque fabrics that characterized dancers' skirts at the turn of the century were replaced by gauzy, semi-transparent fabrics (see Rūḥīyah Fawzī and another unnamed dancer in the 1937 film *al-'Izz Bahdalah* and Bibā Ibrāhīm in the 1938 film *Shaī' Min Lā Shaī'*). Skirts sometimes had slits that exposed the legs (see Taḥīyah Carioca in the 1936 film *Khafīr al-Darak*). Dancers abandoned stockings and performed with legs bare. The combination of revealing skirts and bare legs exposed much more of the dancers' lower bodies than in prior years. Shoe styles evolved to match current European trends. Perhaps the most noteworthy change in the 1930s costume was the disappearance of the ribbon belt among entertainment hall dancers. The ribbon belt, which had been an integral and defining feature of the Egyptian dance costume since the mid–nineteenth century, was replaced by the hip sash/belt.

Dancers' abdomens were almost universally bare, at least among dancers working in the entertainment halls and in the Egyptian cinema. However, it is interesting to note that beginning in the late 1930s, dancers in films began strategically covering their navels—sometimes with a strip of fabric extending from the top to the belt, at other times with low-hanging fringe or jewelry, or with an ornament glued into the navel. This change appears to coincide with the creation of the Ministry of Social Affairs in 1938. This arm of the government took over the administration of film censorship, which had previously been overseen by the Ministry of the Interior (Mansour 2012). While censorship under the Ministry of the Interior was largely concerned with issues of political order and national security, the Ministry of Social Affairs added the protection of social norms and public morality to its purview. Apparently Egyptian censors shared American censors' abhorrence of the female navel. The practice of obscuring dancers' navels would continue in Egyptian cinema until the 1950s, when the Egyptian government instituted a regulation requiring all belly dancers to wear fabric over their abdomens (Roushdy 2009: 40), effectively rendering the various navel-covering strategies of the 1930s and 1940s unnecessary.

There are echoes of earlier costuming in the 1930s *badlah*. Most notably, many of the "bras" or bra-like tops worn by dancers in the 1930s bear a striking similarity to the *ṣudayrī/ṣidrah* worn by Egyptian dancers from the mid–nineteenth century through the 1910s. While some of the *badlah* tops of the 1930s were actual bras, some would be more accurately termed vests. Consider the tops worn by Rūḥīyah Fawzī and another unnamed dancer in the film *al-'Izz Bahdalah* in 1937. Interestingly, these tops were worn *over* bras. They are virtually indistinguishable from some of the early twentieth century vests. The coin-covered *badlah* top worn by Taḥīyah Carioca in the film *Khafīr al-Darak* in 1936 is similarly vest-like, and it bears an unmistakable resemblance to the coin-covered *ṣudayrī/ṣidrah* and *'antarī* worn by Egyptian dancers at the 1889 Exposition Universelle in Paris (*Concert Égyptien* 1889, see images 5, 6, 28, and 29).

The bare-midriff look of the 1930s also had precedents in earlier Egyptian costuming. The chemise that was worn by the dancers of the entertainment halls through the 1910s (and possibly later) was constructed of a sheer fabric that created a near-nude look. Even more convincing, though, are several examples of dancers performing with the abdomen completely exposed well before the 1930s. An 1864 painting by Italian artist Giuseppe Bonnici depicts an Egyptian dancer whose chemise has ridden up to expose her belly; this painting is reproduced on a postcard noted in Chapter Two (Figure 4). Loewenbach's description of the dancer at Cairo's El Dorado in 1907 suggests that she wore no chemise at all: "She is dressed in pink, covered with gaudy trinkets, her belly is bare" (Loewenbach 1908: 220, translated by the author, with assistance from Christine Ferhat). Further, a pair of Underwood and Underwood stereographs clearly illustrates a dancer from Upper Egypt wearing the *ṣudayrī/ṣidrah* without the chemise (*A Nubian Dancing Girl. Upper Egypt.*, *Type Arab Dancing Girl. Upper Egypt.*). Though undated, these stereographs must have been produced sometime between 1880 and 1920, when Underwood and Underwood were actively producing stereographs (University of Chicago Library 2010).

Interestingly, there are hints that the changes to the Egyptian dance costume that become evident in the 1930s may have been driven by

Badī'ah Maṣābnī—or at least were perceived so by the Egyptian public. A 1933 article in the Egyptian women's interest magazine *al-'Arūsah* specifically correlates changes in the Egyptian dance costume with Badī'ah Maṣābnī's start in the troupe of Najīb al-Rīḥānī (*al-'Arūsah* 8 February 1933: 6). Problematically, the author dates this event to 1928, when in fact Badī'ah was already performing with Najīb al-Rīḥānī prior to this time (e.g., *al-Ahrām* 1 January 1926: 5). In fact, Badī'ah and Najīb al-Rīḥānī were briefly married, and they had already separated in early 1926, months before Badī'ah opened her first entertainment hall in Cairo (Adum n.d., *Badia Masabni in 1966 Television Interview* n.d.). However, in a 1928 interview, Najīb al-Rīḥānī and Badī'ah Maṣābnī indicate that they had recently reconciled and that they would be collaborating on a production together (*Segment of 1928 Interview with Nagib El-Rehani* n.d.). Was it in the context of this renewed collaboration that Badī'ah generated costume innovations that would be widely adopted by dancers working in Egypt's entertainment halls? If so, this would be one aspect of the development of *raqṣ sharqī* that could be attributed to the creative impulse of Badī'ah Maṣābnī. However, it is difficult to draw such a conclusion without access to film or images illustrating what Egyptian dancers were wearing in the 1920s, before Badī'ah Maṣābnī became such a prominent figure in the Cairo entertainment scene.

The old turn-of-the-century costume style continued to be depicted periodically by *raqṣ sharqī* performers in Egyptian film. In the 1948 film *Khulūd* (*Immortality*), the dancer Huda Shams al-Dīn and a group of six supporting dancers portray a troupe of *'awālim* performing at a turn-of-the-century wedding celebration in the home of a well-to-do family. They wear the period-appropriate costume of chemise, *ṣudayrī/ṣidrah*, and ankle-length skirt. Huda's vest is decorated with beaded fringe, rendering it more like a *badlah* top (and reinforcing the probable stylistic connection between the early twentieth century vest and the *badlah* top, as noted earlier). However, the later portrayals of turn-of-the-century dancers in the popular biopics of director Ḥassan al-Imām, such as *Bambah Kashar* (1974) and *Shafīqah al-*Qibṭīyah (1963), are decidedly anachronistic, both in terms of dance style and in terms of costuming.

The Question of Foreign Influence

To what degree was the evolution of Egyptian dance costuming influenced by the West? Certainly, Western elements were present in dancers' attire from the latter half of the nineteenth century onward. As noted earlier, Egyptian dancers began wearing European-derived skirts, stockings, and heeled shoes by the end of the nineteenth century. Turn-of-the-century costumes often incorporated European elements such as Edwardian-style lace trims.

However, to suggest that the *badlah* is entirely Western in origin would be to neglect its stylistic precedents in earlier Egyptian dance costuming. Moreover, such a suggestion assumes a uniformity of Western representation of the Egyptian dancer that simply did not exist. There was no single, agreed-upon depiction of the "Oriental dancer," let alone the "Egyptian dancer," in the world of the European music hall or the American vaudeville theater. The costume of the "Oriental dancer," as portrayed by European and American entertainers, generally incorporated a mish-mash of Middle Eastern, North African, and Asian costuming elements.

Consider the four portrayals of the "Oriental dancer" in Figures 21 through 24. These images are roughly contemporary (circa 1900 to 1910), yet each draws together its own unique array of costuming elements to construct an image that evokes the exotic. The dancer in Figure 21 wears a top and pantaloons of a sheer, gauzy fabric with a hip wrap of heavier fabric. Her midriff is not bare, although her sheer clothing does little to hide her body. She manipulates a long scarf—a common cliché in European depictions of "Oriental dance" at this time, and one perhaps derived in equal measures from North African scarf dances (Figure 25) and from the fantasy veil dances of the innumerable European "Salomes." By contrast, the woman pictured in Figure 22 wears a richly decorated vest that is reminiscent of both traditional Algerian dress (Figure 26) as well as dance costuming from Western and Central Asia. Her abdomen is covered. She wears a conical headpiece with similarities to headpieces worn by women in the Maghreb.

The bare-midriff costume of the dancer in Figure 23 is the most *badlah*-like of the four. This dancer wears a crescent necklace, known as a *kirdān*, which is the one feature of her costume that is definitely derived from traditional Arab/Egyptian attire. Her top superficially resembles a bra, though it lacks the structure and support of the modern bra. This bra-like top, with its disc-shaped cups, was adopted by a number of music hall entertainers, including the likes of Mata Hari, La Belle Otero, and Sahary Djeli, and was worn in a range of "Oriental" performance settings, from portrayals of Salome to interpretations of Indian dance. However, it differs in form and construction from the 1930s *badlah* tops, many of which were decidedly vest-like.

Figure 21. European dancer in "Oriental" costume (Maurice Tesson Imprimeur Limoges postcard, *circa* 1900 to 1910).

Figure 22. European in "Oriental" costume (postcard, *circa* 1900 to 1910).

The disc-shaped cups also appear in the costume of French entertainer Tiphaine (Figure 24). Here, instead of forming a bra-like top over bare flesh, they embellish her full-length gown. Interestingly, the disc-shaped cups of these European costumes might have been inspired by the Far East, rather than the Near East: compare with the traditional attire of the Cambodian dancers illustrated in Figure 27.

Figure 23. European in "Oriental" costume (Imprimeries de l'Abeille postcard, *circa* 1900 to 1910).

Some ten to fifteen years later than the time of these images, Vilma Banky, in one of her dance scenes in the American silent film *Son of the Sheik* (1926), wore an ensemble featuring a vest-like top and a skirt of ribbons. This costume is much more evocative of Egyptian dancers' costumes from the 1880s through the 1910s than the European costumes described

Figure 24. French entertainer Tiphaine in "Oriental" costume (Reutlinger postcard, *circa* 1900).

48. - ALGER. - Mauresques, costume d'intérieur - Danse des Almées

Figure 25. Algerian dancers (Collection Régence postcard, *circa* 1900 to 1910).

Figure 26. Algerian woman in traditional costume (Collection Idéale P.S. postcard, *circa* 1900 to 1910).

Figure 27: Cambodian dancers (F. Detaille postcard, 1922) (courtesy of Galerie Detaille).

above. During another of the dance scenes, set in an Arab café, a group of dancers sits onstage as each awaits her turn to perform; their bored expressions and slouching postures are uncannily reminiscent of photos of dancers sitting onstage at Chicago's Columbian Exposition in 1893.

Egyptians were certainly aware of these "Oriental" costumes, and they themselves replicated some of these looks onstage. For example, the disc-shaped bra cups discussed above were integrated into the costuming for an Arabic opera titled *Cleopatra*.[5] Figure 28 shows the ʻUkāshah acting troupe posing in a publicity photo for the production, which took place around the end of the 1920s. The seven female cast members in the foreground, presumably dancers, wear bra-like tops with disc-shaped cups. Interestingly, the singer and actress ʻĀliyah Fawzī, who plays the title role, also wears one of these tops, but her "bra" is worn over a tunic. Still, in spite of the presence of these European-derived "Oriental" stylings on the Egyptian stage in the late 1920s, it would be a mistake to suggest that costumes such as these were the antecedent of the 1930s *badlah*. For, as discussed above, many of the 1930s *badlah* tops bear a closer resemblance to the turn-of-the-century *ṣudayrī/ṣidrah* than to these bra-like tops with their disc-shaped cups.

Egyptian entertainers transacted directly with their European and American counterparts, directly exchanging not only costuming ideas, but actual costume items. In a 1966 television interview, Badīʻah Maṣābnī describes her friendship with the famous French music hall performers Maurice Chevalier and Mistinguett. She states:

Figure 28: The ʻUkāshah acting troupe posing in a publicity photo for *Cleopatra* (newspaper clipping, *circa* 1930).

> Yes, I bought set decorations and costumes from them, after they did shows. They did shows and then discarded those costumes and made new ones. I bought them and gave them to my artists and my dancers, and the set decorations too [*Badia Masabni in 1966 Television Interview* n.d.].

However, Egyptians sometimes supplied costumes to foreigners as well. In 1913, the great Egyptian actor Shaykh Salāmah Ḥijāzī helped a troupe of American actors and technicians from the Vitagraph motion picture studio:

> Mr. Young needed a carload of costumes and properties in Cairo, but there was only one costumer, who politely bowed him out—said he would be busy for years making soldiers' uniforms for the government. Gad Michel, the faithful guide, swore that there was not another maker of costumes, spears, shields and wigs in all Egypt. And again "there was darkness in Egypt"—for a stranded troupe of Thespians, this time....
>
> There was an old sheik living in Cairo—eighty years old and the proprietor of the largest native theater. His name is Sheik Salama Higazi, and he is venerated as the Joe Jefferson of the East. He employs forty principal actors the year round and a pyramid full of "supers."
>
> To him Gad Michel, in fear and trembling—Gad being a religious man and averse to things theatrical—led Effendi Young and Clara Kimball Young, the ripe date of his harem. And these two were received by the venerable magnate with Eastern graciousness, and welcomed as brother actors from across the sea. He promised to look into the matter of costumes, and sent them back to the obdurate costumer, who struck his forehead repeatedly upon the floor this time and accomplished the impossible for them in the matter of a theatrical wardrobe [Wade 1913: 105–106].

The climate of innovation in Egypt's late nineteenth and early twentieth century entertainment halls, together with the ongoing cultural exchanges between Egyptian and non-Egyptian entertainers just described, enabled the stylistic transformations that would produce the modern *badlah*. However, two key issues counter the assertion that the *badlah* originated as a wholesale imitation of an existing Western costume: first, the existence of stylistic precedents for the *badlah* in earlier Egyptian dance costuming, and second, the lack of uniformity in Western representations of the "Oriental dancer." These issues obviate the possibility that the *badlah* was invented in the West and then copied by Egyptians. Rather, any resemblances between the Egyptian *badlah* and certain European and American "Oriental" costumes are better explained by a sort of "feedback loop" wherein each costume style continuously drew upon the other. Western entertainers incorporated miscellaneous Arab and Egyptian elements into their own constructs of the "Oriental dancer." Egyptian entertainers, as they intentionally adopted and integrated aspects of Western theatrical fashion into their own costumes, re-absorbed elements of their own costuming aesthetic that had been passed through a Western lens.

Summary

At the dawn of the nineteenth century, Egypt's professional female entertainers wore essentially the same garments as middle- and upper-class women. However, by the 1860s, specific elements had begun to emerge that differentiated the costuming of the *'awālim* and the *ghawāzī* from everyday dress. By the end of the century, these elements had developed into a distinct dance uniform that was worn both by entertainment hall performers and by many of the *'awālim* and *ghawāzī* who continued to perform at *mawālid*, weddings, and other private celebrations. European fashions, such as skirts, stockings and heeled shoes, introduced into Egyptian dance costuming in the latter half of the nineteenth century, were commonplace in the dance costumes of the turn of the century. The distinctive ribbon belt, first worn *circa* the 1850s or 1860s, became a standard feature of the Egyptian dancer's costume. In the 1910s, Egyptians recognized the ensemble of chemise, *ṣudayrī/ṣidrah* and/or *'antarī*, skirt, stockings, heeled shoes, and ribbon belt as a professional dance costume.

It is clear that precedents for the 1930s *badlah* existed in the turn-of-the-century dance costume. Moreover, the range of representations of the "Oriental dancer" by Westerners at the dawn of the twentieth century erodes the argument that a well-defined *badlah* was invented in the West and then adopted by Egyptian dancers. What seems most likely is that Egyptian dancers integrated appealing aspects of Western theatrical fashion in ways that suited the existing Egyptian costuming style and aesthetic. Thus, while the diaphanous, revealing skirts and glitzy tops and belts of the 1930s suggest a nod to Western theatrical fashion, these elements were absorbed into the existing indigenous costume template of top, bare or barely covered midriff, hip belt, and skirt. Nevertheless, in adopting and integrating aspects of Western theatrical fashion into their own costumes, Egyptian dancers inadvertently re-absorbed elements of their own costuming aesthetic that had been filtered through the lens of Western Orientalist fantasy.

Seven

Raqṣ Sharqī as Part of the Egyptian Cultural Heritage

Chapters One and Two examined the sociocultural and historical factors that enabled and nurtured the emergence and development of *raqṣ sharqī* from the 1890s through the 1920s, and Chapters Three through Six detailed the characteristics of the dance in its early years. *Raqṣ sharqī* was born on the stages of the entertainment halls of Cairo and Alexandria. In the liminal setting of the entertainment hall, where the indigenous intersected with the foreign, and where tradition interfaced with modernity, Egyptians produced and consumed hybrid arts and entertainment that were embraced as culturally authentic. In this context, the dances of Egypt's professional female entertainers, the *'awālim* and the *ghawāzī*, absorbed and integrated new and foreign elements, thus giving rise to a new and distinct dance form.

Like the other forms of entertainment presented in Egypt's turn-of-the-century entertainment halls, *raqṣ sharqī* embodied the struggle to define and assert Egyptian national and cultural identity while under foreign occupation. The history of the dance, as Roushdy states, "has been shaped by the periods in modern Egyptian history when cultural differences ('Western' versus 'Oriental') were being formulated" (Roushdy 2009: 46). Contrary to assertions that *raqṣ sharqī* was defined by the tastes of Westerners, or of a Westernized Egyptian elite, it is quite clear from this study that the development of early *raqṣ sharqī*, like the other forms of popular entertainment presented alongside it, was driven by the interests and concerns of the urban Egyptian masses. *Raqṣ sharqī* was one of many means by which ordinary Egyptians navigated the tension between tradition and innovation and between the native and the foreign. In the same fashion as popular music and theater, *raqṣ sharqī* maintained an enduring connection to tradition, even as it absorbed and integrated new and foreign elements, thus ensuring its appeal with a broad cross-section of the urban Egyptian public.

Over the course of the next several decades, the popularity of *raqṣ sharqī* would extend well beyond the audiences of the urban entertainment halls—even beyond the urban centers of Cairo and Alexandria. This chapter explores how and why audiences outside of the urban entertainment halls of Cairo and Alexandria would come to embrace *raqṣ sharqī* as an authentic Egyptian cultural expression, thus enabling the dance to become part of the cultural heritage of all Egyptians. A key factor was *raqṣ sharqī*'s continuing connection to traditional Egyptian dance. However, the emergence of new technologies—specifically, film and television—was also critical, as these new media permitted the expansion of *raqṣ sharqī* to audiences outside of Egypt's urban entertainment halls. The Egyptian films of the 1930s through the 1960s, brought to the broader Egyptian public via the new medium of television, would have a tremendous impact on defining *raqṣ sharqī* as the accepted representation of Egyptian belly dance and a recognized part of the Egyptian cultural heritage. Meanwhile, the advent of theatrical folk dance companies in the late 1950s and early 1960s, accompanied by the nationalization and professionalization of the entertainment industry, would have profound implications for *raqṣ sharqī* and its position in the public imagination.

The Pan-Egyptian Appeal of Raqṣ Sharqī

The fundamental movements of both *raqṣ sharqī* and the dances of the *'awālim* and the *ghawāzī* clearly emerge from the essential movement vocabulary of *raqṣ baladī*, the social form of belly dance practiced informally throughout Egypt. Men and women of all ages perform *raqṣ baladī* at festive social occasions, particularly wedding celebrations, as an expression of joy and happiness. *Raqṣ baladī* shares with *raqṣ sharqī* and with *'awālim/ghawāzī* dance a core repertoire of torso movements: articulated hip and shoulder movements such as shimmies, circles and "figure eights" of the pelvis, and undulations of the abdomen. It also shares fundamental aesthetic qualities with these dances: the performer of *raqṣ baladī* expresses his or her musical accompaniment through an improvised series of movements and gestures. Further, the performer of *raqṣ baladī* recognizes its seductive qualities and may engage in harmless flirtation while dancing, but he or she avoids overt expressions of sexuality, or other behaviors that would lead to an association with professional performance.

In Arabic, the term *baladī* signifies "indigenous"—"from the land" or "from the country." However, as Roushdy notes, in Egypt, this term carries an additional nuance of meaning:

> Throughout the 20th century, the designation *awalad al-balad* and its *baladi* derivative has acquired a socio-economic, cultural and subjective signification that distinguishes between who and what is perceived as essentially Egyptian and what has been affected, shaped or introduced through foreign, mainly Western, cultural influences [Roushdy 2013: 22].

Within this framework of meaning, *baladī* can carry both positive and negative connotations, particularly when the term is used to describe a person's personality or behavior. On the positive side, *baladī* implies authenticity and a connection to local values and tradition. On the other hand, the term can connote poor taste and a lack of refinement. These subtleties of meaning are highly context-dependent.

The folk form of belly dance bears the name *raqṣ baladī* because it is a pan-Egyptian practice that cross-cuts affiliations of gender, class, religion, etc. Though there are subtle differences in execution that distinguish local variants of the dance, such as urban vs. rural (Roushdy 2013: 23), in general, *raqṣ baladī* is a dance that transcends the differences among its practitioners. Roushdy states:

> As an experience during which boundaries of profession, class, religion, degree of religiosity or gender are dissolved, it primarily materializes collectivity [Roushdy 2013: 30].

In essence, *raqṣ baladī,* as a shared cultural practice that surpasses the internal divisions of Egyptian society, expresses a unified sense of Egyptian identity in a way that ethnic or region-specific dance forms cannot.

The term *sharqī* ("eastern"), like *baladī,* can be used to draw a distinction between Egyptian ideals, values, and practices and those that are foreign. Lorius (1996: 289) notes: "Like *sharqi,* the term [*baladī*] has resonances of an assertion of ethnicity in the face of foreign domination." In short, both *raqṣ baladī,* the folk form of belly dance, and *raqṣ sharqī,* the professional concert dance, are designated by terms that imply the authentic Egyptianness of both dance forms.

Egyptians sometimes use the terms *raqṣ baladī* and *raqṣ sharqī* interchangeably. Roushdy, for example, uses *raqṣ baladī* both for the social style of belly dance and for the professional concert dance (Roushdy 2009, 2013). She notes:

> Among the different dances that are practiced in Egypt, only one form is classified as *baladi.* Though formally referred to as *al-raqs al-sharqi* (Oriental Dance), yet reference to this dance throughout the 20th century and until today has retained its *baladi* attribute. As opposed to region-specific or ethnic dances performed throughout the country, *baladi* dance is not the prerogative of any particular social or ethnic group in Egypt. *Baladi* also refers to both the professional performance and non-professional social practice of Egyptian belly dance [Roushdy 2013: 23].

In fact, before the term *raqṣ sharqī* became definitively tied to the Egyptian concert dance style that forms the focus of this book, the dance was occasionally known as *raqṣ baladī.* For example, in an article from the November 1913 issue of *al-Zuhūr* magazine, the dance of the entertainment halls, which would eventually be known as *raqṣ sharqī,* was variously referred to as *al-raqṣ al-miṣrī* (Egyptian dance) or *al-raqṣ al-baladī* (native dance) by the author (*al-Zuhūr* November 1913). Significantly, the author identifies the dance as indigenous/Egyptian, even though he notes that many performers at the turn of the century were Moroccan, Persian, Syrian, and Tunisian (*al-Zuhūr* November 1913: 359–361). The interchangeability of the terms *raqṣ baladī* and *raqṣ sharqī* in the modern day indicates that *raqṣ sharqī,* like *raqṣ baladī,* is perceived as an authentic cultural practice belonging to all Egyptians. More importantly, the evidence suggests that among some turn-of-the-century Egyptians, the dance was perceived this way from its earliest beginnings.

As noted above, both *raqṣ sharqī* and the dances of the *ʿawālim* and the *ghawāzī* are rooted in the basic technique and aesthetic of *raqṣ baladī.* Yet, in the Egyptian public's imagination, the dances of the *ʿawālim* and the *ghawāzī* remain firmly tied to particular spatial and social contexts. Indeed, even though the terms *ʿālmah* and *ghāziyah* have faded from common usage, the connotations of these terms with regards to performance context are still widely understood. The *ʿawālim* are the performers for the weddings and other celebrations of the urban lower and middle classes, while the *ghawāzī* entertain at the festivities of the rural poor. By contrast, *raqṣ sharqī,* while it is understood to be urban in origin, has transcended its origins to become, like *raqṣ baladī,* a pan-Egyptian dance form. If all of these professional variants of belly dance share core aspects of technique and aesthetic with *raqṣ baladī,* why has only one of them come to be viewed as belonging to all Egyptians?

Part of the answer to this question lies in the nature of the performance environment in which *raqṣ sharqī* was born. As this study has illustrated, *raqṣ sharqī* emerged and developed on the stages of the entertainment halls of Cairo and Alexandria. In these settings, Egyptian arts and entertainment were detached from the traditional social contexts in which they had previously been embedded. The entertainment hall established a setting in which tradition met innovation, and in which the indigenous intersected with the foreign. In this liminal space, Egyptian artists and entertainers drew on foreign ideas and technologies, while simultaneously asserting their connection to traditional Egyptian aesthetics, interests, and values. Their creations were laden with cultural meaning; the colloquial entertainments of the turn of the century made assertions regarding Egyptian nationhood and challenged the contemporary social order. In essence, the stages of the entertainment halls were sites in which Egyptian identity was constructed, negotiated, contested, and performed. As Eve Troutt Powell states:

> Within such a context, then, the staging of any show in Cairo was political, no matter what stance was taken...Questions of national and cultural identity and social mobility were presented to Egyptian audiences every night in 'Azbakiya, their authenticity tested by the amount of applause or laughter they drew [Troutt Powell 2001: 27].

It is vastly significant, then, that in an environment in which important statements were being made regarding Egyptian cultural and national identity, a dance form emerged that was ultimately christened *raqṣ sharqī*. The dance was clearly conceptualized and described as something indigenous—something Egyptian—in spite of its inclusion of foreign techniques.

Still, in its earliest years, *raqṣ sharqī* remained an urban phenomenon, and its audiences were limited to the customers of the entertainment halls. Like other forms of urban entertainment, however, *raqṣ sharqī* would eventually reach audiences far afield from Cairo and Alexandria and offer another illustration of the cultural dominance exerted by Egypt's urban centers over the rest of the nation. The expansion of *raqṣ sharqī* to new audiences would largely hinge on the rise of two new technologies: cinema and television.

The Impact of Cinema and Television

Egypt's first film screening took place in 1896, in a café in Alexandria (el-Charkawi 1963: 3). According to el-Charkawi, by 1908, there were five cinemas in Cairo, three in Alexandria, and one each in Port Sa'īd, Manṣūra, and Asyūṭ (el-Charkawi 1963: 3). Initially, audiences consisted of Europeans and the Egyptian elite. However, film gradually became more accessible to a wider cross-section of the Egyptian public, not only due to the creation of additional cinemas, but also because film screenings were added to the variety programs presented in Egyptian entertainment halls. For example, film screenings were offered at El Dorado in 1907 (Loewenbach 1908: 220), and the March 1, 1903 show at the al-Miṣrī Theater included a motion picture (Figure 2).

Although the earliest films screened in Egypt were produced by foreigners, Egyptians soon began to establish their own production companies and to create films that were targeted towards the interests and aesthetics of the native population. The silent film *Layla,* considered by many to be the first Egyptian feature-length film (el-Charkawi 1963: 5), premiered at Cairo's Metropole Cinema in 1927. A few years later, in 1935, Egyptian businessman Ṭal'at Ḥarb established Studio Miṣr, which would remain an influential force in the Egyptian cinema for years to come (el-Charkawi 1963: 11–13).

Egyptian films from the 1930s onward often contained scenes that provided pretexts for music and dance numbers. Scenes set in nightclubs—the mid–twentieth century incarnation of the entertainment hall—were particularly common and ensured the frequent appearance of *raqṣ sharqī* in film. As Shafik has noted, the Egyptian cinema became "frantically obsessed" with these venues, as well as with the belly dancers who performed within them (Shafik 2006: 163–165). Cinematic portrayals of the nightclubs varied widely. While they were sometimes depicted as dens of vice, in other cases, they provided a path to wealth, fame, and success for an aspiring protagonist. Similarly, film portrayals of *raqṣ sharqī* performers were decidedly mixed. As Dougherty states:

> Female dance stars from the 1930s to the present day have certainly played dancers who were home wreckers, gold-diggers, unreconstructed girlfriends of gangsters, and enslaved, drug-addicted creatures of pimps. But they have also portrayed dancers as loving daughters, faithful wives and partners, good mothers, and successful artists making a contribution to the cultural development of Egyptian society [Dougherty 2005: 153].

These variable depictions reflect Egyptians' complex and conflicted opinions regarding professional dancers, as well as their ambivalent attitudes towards dance in professional entertainment venues, where it is performed without the social justification provided by a festive occasion such as a wedding.

The *raqṣ sharqī* performers who appeared in Egyptian films from the 1930s through the 1960s were generally dancers who got their start in the very venues depicted in such complex and conflicted ways on the silver screen. For example, one of the most prolific dance stars of the twentieth-century Egyptian cinema, Taḥīyah Carioca, started her career working in the entertainment halls of Su'ād Maḥāssan and Badī'ah Maṣābnī (Adum n.d., *Badia Masabni in 1966 Television Interview* n.d.). Similarly, the beloved dancer Sāmiyah Jamāl got her start at Badī'ah Maṣābnī's Casino Opera (Adum n.d., *Badia Masabni in 1966 Television Interview* n.d.).

The *'awālim* and the *ghawāzī* were periodically depicted in Egyptian film; however, they were rarely portrayed by actual *'awālim* and *ghawāzī*. A few notable exceptions exist. For example, a troupe of *'awālim* appears in *al-'Izz Bahdalah* (1937). The famous Muḥammad 'Alī Street *'ālmah* Nazlah al-'Ādil can be seen performing her signature splits to the accompaniment of her finger cymbals in *Qaṣr al-Shūq* (1966). Additionally, the Banāt Māzin *ghawāzī* appear in at least two Egyptian films from the 1960s: *al-Zawjah al-Thāniyah* (1967) and *Anā al-Duktūr* (1968).

These are the exceptions that prove the rule, however. In general, *'awālim* and *ghawāzī* were played by *raqṣ sharqī* performers who, rather than performing *'awālim/ghawāzī* dance, performed *raqṣ sharqī*. For example, in the 1957 film *Tamr Ḥinnah* (*Henna Flower*), the actress and *raqṣ sharqī* dancer Na'īmah 'Ākif plays the title role of the *ghāziyah* Tamr Ḥinnah. Na'īmah 'Ākif was born into a family of circus performers with connections to the entertainers of Cairo's Muḥammad 'Alī Street; she got her start as a dancer in the entertainment halls of urban Cairo. In *Tamr Ḥinnah*, 'Ākif's erect posture, complex traveling steps, frequent spins, and elaborate arm movements bear little resemblance to contemporary *ghawāzī* dance; rather, they reveal her background as a Cairene *raqṣ sharqī* performer.

Similarly, in the 1948 film *Khulūd*, Huda Shams al-Dīn and a group of six supporting dancers portray a troupe of *'awālim* performing at a turn-of-the-century wedding celebration. Some aspects of their dancing reference the *'awālim* style. In general, the performance emphasizes torso-based movement rather than the expansive traveling steps that had become typical of *raqṣ sharqī* by this time. Additionally, the performers' arm movements are minimal; the dancers frequently hold their arms in static positions with bent elbows. Further, each of the supporting dancers balances a small *sham'adān*. Finally, as noted in Chapter Six, all of the dancers wear costumes that would be appropriate to *'awālim* at the turn of the century. However, the supporting dancers perform a rather elaborate group choreography—something entirely alien to the dancing of actual *'awālim*.

Still, it is important to note that many *raqṣ sharqī* performers did have connections to urban *'awālim* culture. As noted in Chapter Two, many of the first dancers to appear in Egypt's entertainment halls were *'awālim* and *ghawāzī*. Throughout the twentieth century, various performers emerged from Cairo's Muḥammad 'Alī Street neighborhood, the area where many *'awālim* continued to be based. For example, Na'amat Mukhtār, a popular dancer who frequently appeared on film in the 1950s and 1960s, resided with her mother in a Muḥammad 'Alī Street flat that they rented from the well-known *'ālmah* Zūbah al-Klūbātīyah (*About Naemet Mokhtar* n.d.). Though she denied any associations with the *'awālim*, the gymnastic backbends that she frequently performed were atypical of *raqṣ sharqī* in her day and suggestive of the *'awālim* style. Another dancer with a style suggestive of *'awālim* connections was Nabawīyah Muṣṭafa, who appeared in many films throughout the 1940s and 1950s. Like Na'amat Mukhtār, she performed flamboyant, gymnastic movements more similar to the *'awālim* style than to contemporary *raqṣ sharqī*. Still, while these examples argue for a continuing connection between the *'awālim* and the performers of *raqṣ sharqī*, the profound stylistic differences between Na'amat Mukhtār and Nabawīyah Muṣṭafa and the vast majority of their contemporaries argue that the ongoing stylistic influence of *'awālim* dance on *raqṣ sharqī* was minimal.

Important implications emerge from *raqṣ sharqī* performers playing varied Egyptian dance roles. A *raqṣ sharqī* dancer, whether playing a Cairo nightclub entertainer, an *'ālmah* dancing at a lower-class Cairo wedding, or a *ghāziyah* performing at a village *mūlid*, danced in a fairly similar manner. The resulting homogeneity of technique and style would begin to shape public perceptions and expectations with regards to professional belly dance. In essence, Egyptian cinema established a unified vision of what constituted good technique, proper costuming, and an interesting and engaging style. Cinema stars such as Taḥīyah Carioca and Sāmiyah Jamāl became the benchmarks against whom other dancers would be measured. In this manner, *raqṣ sharqī* was able to overshadow the dances of the *'awālim* and the *ghawāzī* to become the *de facto* representation of professional belly dance to the Egyptian public.

An illustration of the impact of cinema's homogenization of belly dance is the now widespread acceptance of the *badlah* as the universal costume for Egyptian belly dance, even among many modern-day *'awālim* and the *ghawāzī*. Van Nieuwkerk notes that many of her older informants, women who worked at lower-class weddings and at *mawālid* around the middle of the twentieth century, admitted to wearing the *badlah* (Van

Nieuwkerk 1995: 59). Rabāb, a Muḥammad 'Alī Street *'ālmah* interviewed for the 2006 documentary *The Bellydancers of Cairo*, wore a *badlah*, though she covered her abdomen. Today this style of costuming is widespread among the dancers working at the weddings of the lower and middle classes in Egypt's urban areas. Even rural *ghawāzī* sometimes wear the *badlah*: in 2013, dancer and researcher Sahra C. Kent filmed a *ghāziyah* wearing this style of costuming at a wedding near Qinā in Upper Egypt (Sahra C. Kent, personal communication, July 1, 2013).

Still, because the audiences for the cinema were (and still are) primarily urban (see Shafik 2006: 282–285), the portrayal of *raqṣ sharqī* in Egyptian film had limited impact beyond Egypt's urban centers until the advent of television in the 1960s. Roushdy states:

> What is unquestionably a crucial contribution of Egyptian cinema to the dance culture, not only in Egypt but in the entire Middle East, is the diffusion of the style developed in the nightclubs of Cairo to the public, a style that continues to characterize the structure of the *baladi* dance observed today. Moreover, when television was introduced, these movies entered the Egyptian household and familiarized the wider public with the cabaret style, which was originally limited to a small segment of the population. It played a crucial role in the socialization of young Egyptians into the local dance culture and continues to influence the performance style of professional and non-professional dancers [Roushdy 2009: 38].

As Roushdy and others have noted, the films of the 1930s through the 1960s are still regularly broadcast on Egyptian television, ensuring the continued influence of this cinematic vision of *raqṣ sharqī* on the public imagination. Indeed, many of the *raqṣ sharqī* performers of those early films are still viewed as beloved national icons.

The reverence that many Egyptians continue to express for the dancers of the 1930s through the 1960s is frequently in direct contrast to their feelings about current Egyptian dance stars. An Egyptian man, interviewed anonymously for *The Bellydancers of Cairo*, shares his thoughts on the dancers of the past:

> It is nice for me to watch a dancer who looks beautiful, elegant ... like in the old days during the peak of Eastern dancing ... like Samia Gamal or Naima Akef—they were not very beautiful, and yet most of the population watched them. Their costumes were beautiful, but they did not reveal too much of their body. We used to respect the dancers. Everybody in our society respected Samia Gamal, Naima Akef or Taheya Karioca, or even Nagwa Fuad—who came later [*The Bellydancers of Cairo* 2006].

Contrary to what this man suggests, the dancers of today are no more scantily clad than the dancers of the old Egyptian films. Nor were the latter more respectable or morally upright; for example, Taḥīyah Carioca's numerous marriages were common knowledge to a bemused public (Said 1990). Yet, his statement reflects a widespread perception among Egyptians that the dancers who appeared in Egyptian films from the 1930s through the 1960s were better artists and more respectable women than current dancers.

There are a number of historical factors that have led to this perception. Beginning around 1960, film portrayals of *raqṣ sharqī* underwent a significant change: dancers were increasingly portrayed by non-dancers. According to Dougherty:

> Through my viewing and research I found that in the first three decades of Egyptian cinema, dancers in cinema are portrayed by women who are themselves professional dancers; after about 1960 and ever since, dancers tend to be portrayed by women who are originally actresses and not dancers.... When dancers are portrayed in film by non-dancers, the tendency to present a negative image of the profession is much greater [Dougherty 2005: 167].

The timing of this change corresponds to the nationalization of the Egyptian cinema (1963) and the professionalization of the Egyptian entertainment industry (from the 1960s onward) (Shafik 2006: 108, 282–283; Van Nieuwkerk 1995: 62–63). These processes would create a division between "high" and "low" art, garnering esteem for the newly-established theatrical folk dance companies such as the Riḍā Troupe, while ensuring the marginalization of *raqṣ sharqī* (Van Nieuwkerk 1995: 62–63)—an issue that will be discussed in greater detail below. Public perceptions of *raqṣ sharqī* would continue to decline in the 1970s, as a short-lived economic boom led to an influx of unskilled performers into the dance trade, and, as a result, a substantial and noticeable drop in quality (Van Nieuwkerk 1995: 55–60).

Nevertheless, in spite of the overall downturn in the public perception of *raqṣ sharqī*, many Egyptians continue to hold the dancers of the "old days" in high esteem. This phenomenon reiterates the tremendous impact that the Egyptian films of the 1930s through the 1960s have had on defining professional belly dance for the general Egyptian public. As noted above, the homogenization of Egyptian belly dance via the cinema effectively shaped public perceptions and expectations regarding style, technique, and costuming, and the *raqṣ sharqī* performers of the cinema became the standard against which all Egyptian belly dancers were judged. In this way, *raqṣ sharqī* eclipsed the dances of the *'awālim* and the *ghawāzī* to become, in the eyes of the Egyptian public, the accepted representation of Egyptian belly dance.

Raqṣ Sharqī *and Theatrical Folk Dance: From Parallel Development to Collision Course*

As noted above, a variety of circumstances contributed to a decline in public perception of *raqṣ sharqī* from the 1960s onward. The emergence of theatrical folk dance companies in the late 1950s and early 1960s, accompanied by the nationalization and professionalization of the entertainment industry, had a particularly profound impact on the position of *raqṣ sharqī* in the public imagination. In fact, the genre of theatrical folk dance represented by the Firqah Riḍā (the Riḍā Troupe) and the Firqah al-Qawmīyah lil-Funūn al-Sha'bīyah (the National Troupe of Folk Arts) offers interesting parallels to the history of *raqṣ sharqī*, and therefore merits further consideration. Like *raqṣ sharqī*, the theatrical folk dance of these two troupes emerged at a time of intense nationalistic sentiment. Also like *raqṣ sharqī*, this new genre hybridized Egyptian and non-Egyptian elements. However, the nationalist movement of the mid-twentieth century was very different in character from that of the turn of the century, and the process of the development of theatrical folk dance was quite distinct from the process that gave rise to *raqṣ sharqī*. As a consequence, the theatrical folk dance of these troupes would express Egyptian identity in a different way from *raqṣ sharqī*, and the success of the former would have dire implications for the latter.

On July 23, 1952, Egypt witnessed its second revolution of the twentieth century, when a group of young military officers overthrew the Egyptian monarchy. While the 1952 revolution shared the anti-British orientation of the 1919 revolution, the class divisions brought to the fore in 1952 established a stark contrast to the cross-class unity that characterized the revolution of 1919. The Revolutionary Command Council that assumed control of Egypt instituted a six-point plan advocating the following:

1. the purification of political life;
2. the establishment of democracy;
3. the promotion of social justice;
4. the abolition of the remnants of feudalism;
5. the creation of a strong national army; and
6. the assertion of full Egyptian independence and sovereignty (Beinin and Lockman 1998: 418).

Under the presidency of Jamāl 'Abd al-Nāṣir (1953–1970), the wealth and influence of foreigners and of Egypt's landed aristocracy were effectively dissolved through the institution of state socialism, and Egyptian nationalism was linked to a broader vision of pan-Arab unity.

In this context, Maḥmūd Riḍā founded the theatrical folk dance troupe that bears his name. Maḥmūd Riḍā was born in 1930 into a middle-class Cairo family (Fahmy 1987: 17–19). An athlete, Riḍā represented Egypt as a gymnast in the 1952 Olympic Games in Helsinki. In 1954, he joined an Argentinean dance troupe and toured with them in Europe; while performing in Paris, he attended classes in ballet and choreography. It was during this time that Riḍā first formulated his vision for an Egyptian folk dance troupe (Shay 2002: 147).

With the Riḍā Troupe, founded in 1959 and nationalized in 1961, Riḍā envisioned a new genre of theatrical folk dance, one built upon the indigenous dance traditions and movement qualities of the Egyptian people. Farida Fahmy, the principal dancer of the troupe, writes:

> Mahmoud Reda's goal was creating a new theater dance form rather than transplanting dances from their local setting onto the stage. His works were never direct imitations or accurate reconstructions. They were his own vision of the movement qualities of the Egyptians. His choreographies remain to this day his personal interpretations of the essential ingredients of the posture, carriage, and gesture of his country's men and women, whether it be in dance or in everyday activities [Fahmy 1987: 24].

Riḍā's middle-class origins and his personal experiences would shape his stage portrayal of the Egyptian folk. Riḍā's dance style was informed by his athletic background, as well as his Western dance training. Further, as Shay notes, Riḍā traveled to and performed in the Soviet union, and it is quite likely that the Soviet Moiseyev Dance Company served as the conceptual model for his troupe (Shay 2002: 144–145).

The dance style that Riḍā created differs profoundly from traditional Egyptian dance in both aesthetic and technique. First, Riḍā wholeheartedly embraced choreography in the Western sense, creating carefully choreographed and staged productions completely lacking in the improvisational character so typical of traditional Egyptian dance. Additionally, Riḍā imbued many of his works with narrative structure—narratives that echo the story lines of nineteenth-century European ballets. As Shay (2002: 152) points out: "...the story lines of Mahmoud Reda's choreographies follow the format of nineteenth-century fairy tale ballets such as *Sleeping Beauty* and *Giselle*, and has no precedent in traditional Egyptian storytelling and narration practices." Finally, though he included the movements of *raqṣ baladī*, Riḍā either removed or modified movements that he deemed too sexually suggestive. These sanitized torso-based movements came to be embedded within a broad array of balletic footwork, turns, and spins.

Yet, the hybrid nature of Riḍā's work has been denied or downplayed by the troupe members themselves. Principal dancer Fahmy writes:

> In his formative years as a choreographer, Mahmoud Reda understood the dangers of allowing himself to succumb to Western influences, especially in the content of his art medium. He realized that the abundance of music and dance that were rooted in Egypt was to be the basis for his choreography, and the starting point for his creations [Fahmy 1987: 15].

In making her case for the "Egyptianness" of the Riḍā Troupe, Fahmy points to the "Westernness" of the Riḍā Troupe's counterpart, the National Troupe of Folk Arts. The National Troupe was founded in 1961, when the Egyptian government hired Boris Ramazin, a former Moiseyev Dance Company member, to create an Egyptian folk dance company in the mold of the Riḍā Troupe. Fahmy writes:

> Soon after the Reda Troupe appeared in the theaters of Cairo, the Ministry of Culture imported Russian experts to teach and establish an Egyptian folk dance company. These experts were former members of the Moiseyev Ensemble. Three years later, the author of this thesis, while attending the company's opening night, noticed a suspiciously close resemblance in movement content, gesture, and themes to the performances of the Moiseyev Dance Ensemble [Fahmy 1987: 15].

Nevertheless, as Shay notes, the National Troupe is similar to the Riḍā Troupe "in almost every element" (Shay 2002: 155), which lends a certain irony to Fahmy's criticisms.

The denial of the clearly Western features of this new genre of theatrical folk dance reflects the anti-elite, anti-Western spirit that dominated Egypt at mid–twentieth century. Shay writes:

> [I]n the Egypt of the 1950s, nationalist rhetoric precluded any claims for non-Egyptian inspiration. With all of [Riḍā's] use of ballet, show dancing, and other Western choreographic strategies, it was important to appear Egyptian [Shay 2002: 146].

Consequently, the Riḍā Troupe deliberately represented Egyptian folk dance as something pristine and untouched by Western influences, even as its performances were built upon the Western concert dance idioms of narrative and choreography. Lauren Siebert notes:

> Reda is defining the folk as a group untouched by the influences of the Westernization and modernization with which members of Reda Troupe and its audiences coped on a daily basis. The folk are defined as a "baseline" of Egyptian identity, in a preserved, ahistorical state: premodern and pre-Westernized, quaint and timeless [Siebert 2002: 57–58].

In this manner, she argues, the Riḍā Troupe helped to construct a vision of a unified Egypt:

> Because of the care taken to remove all identifiably "Western" elements from the choreographies, the folk pageant seemed to be preserved and unadulterated. Brought together under the patriotic theme of the 1952 revolution, the imagery of a unified nation was only accentuated [Siebert 2002: 59].

The regime of 'Abd al-Nāṣir had a vested interest in such unifying portrayals of Egyptian nationhood. With its embrace of Arab socialism in 1960, the Egyptian government espoused an ideology of popular unity that celebrated the important role of the ordinary folk—the lower class and the peasantry—in Egyptian society:

> According to the theory of Arab socialism, Egypt's revolutionary transformation was to be led by a "bloc of popular forces" that included workers, peasants, soldiers, intellectuals, and "national capital." In reality, the social strata referred to in this slogan did not equally exercise state power, or ultimately share the same interests, nor was the regime's refusal to acknowledge this the result of willful ignorance [Beinin and Lockman 1998: 457].

In the entertainment industry, the state found an important mechanism for spreading its vision of Egyptian national identity. The Egyptian government sanctioned and supported arts and entertainment enterprises that represented Egyptian music, song, and dance in a manner consistent with the state's ideology. Additionally, the state supported institutional forms of training in the arts. Both the Riḍā Troupe and the National Troupe were under the sponsorship of the Ministry of Culture from 1961 onward. Additionally, provincial troupes in the mold of these Cairo-based folk dance groups were founded at the various "Palaces of Culture" throughout Egypt; to this day, these institutions propagate the cultural policies of the Ministry of Culture at the local level (Saleh 1979: 33). Saleh, writing in 1979, describes how the theatrical folk dance genre became so pervasive that it even began to impact the source dances upon which it was based:

> As concerns the status of dance, it is worthy of note that for the past twenty years they have been subjected to a concentrated campaign bent on "improving" them, to make them more befitting to the new image of Egypt. The result to date has been a proliferation of theatricalized versions of a number of dances. These have, in their transition to stage and night-club, almost lost any resemblance to the authentic material, whether in regard to pattern, gesture, costume, music, or custom. The regrettable tendency of these innovations is then, by means of the vast media network and Palaces of Culture, to revert to their home base, there affecting the source of original inspiration [Saleh 1979: 462].

As the current study has revealed, the origin and development of *raqṣ sharqī* contrasts markedly with the history just described. First, from its inception, the hybrid nature of *raqṣ sharqī* was neither downplayed nor denied. At the turn of the nineteenth and twentieth centuries, modern and foreign innovations—even Western ones—were acceptable, as long as they could be repurposed towards Egyptian interests and concerns. Second, *raqṣ sharqī* emerged organically from traditional Egyptian dance, as historical circumstances led Egypt's *'awālim* and *ghawāzī* to transition from traditional performance contexts to the formalized performance setting of the entertainment hall. By contrast, the Riḍā Troupe was largely the brainchild of a single individual, and both the Riḍā Troupe and the National Troupe, as state-sponsored entities, presented a vision of the Egyptian folk that aligned with the concerns and interests of the Egyptian government.

As noted earlier, the processes of nationalization and professionalization adversely impacted *raqṣ sharqī.* The professionalization of the entertainment industry—in particular, the institutionalization of training—created a split between "high" and "low" art. The theatrical folk dance troupes, which embraced a formalized mode of classroom training based on the Western ballet model (see, for example, Fahmy 1987: 25–27), fit well within an institutional structure. Artists and entertainers with institutional training found themselves with more and better employment opportunities than those without formal training.

> For [belly] dancers, professionalization has generally had an unfavorable effect. From the 1960s, the Ministry of Culture has patronized ballet and folk-dance groups, such as the Reḍa Troupe and the National Troupe of Folk Arts. Belly dancing has been left without any form of schooling or recognition [Van Nieuwkerk 1995: 63].

Raqṣ sharqī, which generally followed a more traditional mode of learning centered on individual training and mentoring by an experienced performer, would be effectively marginalized by an entertainment industry that favored institutionally-trained, credentialed theatrical folk dancers representing a state-supported vision of wholesome Egyptianness. There would be no academies or institutes for *raqṣ sharqī*, nor would there be state sponsorship; for, under the 'Abd al-Nāṣir regime, "Belly dancers were seen as bad advertisement for Arabic Muslim womanhood" (Van Nieuwkerk 1995: 48).

The theatrical folk dance troupes that emerged at mid-century eventually impacted *raqṣ sharqī* in another significant way. As mentioned in Chapter Four, in the latter decades of the twentieth century, former members of the Riḍā Troupe and the National Troupe of Folk Arts would enter the world of *raqṣ sharqī* as solo performers and as trainers/choreographers.

Rāqīah Ḥassan, a former company dancer of the Riḍā Troupe, is a trainer and choreographer to some of the most celebrated *raqṣ sharqī* performers of the present day, including Dīnā Ṭal'at, perhaps the most stylistically influential Egyptian belly dancer of the last twenty years. Notably, Ṭal'at, like Ḥassan, began her dance career as a theatrical folk dancer before turning to *raqṣ sharqī*. Rāqīah Ḥassan and 'Ā'idah Nūr, another former Riḍā Troupe dancer, host competing *raqṣ sharqī* festivals targeted at non-Egyptian dancers, thus taking advantage of the widespread popularity of belly dance outside of Egypt (Roushdy 2009: 45). Moreover, former members of the theatrical folk dance troupes, as well as protégés of trainers such as Rāqīah Ḥassan, tour and train dancers around the world. Through these individuals, the theatrical folk dance genre has had a profound impact on the technique and aesthetic of *raqṣ sharqī* in the modern day.

Summary

This chapter has examined the process whereby *raqṣ sharqī* became part of the Egyptian cultural heritage. Like other modes of professional entertainment at the turn of the nineteenth and twentieth centuries, this dance form was forged in a climate of intense Egyptian nationalism. As a consequence, *raqṣ sharqī* embodied the persistent tension between tradition and innovation as Egyptians struggled to define themselves as a nation. Thus, though the dance readily absorbed and integrated new and foreign elements, it also maintained its connection to tradition, which ensured its appeal with a broad cross-section of the Egyptian public.

Like other forms of popular entertainment presented on the stages of Egypt's entertainment halls, *raqṣ sharqī* transcended its urban origins and found appeal among Egyptians beyond Alexandria and Cairo. The emergence of new technologies—film and television—was a critical factor in the dissemination of *raqṣ sharqī* to audiences outside of Egypt's urban entertainment halls. In addition, *raqṣ sharqī*'s continuing connection to traditional Egyptian dance enabled its widespread and enduring appeal with Egyptian audiences throughout the nation.

Today, *raqṣ sharqī* is firmly situated within the heritage of Egyptian culture. This is well-illustrated in the following statements by some of the most famous and influential practitioners of the dance in modern times. Rāqīah Ḥassan states: "I am Egyptian! Oriental dancing is something inside every Egyptian" (MacFarquhar 2004). Similarly, in the words of the late trainer and choreographer Ibrāhīm 'Ākif: "Belly dance is in the blood of every Egyptian" (*Cairo Unveiled* 1992). The celebrated Egyptian dancer Lucy, during an interview for the documentary *The Bellydancers of Cairo*, asserts of the dance: "This is my heritage" (*The Bellydancers of Cairo* 2006). Finally, Randā Kāmal, another popular Egyptian dancer, when asked what advice she could give to an aspiring dancer, stressed the importance of visiting and training in Egypt, because "Egypt was the mother of the dance" (*Interview to Randa Kamel Ahlan Wa Sahlan Festival* 2008). *Raqṣ sharqī* has evolved from its beginnings as turn-of-the-century urban entertainment to become a part of the heritage of all Egyptians.

Conclusion

As a teenage boy living in Cairo, the Palestinian-American intellectual Edward Said had the opportunity to witness a performance by the famous Egyptian belly dancer Taḥīyah Carioca. It was an experience that he recalled for the rest of his life with "startling vividness."

> Tahia suddenly revealed herself a few feet behind the singer's chair. We were sitting about as far from the stage as it was possible to sit, but the shimmering, glistening blue costume she wore simply dazzled the eye, so bright were the sequins and spangles, so controlled was her quite lengthy immobility as she stood there with an entirely composed look about her. As in bullfighting, the essence of the classic Arab belly-dancer's art is not how much but how little the artist moves: only the novices, or the deplorable Greek and American imitators, go in for the appalling wiggling and jumping around that passes for "sexiness" and harem hootchy-kootch. The point is to make an effect mainly (but by no means exclusively) through suggestiveness, and—in the kind of full-scale composition Tahia offered that night—to do so over a series of episodes knitted together in alternating moods, recurring motifs [Said 1990: 6–7].

Edward Said's rhapsodic description of Taḥīyah's dance helps to explain the enduring fascination of *raqṣ sharqī* among Egyptians and non-Egyptians alike. The deliberate, sensual movements attuned to the ebb and flow of the accompanying music; the dazzling costume; the individual performer's unique style and presentation: all merge in the moment to create something unique, elusive, beautiful, and spellbinding.

The dance's captivating qualities have inspired numerous admirers outside of Egypt and the Middle East. Unfortunately, the widespread popularity of *raqṣ sharqī* has been coupled with a commonplace tendency to detach it from its cultural context and to manipulate and distort its history towards the needs, interests, and agendas of its non-Egyptian practitioners. As a consequence, the origins and early development of the dance have been obscured by an array of myths and fantasies that are steeped in Orientalist attitudes toward the Middle East, its peoples, and its cultures.

As I stated at the outset of this work, one of the most widely accepted narratives regarding the origin of *raqṣ sharqī* asserts that the dance was created by Egyptians in response to Western influences and desires. This narrative argues that Egyptian entertainment hall owners, catering to the tastes of Euro-American and upper-class Egyptian audiences, created a dance and associated costuming style that embodied Westerners' Orientalist fantasies of Middle Eastern dance. Within this narrative framework, Badī'ah Maṣābnī, the Syrian entertainer and entrepreneur who owned several entertainment halls in Cairo and Alexandria from the 1920s through the 1940s, is frequently invoked as the prime creative force behind the dance.

An examination of primary sources from the late nineteenth and early twentieth centuries contradicts this accepted narrative. The assertion that Egyptian entertainment hall owners were targeting their programs specifically to Europeans, Americans, and the Egyptian elite is simply false. Both foreign and indigenous sources from turn-of-the-century Egypt reveal that many popular venues were frequented by indigenous Egyptian audiences from a broad range of social strata and that Egyptian, Middle Eastern, and North African entertainment was in high demand at these establishments. Moreover, although Egyptian artists and entertainers were open to foreign innovations, these foreign elements were adapted and repurposed to suit indigenous interests and aesthetics. Furthermore, the overwhelming importance assigned to Badī'ah Maṣābnī ignores the history of Egyptian entertainment halls prior to the 1930s and the influence of earlier entertainers and business owners on the development of *raqṣ sharqī*. In reality, essential features that differentiate *raqṣ sharqī* from the dances of the *'awālim* and *ghawāzī* were in place in Egyptian entertainment halls as early as the 1890s.

The narrative described above embodies the Orientalist paradigm that pervades European and American understandings of the Arab world. To suggest that Egyptians created *raqṣ sharqī* to please Westerners not only ignores the substantial primary source evidence available, but also reduces Egyptians to acquiescent subjects who create only in response to the impulse of Western influence. Egyptian dance is framed as being static and unchanging until the innovations of the West are brought to bear on it, and Egyptians are rendered largely irrelevant to the process.

Such a simplistic explanation can not adequately account for the seemingly contradictory nature of *raqṣ sharqī*, a dance form that Egyptians embrace as an authentic part of their cultural heritage, even though it clearly incorporates non-Egyptian features. An understanding of how this dance form came to be, and how it came to be viewed as authentically

Egyptian in spite of its non-Egyptian elements, requires a consideration of cultural hybridity and its relationship to cultural identity. Postcolonial scholarship has drawn attention to the productive nature of cultural identity, highlighting the creative and deliberate ways in which colonized peoples absorb and integrate elements of colonizing cultures into the construction of their own identities. When cultural identity is viewed as a process, rather than a product, hybridity can be viewed as an outcome of colonized peoples actively constructing, negotiating, contesting, and performing their cultural identities in the face of colonial domination, rather than as a corruption of a pure and primordial cultural identity. In the words of Homi Bhabha: "The social articulation of difference, from the minority perspective, is a complex, on-going negotiation that seeks to authorize cultural hybridities that emerge in moments of historical transformation" (Bhabha 1994: 2). This view of hybridity resolves the seeming contradiction posed by *raqṣ sharqī*. The hybrid nature of the dance can be viewed as the product of Egyptian agency, rather than a distortion of pure indigenous dance imposed by Westerners.

In this work, I have approached *raqṣ sharqī* as a hybrid cultural expression emerging from the process of Egyptian cultural and national identity production. I have positioned the emergence of the dance within the context of larger trends in turn-of-the-century Egyptian arts and entertainment. In doing so, I have demonstrated that the development of *raqṣ sharqī* parallels developments in other aspects of Egyptian arts and entertainment, where foreign ideas and influences were embraced, but always on Egyptian terms and toward Egyptian ends. I have illustrated how these processes were enabled and nurtured by the emergence of formalized performance spaces in nineteenth century Egypt, as well as by the growing nationalist sentiment among the Egyptian people. This study has revealed that *raqṣ sharqī* emerged as a product of Egyptians actively defining and asserting their cultural and national identity while under the domination of a foreign occupying power. As a result, this complex hybrid of Egyptian and non-Egyptian inspirations could be embraced by Egyptians as an authentic expression of their identity.

Egyptian Arts and Entertainment at the Turn of the Century

As this study has demonstrated, the origin and development of *raqṣ sharqī* cannot be adequately understood without examining the arts and entertainment milieu in which the dance emerged and evolved. In Egypt, the late nineteenth and early twentieth centuries were a time of tremendous innovation in arts and entertainment. This period witnessed unprecedented growth in indigenous literature, music, and theater, and the birth of the Egyptian cinema. It is impossible to consider these developments without acknowledging the expanding European presence in Egypt throughout the nineteenth century. The fact that indigenous Egyptian arts and entertainment were impacted by this foreign presence cannot be denied. However, turn-of-the-century developments in Egyptian arts and entertainment can not be reduced to a simple reaction to Western influence, or an imitation of Western ideals.

On the contrary, this study has revealed the complex and intentional ways that Egyptian artists and entertainers repurposed foreign influences toward their own interests and agendas. Egyptians very deliberately adopted and adapted foreign ideas and technologies to create hybrid cultural expressions that would be embraced as authentically Egyptian. These cultural expressions, rather than being targeted toward Western or elite Egyptian audiences, were frequently geared toward the Egyptian lower and middle classes. Indeed, turn-of-the-century Egyptian arts and entertainment were firmly grounded in the growing nationalist sentiment of the Egyptian masses, and they were important means by which Egyptians attempted to define and assert their cultural and national identity during the British occupation.

The entertainment halls of Cairo and Alexandria enabled and nurtured these developments. These liminal spaces—at the interface of indigenous and foreign, traditional and modern—represented a fundamental break from traditional Egyptian modes of entertainment. By disconnecting entertainment from its traditional social contexts, they established dedicated spaces in which ordinary Egyptians could enjoy art and entertainment. With their variety-show format, they brought together a diverse range of artists and entertainers—singers, dancers, composers, actors and actresses, etc. in a "melting pot" of invention and innovation. On their stages, Egyptians broke new ground in song, dance, comedy, drama, and more, by absorbing and adapting foreign ideas and technologies. These hybrid cultural productions continued to be rooted in traditional Egyptian aesthetics, interests, and values, ensuring that they would be embraced by Egyptian audiences as authentic. The accessibility and popularity of these venues with a broad cross-section of Egyptians—both men and women, of all social classes—gave mass appeal to the entertainment created within their walls and supported the growing sense of national unity and pride among Egyptians. It was in this context that the dances of Egypt's professional female entertainers, the *'awālim* and the *ghawāzī*, were transformed into the new Egyptian dance form known as *raqṣ sharqī*.

The Entertainment Hall and the Emergence of Raqṣ Sharqī

Throughout the nineteenth century, the *'awālim* and the *ghawāzī* endured the challenges posed by a capricious government, a public that was sometimes conflicted about their art, and an intrusive and exploitative foreign presence in Egypt. By the end of the century, a combination of increasingly systematic governmental regulation and shifting performance opportunities led these women to seek employment in the newly-established entertainment halls of Cairo and Alexandria. The move from traditional performance settings such as weddings and *mawālid* to the stages of the entertainment halls initiated the transition of the traditional dances of the *'awālim* and the *ghawāzī* into the concert dance form that would come to be known as *raqṣ sharqī*. By definition, concert dance is entertainment for a non-participating audience, and two essential features that mark *raqṣ sharqī* as a concert dance and differentiate it from the dances of the *'awālim* and the *ghawāzī* are 1. Performance for the sake of performance, and 2. Performance for a primarily non-participating audience. These features were in place as early as the 1890s, indicating that the development of *raqṣ sharqī* was well underway by the end of the nineteenth century.

Beyond establishing these defining features, the move to the entertainment hall enabled several additional factors that would eventually shape *raqṣ sharqī* into its recognizable modern-day form. First, it led to the mingling of Egyptian dancers with performers of other nationalities, creating the opportunity for Egyptian dance to absorb technical and aesthetic elements from non-Egyptian dance styles. Second, it brought dancers and their accompanying musical ensembles into a setting where Egyptian music was being actively transformed through the deliberate adaptation of Western musical principles and technologies to the Egyptian musical tradition. Finally, it introduced Egyptian dancers to various features of the contemporary Western music-hall, such as the use of choreography and chorus lines, as well as current trends in Western theatrical costuming.

Over a period of roughly forty years—from the 1890s through the

1920s—*raqṣ sharqī* evolved into the dance form that is recognized today. The term *raqṣ sharqī* did not become definitively tied to this emergent concert dance style until the end of this period—in the late 1920s or early 1930s. The fact that *sharqī*—Eastern, i.e., Middle Eastern—would become the defining descriptor of the dance is of tremendous significance, as it indicates that the dance came to be firmly identified by Egyptians as indigenous, rather than *afrankī/afranjī*—Western.

Describing Early Raqṣ Sharqī

What were the characteristics of *raqṣ sharqī* during this early period? As this study has revealed, a number of lines of evidence allow for a fairly detailed reconstruction of *raqṣ sharqī* from the 1890s through the 1920s. Available primary sources include both foreign sources, such as the textual descriptions derived from travelers' accounts and travel guide books, photographs, and picture postcards, as well as indigenous Egyptian sources, such as Arabic-language advertisements and flyers targeted at the local Egyptian population. Secondary sources, such as observations and film footage of Egyptian *'awālim* and *ghawāzī* from the 1930s through the present day, as well as film footage of *raqṣ sharqī* performers in the mid-to-late 1930s, supplement the primary evidence and allow some extrapolation. Taken together, these sources paint a coherent picture of the technique, aesthetic, performance format, and costuming of early *raqṣ sharqī.*

The available evidence allows several conclusions regarding the dance's technique. In general, *raqṣ sharqī* was performed solo until the innovation of choreographed group dance and chorus lines sometime prior to the mid–1930s. As with the dances of the *'awālim* and *ghawāzī*, primary movements were focused in the torso, and footwork was nominal. Early *raqṣ sharqī* was performed to the accompaniment of a small traditional *takht,* which gave way to a larger, more varied *firqa* beginning in the 1930s. Dancers frequently accompanied themselves with finger cymbals.

The early performers of *raqṣ sharqī* were open to incorporating features of non-Egyptian dance genres into their repertoires. It is clear that *raqṣ sharqī* absorbed certain technical elements from European and American music and dance. By the mid–1930s, Egyptian *raqṣ sharqī* had integrated the Western features of choreographed group dance and chorus lines. Additionally, consistent with contemporary trends in Egyptian music, dancers were increasingly accompanied by a large musical ensemble that included a mix of indigenous and Western instrumentation. Western influences on dance posture and alignment also become apparent in the 1930s. Other non-native elements that eventually became part of *raqṣ sharqī* include elaborate traveling steps and complex arm movements; these are generally considered to be derived from ballet and ballroom dance technique. However, these features are not immediately evident in footage of *raqṣ sharqī* performers from the 1930s.

In discussing foreign influence, it is critical to consider the likely impact of other Middle Eastern and North African dance styles on early *raqṣ sharqī*. As discussed in Chapter Three, performers from all over the Middle East, North Africa, and Turkey appeared on the stages of Egypt's turn-of-the-century entertainment halls, and dance styles from throughout the region were presented as part of an evening's program. The important implication is that divergence of *raqṣ sharqī* from the dances of the *'awālim* and *ghawāzī* may owe as much to the incorporation of elements of Turkish and other Middle Eastern/North African dance styles as to the assimilation of Western dance technique.

Regarding the aesthetic of *raqṣ sharqī*, a careful examination of primary source materials in light of present-day Egyptian perspectives reveals several important features. First, improvisation was the preferred mode of performance—even after the introduction of choreographed group dance—because improvisation is conducive to the expression and evocation of feeling. Second, dance performance was closely tied to effective musical interpretation. Finally, the dance periodically assumed an erotic character, but the presence or absence of this quality was dependent on the performer and the performance context. Notably, though early *raqṣ sharqī* seems to have lacked the explicit eroticism sometimes present in *'awālim/ghawāzī* dance, the dance's disconnection from traditional performance contexts, combined with the widespread practice of *fatḥ* in the entertainment halls where it was performed, greatly impacted Egyptians' perceptions of the propriety—or lack thereof—of *raqṣ sharqī* and its performers.

In short, from the 1890s through the 1920s, in the liminal setting provided by the entertainment halls, the traditional dances of the *'awālim* and *ghawāzī* absorbed and integrated the elements that would result in the development of a new and distinct dance form. Nevertheless, the evidence demonstrates that *raqṣ sharqī* continued to share core aesthetic and technical elements with *'awālim/ghawāzī* dance. This enduring connection to traditional Egyptian dance would reaffirm the cultural authenticity of *raqṣ sharqī* in spite of its hybrid nature.

What can be concluded regarding a typical *raqṣ sharqī* performance at the turn of the century? A careful examination of the primary sources provides valuable insights into the characteristics of a typical Egyptian dance show at a turn-of-the-century Egyptian entertainment hall. Despite the challenges posed by both the foreign and the indigenous source materials, they yield important information regarding a typical performance, including the characteristics of the entertainment halls that presented dance, the organization of the show, and the nature and extent of interaction between audience and performers.

The entertainment halls that presented dance ranged from modest music-hall style venues to grand theaters. Admission was affordable—and remarkably stable over a period of several decades—allowing Egyptians from a broad range of social backgrounds to patronize these establishments. Many venues offered ladies-only and family-oriented shows, which enabled all Egyptians—men and women, young and old—to enjoy dance performances. In some cases, *raqṣ sharqī* was the venue's main attraction, while in others, the dance was integrated into a larger program focused on a play or a musical performance. Dancers who performed during intermissions or before/after the main act were frequently identified by name in contemporary advertisements and flyers, suggesting that these women had achieved some degree of celebrity. In the performance environment of the entertainment hall, dancers were separated spatially and socially from their audiences. Nevertheless, Egyptian entertainers continued to break the "fourth wall" during performance—a vestige of traditional modes of entertainment, in which the relationship between entertainers and their patrons was informal and friendly. Beyond this, interaction between dancers and their audiences was limited to two types of exchanges: tip collection and *fatḥ*. As previously noted, the practice of *fatḥ* contributed to the Egyptian public's conflicted perceptions of *raqṣ sharqī* performers.

Finally, what can be concluded regarding costuming for early *raqṣ sharqī*? As with other aspects of the origin and development of the dance, the history of costuming for *raqṣ sharqī* reveals a deliberate integration of foreign elements into an existing indigenous costuming aesthetic, rather than Egyptians simply copying a pre-existing Western fantasy costume. An examination of primary source materials from the dawn of the nineteenth century until the end of the 1930s suggests that the basic template of the modern-day *raqṣ sharqī* costume, known as the *badlah*, evolved from an indigenous (though Ottoman-influenced) costuming style, while absorbing foreign innovations, such as European shoes, stockings, and new fabric choices and design elements. This evolution of costuming is consistent with the broader trend of adapting and integrating foreign ideas and influences into a native Egyptian aesthetic.

Raqṣ Sharqī *as Part of the Egyptian Cultural Heritage*

In similar fashion to the other modes of entertainment presented on the stages of Egypt's turn-of-the-century entertainment halls, *raqṣ sharqī* transcended its urban origins to find broad and enduring appeal among Egyptians outside Alexandria and Cairo. *Raqṣ sharqī*'s continuing connection to traditional Egyptian dance was key to allowing this urban concert dance genre to be accepted and enjoyed throughout the nation. However, the emergence of new technologies—film and television—was also critical to the expansion of the dance to audiences outside of Egypt's urban entertainment halls. The Egyptian films of the 1930s through the 1960s, brought to the wider Egyptian public through the new medium of television, would have the effect of homogenizing Egyptian belly dance, thus shaping public perceptions and expectations regarding style, technique, and costuming. In this way, *raqṣ sharqī* would overshadow the dances of the *'awālim* and the *ghawāzī* to become the accepted representation of Egyptian belly dance in the eyes of the Egyptian public. At the same time, the emergence of theatrical folk dance companies in the middle of the twentieth century, together with the nationalization and professionalization of the entertainment industry, would have significant implications for the position of *raqṣ sharqī* in the public imagination. *Raqṣ sharqī* would find itself marginalized by an entertainment industry that favored institutionally-trained, credentialed theatrical folk dancers representing a state-supported ideal of wholesome Egyptianness. Further, as former members of the Riḍā Troupe and the National Troupe of Folk Arts entered the world of *raqṣ sharqī* as solo performers, trainers, and choreographers, the theatrical folk dance genre would come to impact the technical and aesthetic direction of *raqṣ sharqī*.

Reassessing the Role of Badī'ah Maṣābnī

What of Badī'ah Maṣābnī? As I noted earlier, a popularly-held belief among practitioners and aficionados of *raqṣ sharqī* is that Badī'ah Maṣābnī was the prime creative force behind the emergence and development of the dance. Badī'ah Maṣābnī rose from difficult circumstances to find fame as an entertainer and entrepreneur (Adum n.d., *Badia Masabni in 1966 Television Interview* n.d., Danielson 1997: 48, Dougherty 2000, Van Nieuwkerk 1995: 46). Born in Syria, she began her career in the entertainment industry during a brief stint in Egypt, where she found work as an actress. Returning to the Levant, she built her career working as a singer and a dancer in the cafés and entertainment halls of Lebanon and Syria. Moving back to Egypt in the early 1920s, Badīʿah eventually found work in the troupe of Najīb al-Rīḥānī, to whom she was briefly married in the mid–1920s. In 1926, months after her separation from al-Rīḥānī, Badīʿah opened her first entertainment hall, Ṣālah Badīʿah Maṣābnī, on Cairo's ʿImād al-Dīn Street. Badīʿah would go on to establish several additional venues, including a short-lived establishment in Alexandria (opened in 1928), a casino in Giza (opened in 1930), and, perhaps her most famous establishment of all, the grand Casino Opera, located next to the Khedivial Opera House in central Cairo (opened in 1940) (Adum n.d.).

Badīʿah Maṣābnī launched the careers of many of the most famous *raqṣ sharqī* performers of the twentieth century, and for this reason alone, she is rightly considered to be a profoundly influential figure in the history of *raqṣ sharqī*. However, many problematic assertions about Badīʿah and her entertainment halls continue to be repeated without scholarly analysis, and the true nature and degree of her influence on *raqṣ sharqī* have been distorted. Buonaventura, in her oft-cited volume *Serpent of the Nile*, asserts:

> The first Egyptian cabaret, the Casino Opera, was opened in 1926 in Cairo by Syrian actress-dancer Badia Masabni. Badia's offered a varied bill of all-around entertainment, including an innovatory 6 'clock matinee for women only, which was packed out every evening. With an eye on Western entertainment, she then decided to broaden the scope of Egyptian *baladi* [Buonaventura 1998: 149].

Buonaventura's statement captures the most commonly repeated distortions (besides conflating Badīʿah's Casino Opera with her earlier Ṣālah Badīʿah Maṣābnī). Badīʿah is frequently credited with each of the following innovations:

1. Founding the first "cabaret" or entertainment hall in Egypt
2. Establishing the first "ladies-only" entertainment programs
3. Being the first to merge Arabic and foreign elements in music and dance

However, as this study has revealed, these innovations are not attributable to Badīʿah Maṣābnī. On the contrary, each of these elements was in place in the Egyptian entertainment industry long before Badīʿah opened her first establishment.

Confronting the First Misconception: "Badī'ah Maṣābnī founded the first 'cabaret' or entertainment hall in Egypt"

It is quite clear from the current study that Badī'ah Maṣābnī was not the first to open a professional entertainment venue in Egypt. Chapter One has revealed the long history of the entertainment hall in Egypt's urban centers. Many of these venues were established in Cairo and Alexandria in the latter half of the nineteenth century. For example, the El Dorado entertainment hall was in existence as early as 1870 (Académie Royale des Sciences, des Lettres et des Beaux-Arts de Belgique 1870: 51). Similarly, the Azbakīyah Garden Theater was built sometime prior to 1872 (Sadgrove 1996: 65).

Further, Badī'ah was not the first to open an entertainment hall featuring performances of Egyptian dance. As Chapters Two and Five have clearly demonstrated, numerous entertainment halls were presenting Egyptian dance on their stages as early as the 1890s. Many sources mention and/or describe the Egyptian dance performances at El Dorado in the 1890s and 1900s, for example (e.g., Baedeker 1898: 24, Loewenbach 1908: 218–220, Reynolds-Ball 1898a: 12).

Additionally, it is worth noting that Badī'ah was not the first to feature a solo dancer in her programming. Again, Chapters Two and Five have revealed numerous examples of entertainment halls featuring solo dance performers, particularly in the mid-to-late 1920s. For example, Cairo's Kāzīnū al-Būsfūr presented a "marvelous" dance by Fatḥīyah al-Maghribīyah in December 1924, nearly two full years before Badī'ah Maṣābnī opened her first establishment (Adum n.d., *al-Ahrām* 19 December 1924: 7, *al-Ahrām* 4 November 1926: 3).

Confronting the Second Misconception: "Badī'ah Maṣābnī established the first 'ladies-only' entertainment programs"

Badī'ah was certainly not the first to schedule ladies-only or families-only shows at her establishments. As noted in Chapters One and Five, there are numerous examples of venues providing these sorts of shows from the 1910s onward. In 1919, the Egypsiana Theater offered ladies-only shows on Tuesdays and Wednesdays and family-oriented shows on Thursdays, Fridays, and Sundays (*al-Ahrām* 16 September 1919: 3). Fahmy cites examples from earlier in the 1910s (Fahmy 2011: 122, 207 n. 116). The evidence demonstrates that Badīʿah was following established practice when she began offering ladies-only shows at her establishments.

Confronting the Third Misconception: "Badīʿah Maṣābnī was the first to merge Arabic and foreign elements in music and dance"

The idea that Badīʿah Maṣābnī was the first to integrate Arabic and foreign elements in music and dance is partially attributable to statements made by Badīʿah herself. As noted in Chapter Three, Badīʿah stated in a 1966 television interview that she was the first to mix Arabic and foreign music (*Badia Masabni in 1966 Television Interview* n.d.). However, it is clear that she was not the first to do so. As explained in Chapter Three, it is possible that Badīʿah meant that she was the first to merge Arabic and foreign music as accompaniment for *raqṣ sharqī*, which is indeed possible, but not proven by the evidence that is currently available.

What of Badīʿah's role in incorporating elements of foreign dance styles into indigenous Egyptian dance? As detailed in Chapters One and Three, dancers and dance styles from all over the world were appearing on the stages of Egypt's entertainment halls well before Badīʿah opened her first venue. Given the climate of innovation in the turn-of-the-century Egyptian entertainment halls, it is improbable that Badīʿah was the first to absorb and adapt non-native elements into Egyptian dance. Rather, Badīʿah was following general trends when she decided to integrate features of Latin, Turkish, and Persian dance into *raqṣ sharqī*.

What seems probable is that Badīʿah's innovations were more deliberate, more comprehensive, and/or more attractive to audiences than those of her predecessors, or—more importantly—those of her contemporaries, allowing her innovations to become the norm, and positioning Badīʿah as the most influential person in the development of early-to-mid twentieth century *raqṣ sharqī*. This would help to explain why a 1933 article in the Egyptian women's interest magazine *al-ʿArūsah* attributes the development of the 1930s *badlah* to Badīʿah Maṣābnī (*al-ʿArūsah* 8 February 1933: 6), even though, as revealed in Chapter Six, the Egyptian dance costume had been steadily absorbing elements from European fashion since the second half of the nineteenth century. Perhaps Badīʿah introduced the bare-legged, sheer-skirted look that was so widespread in the 1930s *badlah*. However, until films or images come to light that illustrate what *raqṣ sharqī* performers were wearing in the 1920s, before Badīʿah Maṣābnī became such a prominent figure in the Cairo entertainment scene, it is difficult to draw firm conclusions regarding her role in the development of the modern *badlah*.

Final Thoughts about Badīʿah

Did Badīʿah Maṣābnī create *raqṣ sharqī*? No. As this study has demonstrated, the essential features that mark *raqṣ sharqī* as a concert dance and that differentiate it from the dances of the *ʿawālim* and the *ghawāzī* were in place in Egyptian entertainment halls as early as the 1890s. By the time Badīʿah emerged on the scene, Egyptian dance was being performed on Egyptian entertainment hall stages for roughly four decades.

Did Badīʿah Maṣābnī influence the development of *raqṣ sharqī*? Yes, unquestionably. Badīʿah was a creative artist and an excellent businesswoman; she was skilled not only at positioning herself on the cutting edge of trends in Egyptian arts and entertainment, but also at out-doing her competitors. When she opened Ṣālah Badīʿah Maṣābnī and began offering variety entertainment, she was following the precedent set by earlier venues such as El Dorado. As noted in Chapter Five, dancers were initially not part of the program at Ṣālah Badīʿah Maṣābnī. However, as other establishments in Cairo featured well-known solo dancers, Badīʿah was compelled to follow suit. Badīʿah did not set out to create a new dance form; rather, she attempted—quite successfully—to out-do her competitors in an already proven model for variety entertainment that included dance. Although Badīʿah's entertainment halls were neither the first nor the only such venues to feature *raqṣ sharqī*, thanks to Badīʿah's business acumen and her success at launching the careers of many famous dancers, the particular brand of *raqṣ sharqī* that she presented on her stages became the "industry standard." Yet, it is critical to remember that Badīʿah Maṣābnī's establishments would never have existed without the precedent of earlier entertainment halls such as El Dorado.

Directions for Future Research

As I stated in the introduction to this work, I hope that this study will encourage others to conduct their own empirically-based research that will build upon the foundation that I have provided. In particular, I hope that others will join me in investigating what more the Arabic-language source materials from the late nineteenth and early twentieth centuries reveal regarding early *raqṣ sharqī*. I have no doubt that there is still a great more to be learned from these sources.

For example, as noted in Chapter Six, I have not yet been able to locate well-sourced photographs or film footage of *raqṣ sharqī* performers in costume during the 1920s. Further research into the Arabic-language sources from this period may shed light on what dancers were wearing during this decade and help to clarify the development of the Egyptian dance costume from the 1910s to the 1930s. Such evidence would resolve the nature and extent of Badī'ah Maṣābnī's influence on the development of the 1930s *badlah*.

Additionally, the Arabic-language primary sources have the potential to reveal details regarding individual dancers from this early period. Many of these early *raqṣ sharqī* pioneers remain a mystery. The Turkish dancer Afrānza Hānim, for example, was clearly a very popular performer in the 1920s. Yet, to date, I have encountered neither photos nor film footage of Afrānza, even though she was performing in the entertainment halls of Cairo until 1930 (and possibly later).

The presence of the Turkish dancer Afrānza Hānim and other Middle Eastern and North African performers on the stages of Egypt's entertainment halls points to another important issue that requires investigation. Some of these dancers were celebrities in Turkey, Syria, and elsewhere—areas that had their own developing entertainment industries. Indeed, the entertainment halls of Egypt had counterparts in both Turkey and Syria. For example, Metin And describes nineteenth-century professional entertainment venues in Turkey as follows:

> Until the end of the 19th century, many playhouses were built in Istanbul. There were two kinds, theatres and music halls. Cafés-chantants were included in the latter class and in these, "variety" entertainment was given; some of these cafés having gardens and beer shops attached to them [And 1963: 67].

He goes on to list several of these venues by name. Understanding the style of performance in the professional entertainment venues of Turkey and Syria may enable a more comprehensive understanding of the manner in which other Middle Eastern dance styles influenced the technique of early *raqṣ sharqī*.

In Conclusion

When I began my research into the history of *raqṣ sharqī* in 2009, I did so to address my personal dissatisfaction, as a student and instructor of the dance, with the limited scholarly attention to this issue. I was—and continue to be—greatly frustrated by the many unsourced narratives that continue to circulate among practitioners and aficionados of the dance. In particular, I wanted to address the tendency of these narratives to detach this dance form from its cultural context. I chose to focus on the oft-cited issue of "Western influence" because it encapsulates the Orientalist bias that pervades current understandings of the history of the dance. I wished to debunk, once and for all, the simplistic suggestion that Egyptian entertainment hall owners, catering to Western audiences and to upper-class Egyptian audiences with Western tastes, created a dance and associated costuming style that embodied a Western Orientalist vision of Middle Eastern dance.

In this work, I have brought together evidence from a broad array of primary sources in order to counter this widely-accepted narrative. As I have shown, the emergence and development of *raqṣ sharqī* parallels developments in other aspects of turn-of-the-century Egyptian arts and entertainment. In the late nineteenth and early twentieth centuries, Egyptians actively adopted and adapted foreign ideas and technologies, but always on Egyptian terms and toward Egyptian ends. Rather than being passive reactors to powerful Western influences, turn-of-the-century Egyptians were active innovators, repurposing foreign concepts and technologies towards Egyptian interests. Within the climate of late nineteenth and early twentieth century nationalism, Egyptian art and entertainment were one of the mechanisms through which Egyptians discussed, debated, and defined their cultural and national identity. *Raqṣ sharqī* was born in this complex climate, at the nexus of tradition and innovation. Although it emerged as a hybrid of Egyptian and non-Egyptian inspirations, *raqṣ sharqī* is, and will remain, fundamentally and authentically Egyptian.

Chapter Notes

Introduction

1. One popular text encapsulates this trend in its very title: *The Belly Dance Book: Rediscovering the Oldest Dance* (Richards 2000).

2. It is important to note, however, that Egyptians sometimes use the terms *raqṣ baladī* and *raqṣ sharqī* interchangeably, not only when referring to the informal, social form of belly dance, but also when discussing the professional concert dance that forms the focus of this work. For example, Roushdy uses *raqṣ baladī* for both dance forms (Roushdy 2009, 2013). In the interest of clarity, I use *raqṣ baladī* to refer specifically to the informal, social form of the dance and *raqṣ sharqī* to refer specifically to the professional concert dance that originated at the turn of the nineteenth and twentieth centuries.

3. The literacy rate differed substantially between men and women (Fahmy 2011: 33). In 1897, the literacy rate was 0.7 percent for women, compared to 9.1 percent for men. In 1927, the rate was 3.9 percent for women, and 19.6 percent for men.

Chapter One

1. The Dinshawāy Incident was a confrontation between British military officers and Egyptians from the village of Dinshawāy. The officers sparked local outrage by hunting for sport the pigeons that were an important food source for the village residents. In the ensuing altercation, a British officer fled the scene and died, most likely due to heat stroke. Although the villagers likely did not cause the officer's death, the British, fearing a larger insurrection, used the death as a pretense to mete out exemplary punishments to the Dinshawāy villagers. After a cursory trial, several villagers were convicted of punishments ranging from death by hanging to flogging and imprisonment.

2. The primary unit of Egyptian currency at the turn of the century was the Egyptian pound (*al-jinīh al-miṣrī*). The pound was divided into 100 piasters (*qurūsh*, singular *qirsh*).

Chapter Two

1. Egyptians of the lower classes did periodically witness performances of the *'awālim*. For example, during the royal wedding of Zaynab Hānim in 1845, the palace *ḥarīm* was open to all female citizens of Cairo, regardless of class (Lane-Poole 1846: 126).

2. Contrary to frequent assertions by Dinicu that the *ghawāzī* are "Sinti" (e.g., Dinicu 2011: 46), I have found no evidence to indicate an association between the *ghawāzī* and the Sinti Gypsies of Europe.

3. Confusingly, Egyptians also use the term *ghajar* generically to refer to all Egyptian Gypsies.

4. The -īn and -ūn suffixes represent accusative/genitive and nominative cases, respectively. Note also that in Arabic, there are two spellings for the word for male dancer: in the singular, *raqqāṣ* (رقّاص) and *rāqiṣ* (راقص), and in the plu-

ral, *raqqāṣīn/raqqāṣūn* (رقاصون/رقاصين) and *rāqiṣīn/rāqiṣūn* (راقصون/راقصين). See also Wehr (1976: 354).

5. The *al-Hilāl* article also notes that the ban only applied to Egyptian dancers, not to foreigners; this inequity mirrors discrepancies in the regulation of Egyptian and foreign prostitutes as a result of the Capitulations (Tucker 1985: 153–154).

6. Rizk (2000) dates the Theatre Law to 1911, while Van Nieuwkerk (1995: 42–43) dates the law to 1904 and states that amendments to the law were passed in 1911.

7. Writing of audience behavior during musical performance, Danielson notes: "In its immediate context, listening, in Egypt, is usually participatory: audience members call out subtle compliments or loud encouragement to performers. Silence is interpreted as disinterest or dislike. Some audiences express vociferous displeasure as well. Performances are ultimately shaped by repetitions encouraged by audience requests." (Danielson 1997: 9)

8. Here I am not including liaisons between entertainers and customers that sometimes took place outside of the context of the entertainment hall. *Fatḥ* was sometimes the prelude to prostitution, but it would be a mistake to suggest that all dancers who engaged in the former were also practicing the latter (see Van Nieuwkerk 1995: 44–46).

9. The plural of *rāqiṣah* (راقصة) is *rāqiṣāt* (راقصات), and the plural of *raqqāṣah* *(رقاصة) is raqqāṣāt (رقاصات)*. See also Wehr (1976: 354).

10. Each postcard has an undivided back; this style of card was replaced by cards with divided backs in 1906 (Staff 1979: 66). Each postcard also includes the words "Union Postale Universelle" on the back, indicating that these cards were printed after the creation of the Universal Postal Union in 1878 (Staff 1979: 53, 87).

Chapter Three

1. Bambah Kashar, a famous early twentieth century *'ālmah*, is purported to have appeared in this film (el-Charkawi 1963: 5).

2. Magda Saleh's 1979 doctoral dissertation is supplemented by a documentary film, *Egypt Dances*, which includes footage of the dances described in the text; however, I did not have access to this film while researching and writing this book.

3. Taḥīyah Carioca could certainly play finger cymbals, however; she can be seen playing them in several of her later films.

4. Magda Saleh, who witnessed performances by Muḥammad 'Alī Street *'ālmah* Nazlah al-'Ādil, notes that along with traditional movements, Nazlah performed a rendition of the Charleston (which she termed "Char-lis-toon") and a spin that she termed "Birwit" (pirouette) (Saleh 1979: 119).

Chapter Four

1. Notably, a frequent critique lodged against non-Egyptian performers of *raqṣ sharqī* is that they lack the requisite feeling (e.g., Evanoff 2012).

2. The "springing bounds" mentioned here likely represent the hopping steps that are a distinctive feature of Upper Egyptian folk dance. The present-day *ghawāzī* of Upper Egypt can be observed periodically performing these steps, in addition to their more typical torso-focused repertoire. See, for example, footage of the Banāt Māzin in *Dances of Egypt* (2006).

Chapter Five

1. The *Wāsa'a* ("wide area") was known to English-speaking tourists as the "Fish-market" because this was the area's original function (Dunn 2011).

2. According to Baedeker's 1929 guide book, the Thousand and One Nights Theater was eventually relocated to 'Imād al-Dīn Street (Baedeker 1929: 43).

3. In 1924, Tawḥīdah published a songbook of the tunes that she performed at this venue (Tawḥīdah 1924). According to Danielson, Tawḥīdah was married to the owner of the Thousand and One Nights Theater and took it over after his death (Danielson 1991: 295).

Chapter Six

1. The terms *'antarī* and *yelek* likely derive from Turkish *entari* and *yelek*, respectively. However, in Turkish, these terms describe different garments. Both *'antarī* and *shintiyān* appear in Hans Wehr's Arabic dictionary: the *'antarī* is defined as a brassiere or bodice (Wehr 1976: 648), and *shintiyān* are defined as loose trousers worn by women (487). See also Tilke (1922) for another illustration of the *yelek* and *shintiyān*.

2. The term *ṣafa* is likely derived from the Arabic verb *ṣafa*, meaning "to set up in a row or line, line up, align, array, arrange, order" (Wehr 1976: 516).

3. Note that most of the models for photographs and *cartes de visite* in the mid-to-late nineteenth century were dancers and/or prostitutes, as most ordinary Egyptian women would not have been willing to pose in interior garments for a male photographer.

4. However, the *yelek* seems to have persisted longer outside the urban centers of Cairo and Alexandria; Klunzinger (1878: 31, 189) describes dancers wearing this garment in Upper Egypt in the 1860s or 1870s.

5. This was not the *Cleopatra* composed by Sayyid Darwīsh and Muḥammad 'Abd al-Wahāb. This *Cleopatra* was composed by Dāwūd Ḥusnī, with a libretto by Ḥusayn Fawzī.

Bibliography

Text Sources

'Abd al-Wahāb, Aṭfi. 2001. *al-Masraḥ al-Miṣrī. 1917–1918*. al-Qāhirah: Wizārat al-Thaqāfah, al-Markaz al-Qawmī lil-Masraḥ wa-al-Mūsīqī wa-al-Funūn al-Sha'bīyah.

Abou Saif, Laila. 1973. "Najīb Al-Rīḥānī: From Buffoonery to Social Comedy." *Journal of Arabic Literature* (IV): 1–17.

About Naemet Mokhtar. n.d. Translation by Priscilla Adum. *All About Belly Dancing, by Shira*. http://www.shira.net/about/bio-naemet-mokhtar.htm.

Académie Royale des Sciences, des Lettres et des Beaux-Arts de Belgique. 1870. *Bulletins de l'Académie Royale des Sciences, des Lettres et des Beaux-Arts de Belgique. Ser. 2 T.* 29. Bruxelles: F. Hayez.

Adra, Najwa. 2005. "Belly Dance: An Urban Folk Genre." In *Belly Dance: Orientalism, Transnationalism, and Harem Fantasy*, edited by Anthony Shay and Barbara Sellers-Young, pp. 28–50. Costa Mesa, California: Mazda Publishers, Inc.

Adum, Priscilla. n.d. "Badia Masabni: The Lady and Her Clubs." *All About Belly Dancing, by Shira*. http://www.shira.net/about/badia-lady-and-clubs.htm.

_____. 2015. "Translations of 1930s Gossip Column in a Local Cairo Paper." *The Gilded Serpent*. 8 October. http://www.gildedserpent.com/cms/2015/10/08/translations-of-1930s-gossip-column-in-a-local-cairo-paper.

al-Ahrām. Egyptian Daily Newspaper, 1888–1931.

And, Metin. 1963. *A History of Theatre and Popular Entertainment in Turkey*. Ankara: Forum Yayınları.

Arnold, Julian T. Biddulph. 1882. *Palms and Temples; Being Notes of a Four Months' Voyage Upon the Nile*. London: Tinsley Brothers.

al-'Arūsah. 1933. "al-Kawāthib Tataḥadith 'An al-'Uhur wa al-Baghā' Litusi' Illa al-Miṣriyīn wa Turḍī al-Musta'mirīn." 8 February: 6.

_____. 1933. Advertisement. 26 April: 18.

Badawi, M.M. 1988. *Early Arabic Drama*. Cambridge: Cambridge University Press.

Badia Masabni in 1966 Television Interview. n.d. Translation by Priscilla Adum. *All About Belly Dancing, by Shira*. http://www.shira.net/about/badia-interview-1966.htm.

Baedeker, Karl. 1878. *Egypt, Handbook for Travellers. Part First: Lower Egypt, with the Fayûm and the Peninsula of Sinai*. Leipsic: K. Baedeker; London: Dulau and Co.

_____. 1885. *Egypt, Handbook for Travellers. Part First: Lower Egypt, with the Fayûm and the Peninsula of Sinai. 2nd Edition, Revised and Augmented*. Leipsic, London: K. Baedeker.

_____. 1898. *Egypt: Handbook for Travellers. 4th Remodelled Edition*. Leipsic: K. Baedeker.

_____. 1914. *Egypt and the Sudan: Handbook for Travellers*. 7th Remodelled Edition. New York: K. Baedeker.

_____. 1929. *Egypt and the Sudan: Handbook for Travellers.* Eighth Revised Edition. Leipzig: Karl Baedeker.
Baer, Gabriel. 1964. *Egyptian Guilds in Modern Times.* Jerusalem: The Israel Oriental Society.
Bartlett, William Henry. 1850. *The Nile Boat.* Second Edition. London: Arthur Hall, Virtue, and Company.
Beinin, Joel, and Zachary Lockman. 1998. *Workers on the Nile: Nationalism, Communism, Islam, and the Egyptian Working Class, 1882–1954.* Cairo: American University in Cairo Press.
Bhabha, Homi K. 1994. *The Location of Culture.* London: Routledge.
Bocthor, Ellious. 1828. *Dictionnaire Français-Arabe.* Paris: Chez Firmin Didot.
Bordelon, Candace. 2013. "Finding 'The Feeling': Oriental Dance, *Musiqa al-Gadid,* and *Tarab.*" In *Belly Dance Around the World: New Communities, Performance, and Identity,* edited by Caitlin E. McDonald and Barbara Sellers-Young, pp. 33–47. Jefferson, North Carolina: McFarland.
The Brooklyn Daily Eagle. 1927. "Mrs. Palmer Sees New Day for Women Dawning in Egypt." 23 April: 3.
Brunyate, W.E. 1906. "Egypt." *Journal of the Society of Comparative Legislation* 7(1): 55–65.
Buonaventura, Wendy. 1998. *Serpent of the Nile: Women and Dance in the Arab World.* New York: Interlink Books.
Carlton, Donna. 1994. *Looking for Little Egypt.* Bloomington: IDD Books.
Castle, Vernon. 1914. *Modern Dancing.* New York: World Syndicate Co.
Chabrol, M. de. 1822. *Essai sur les Moeurs des Habitans Modernes de l'Égypte.* In *Description de l'Égypte.* État Moderne, Tome 2, Partie 2. Paris: l'Imprimerie Royale.
Chalcraft, John T. 2005. *The Striking Cabbies of Cairo and Other Stories: Crafts and Guilds in Egypt, 1863–1914.* Albany: State University of New York Press.
el-Charkawi, Galal. 1963. *The Present Situation and Trends of the Arab Cinema.* UNESCO Report. Paris: UNESCO.
Charmes, Gabriel. 1883. *Five Months at Cairo and in Lower Egypt.* London: Bentley.
Chennells, Ellen. 1893. *Recollections of an Egyptian Princess, by Her English Governess.* Edinburgh and London: William Blackwood.
Christout, Marie-Françoise. 1998. "Music Hall: French Traditions." In *International Encyclopedia of Dance, Volume 4,* edited by Selma Jeanne Cohen, pp. 523–524. Oxford: Oxford University Press.
Clot-Bey, A.B. 1840a. *Aperçu Général sur l'Égypte.* Tome Premier. Paris: Fortin, Masson et Cie.
_____. 1840b. *Aperçu Général sur l'Égypte.* Tome Deuxième. Paris: Fortin, Masson et Cie.
Cohen, Selma Jeanne. 1998. "Genres of Western Theatrical Dance." In *International Encyclopedia of Dance, Volume 3,* edited by Selma Jeanne Cohen, pp. 130–131. Oxford: Oxford University Press.
Collett, Herbert Brayley. 1922. *The 28th: A Record of War Service in the Australian Imperial Force, 1915–19, Vol. I.* Perth: The Public Library, Museum, and Art Gallery of Western Australia.
Cooper, Elizabeth. 1914. *The Women of Egypt.* London: Hurst and Blackett.
Cunningham, Alfred. 1912. *To-Day in Egypt.* London: Hurst and Blackett.
Danielson, Virginia. 1991. "Artists and Entrepreneurs: Female Singers in Cairo During the 1920s." In *Women in Middle Eastern History: Shifting Boundaries in Sex and Gender,* edited by Nikki R. Keddie and Beth Baron, pp. 292–309. New Haven: Yale University Press.
_____. 1997. *The Voice of Egypt: Umm Kulthūm, Arabic Song, and Egyptian Society in the Twentieth Century.* Chicago: The University of Chicago Press.
_____. 1999. "Moving Toward Public Space: Women and Musical Performance in Twen-

tieth Century Egypt." In *Hermeneutics and Honor: Negotiating Female "Public" Space in Islamic/ate Societies*, edited by Asma Afsaruddin, pp. 116–139. Cambridge: Harvard University Press.

Denon, Vivant. 1803. *Travels in Upper and Lower Egypt.* Volume I. Trans. Arthur Aikin. New York: Heard and Forman.

Didier, Charles. 1860. *Les Nuits du Caire.* Paris: Hachette.

Dinicu, C. Varga. 2011. *You Asked Aunt Rocky: Answers and Advice About Raqs Sharqi and Raqs Shaabi.* Virginia Beach: RDI Publications.

Dinning, Hector William. 1920. *Nile to Aleppo, with the Light-Horse in the Middle-East.* London: George Allen & Unwin Ltd.

Dougherty, Roberta L. 2000. "Badi'a Masabni, Artiste and Modernist: The Egyptian Print Media's Carnival of National Identity." In *Mass Mediations: New Approaches to Popular Culture in the Middle East and Beyond*, edited by Walter Armbrust, pp. 243–268. Berkeley: University of California Press.

_____. 2005. "Dance and the Dancer in Egyptian Film." In *Belly Dance: Orientalism, Transnationalism, and Harem Fantasy*, edited by Anthony Shay and Barbara Sellers-Young, pp. 145–171. Costa Mesa, California: Mazda Publishers, Inc.

Duff Gordon, Lucie, Lady. 1865. *Letters from Egypt, 1863–65.* London: Macmillan.

_____. 1875. *Last Letters from Egypt.* London: Macmillan.

Dunn, Michael Collins. 2011. "Historical Discursus for April 2: The First Battle of the Wasa'a or Wozzer." *Middle East Institute Editor's Blog: A Blog by the Editor of the Middle East Journal.* http://mideasti.blogspot.com/2011/03/historical-note-for-april-2-first.html.

Ebers, Georg. 1887. *Egypt: Descriptive, Historical, and Picturesque.* Trans. Clara Bell. London: Cassell & Co.

L'Égypte Nouvelle. 1924. "Nouveau Théâtre Printania." 5 April: I.

_____. 1924. "Au Ramsès: Troupe Wahbi." 27 December: II

Evanoff, Caroline. 2012. "Nelly, Beloved Star of Egypt." *The Gilded Serpent.* 4 February. http://www.gildedserpent.com/cms/2012/02/05/caroline-interview-nelly-fouad.

Fahim, Hussein M. 1998. "European Travellers in Egypt: The Representation of the Host Culture." In *Travellers in Egypt*, edited by Paul Starkey and Janet Starkey, pp. 7–12. London: I.B. Tauris.

Fahmy, Farida. 1987. "The Creative Development of Mahmoud Reda, a Contemporary Egyptian Choreographer." Unpublished MA thesis, University of California, Los Angeles.

Fahmy, Ziad. 2011. *Ordinary Egyptians: Creating the Modern Nation Through Popular Culture.* Stanford: Stanford University Press.

Falkland, Viscountess. 1857. *Chow-Chow; Being Selections from a Journal Kept in India, Egypt, and Syria.* Second Edition. Vol. II. London: Hurst and Blackett.

al-Faruqi, Lois Ibsen. 1978. "Dance as an Expression of Islamic Culture." *Dance Research Journal* 10(2): 6–13.

Fonder, Nathan Lambert. 2013. *Pleasure, Leisure, or Vice? Public Morality in Imperial Cairo, 1882–1949.* Unpublished PhD dissertation, Harvard University, Cambridge.

Fraser, Kathleen. 2002. "Public and Private Entertainment at a Royal Egyptian Wedding: 1845." *Habibi* 19(1). http://thebestofhabibi.com/vol-19-no-1-feb-2002/royal-egyptian-wedding.

_____. 2015. *Before They Were Belly Dancers: European Accounts of Female Entertainers in Egypt, 1760–1870.* Jefferson, North Carolina: McFarland.

Friend, Robyn. 1996. "The Exquisite Art of Persian Classical Dance." *Habibi* 15(2). http://thebestofhabibi.com/vol-15-no-2-spring-1996/1132–2.

Giffin, Etta Josselyn. 1911. "Report of the International Congress for the Amelioration of the Lot of the Blind, Held at Cairo, Egypt, February, 1911." In *Eleventh Convention of the American Association of Workers for the Blind*, pp. 37–40. Philadelphia: American Association of Workers for the Blind.

Gran, Peter. 2005. "Rediscovering Al-'Attar." *Al-Ahram Weekly Online* (770). http://weekly.ahram.org.eg/Archive/2005/770/cu4.htm.

Habeiche, Joseph J. 1890. *Dictionnaire Français-Arabe. Première Édition.* Le Caire: Imprimerie du Journal "al-Mahroussa."

Habiba. 2005. "The Legacy of the Ghawazi." *Habibi* 20(4): 38–46.

Hall, Stuart. 1990. "Cultural Identity and Diaspora." In *Identity: Community, Culture, Difference*, edited by Jonathan Rutherford, pp. 222–237. London: Lawrence and Wishart.

Hanna, Nabil Sobhi. 1982. "Ghagar of Sett Guiranha: A Study of a Gypsy Community in Egypt." *Cairo Papers in Social Science* 5(1).

Hassan, Fayza. 1998. "How Green Was This Valley." *Al-Ahram Weekly Online* (400). http://weekly.ahram.org.eg/Archive/1998/400/feature.htm.

_____. 1999. "Well May They Weep." *Al-Ahram Weekly Online* (427). http://weekly.ahram.org.eg/Archive/1999/427/special.htm.

al-Ḥifnī, Ratībah. 2001. *al-Sulṭānah Munīrah al-Mahdīyah wa al-Ghinā' fī Miṣr Qablahā wa fī Zamānihā.* al-Qāhirah: Dār al-Shurūq.

Al-Hilāl. 1894. "Abṭāl al-Raqṣ." 1 August: 729.

_____. 1901. "al-Mar'ah al-Sharqiyah wa al-Raqṣ." 10 April: 410–413.

_____. 1901. "al-Raqṣ al-Afranjī wa al-Ṣaḥah." 1 May: 437–439.

Hopkinsville Kentuckian. 1899. "In an Arab Music Hall." 30 May: 7.

The Horsham Times [Horsham, Victoria, Australia]. 1929. "Café Life in Cairo." 12 November: 4.

al-Jabartī, 'Abd al-Raḥmān. 1904. *'Ajā'ib al-Athār fī al-Tarājim wa al-Akhbār.* al-Qāhirah: al-Maṭba'ah al-'Āmirah al-Sharafīyah.

Jacobson, Ken. 2007. *Odalisques and Arabesques: Orientalist Photography 1839–1925.* London: Bernard Quaritch Ltd.

Jankowski, James. 1991. "Egypt and Early Arab Nationalism, 1908–1922." In *The Origins of Arab Nationalism*, edited by Rashid Khalidi et al., pp. 243–270. New York: Columbia University Press.

Jollois, M. 1822. *Notice sur la Ville de Rosette.* In *Description De L'ÉGypte.* État Moderne, Tome 2, Partie 2. Paris: l'Imprimerie Royale.

Jomard, M. 1822. *Description Abrégée de la Ville et de la Citadelle du Kaire.* In *Description de l'ÉGypte.* État Moderne, Tome 2, Partie 2. Paris: l'Imprimerie Royale.

Kealiinohomoku, Joann. 2001. "An Anthropologist Looks at Ballet as a Form of Ethnic Dance." In *Moving History/Dancing Cultures: A Dance History Reader*, edited by Ann Dils and Ann Cooper Albright, pp. 33–43. Middletown, Connecticut: Wesleyan University Press.

Kholoussy, Hanan. 2010. *For Better, for Worse: The Marriage Crisis That Made Modern Egypt.* Stanford: Stanford University Press.

Klunzinger, C.B. 1878. Upper Egypt: Its People and Its Products. London: Blackie and Son.

Knox, Thomas Wallace. 1879. *The Oriental World; Or, New Travels in Turkey, Russia, Egypt, Asia Minor, and the Holy Land.* San Francisco: Hawley, Rising, and Stiles.

Lagrange, Frédéric. 1994. "Musiciens et Poetes en Égypte au Temps de la *Nahda*." Unpublished PhD dissertation, Universite de Paris VIII a Saint-Denis.

_____. 2009. "Women in the Singing Business, Women in Songs." *History Compass* 7/1: 226–250.

Lamplough, A.O. 1907. *Egypt and How to See It.* New York: Doubleday, Page and Co.

Lane, Edward. 1860. *An Account of the Manners and Customs of the Modern Egyptians.* Fifth Edition. London: John Murray.

_____. 2005 [1836]. *Manners and Customs of the Modern Egyptians.* New York: Cosimo Classics.

Lane-Poole, Sophia. 1846. *The Englishwoman in Egypt: Letters from Cairo. (Second Series).* London: Charles Knight and Co.

Leeder, S.H. 1913. *Veiled Mysteries of Egypt and the Religion of Islam*. New York: Charles Scribners' Sons.

_____. 1918. *Modern Sons of the Pharaohs*. London, New York: Hodder and Stoughton.

Leland, Charles. 1873. *The Egyptian Sketch Book*. London: Strahan and Co., Trubner and Co.

Linden, J. 1884. *L'Illustration Horticole*. V. 31. Gand, Belgium: Compagnie Continentale D'Horticulture (Société Anonyme).

Loewenbach, Lothaire. 1908. *Promenade Autour de l'Afrique, 1907*. Paris: Ernest Flammarion.

Lorius, Cassandra. 1996. "'Oh boy, you salt of the Earth': Outwitting Patriarchy in *Raqs Baladi*." *Popular Music* 15/3: 285–298.

Lott, Emmeline. 1867. *The English Governess in Egypt: Harem Life in Egypt and Constantinople*. Fourth Edition. London: Richard Bentley.

Lüscher, Barbara. 2000. "The Golden Age of Egyptian Oriental Dance." In *The Belly Dance Book: Rediscovering the Oldest Dance*, edited by Tazz Richards, pp. 18–23. Concord, California: Backbeat Press.

MacFarquhar, Neil. 2004. "Symphony in Motion? Ancient Tradition? Or Just Tacky?" *New York Times*. 20 January. http://www.nytimes.com/2004/01/20/world/cairo-journal-symphony-in-motion-ancient-tradition-or-just-tacky.html.

Mansour, Dina. 2012. "Egyptian Film Censorship: Safeguarding Society, Upholding Taboos." *Alphaville Journal of Film and Screen Media* 4. http://www.alphavillejournal.com/Issue%204/HTML/ArticleMansour.html.

Marsh, Adrian. 2000. "Gypsies and Non-Gypsies of Egypt: The Zabaleen and Ghagar Communities of Cairo." *KURI Journal* 1(3). http://www.domresearchcenter.com/journal/13/ghagar13.html.

Marsot, Afaf Lutfi Al-Sayyid. 1985. *A Short History of Modern Egypt*. Cambridge: Cambridge University Press.

Mendoza, Carlos. 1900. "El Teatro Egipcio en la Exposicion de 1900." *Iris*. 18 August (No. 67).

Mitchell, Timothy. 1988. *Colonising Egypt*. Berkeley: University of California Press.

Moseley, Sydney A. 1917. *With Kitchener in Cairo*. New York: Cassell and Company.

Moulton, Robert D. 1998. "Precision Dancing." In *International Encyclopedia of Dance, Volume 5*, edited by Selma Jeanne Cohen, pp. 246–247. Oxford: Oxford University Press.

Murray, John. 1888. *A Handbook for Travellers in Lower and Upper Egypt*. London: John Murray.

Nearing, Edwina. 1993. "Ghawazi on the Edge of Extinction." *Habibi* 12(2). http://thebestofhabibi.com/2-vol-12-no-2-spring-1993/ghawazi.

_____. 2004a. "Khairiyya Mazin Struggles to Preserve Authentic Ghawazi Dance Tradition." *The Gilded Serpent*. 3 January. http://www.gildedserpent.com/articles25/edwinakhairiyyastruggles.htm.

_____. 2004b. "Sirat al-Ghawazi." *The Gilded Serpent*. 11 February. http://www.gildedserpent.com/articles25/edwinaghawazich1.htm.

Newbold, Capt. 1856. "The Gypsies of Egypt." *Journal of the Royal Asiatic Society of Great Britain and Ireland* 16: 285–312.

Ninde, Mary L. 1886. *We Two Alone in Europe*. Chicago: Jansen, McClurg, and Company.

Nugent, Marilee. n.d. "Fatima's Coochee-Coochee Dance (1896): A Film by Thomas Edison." *All About Belly Dancing, by Shira*. http://www.shira.net/about/fatima-coochee-coochee.htm.

Penfield, Frederic Courtland. 1899. *Present-Day Egypt*. London: Macmillan.

Poffandi, Stefano G. 1904. *L'Indicateur Égyptien Administratif et Commercial*. Alexandria: Imprimerie Générale A. Mourés et Cie.

Prime, William Cowper. 1874. *Boat Life in Egypt and Nubia*. New York: Harper and Brothers.

Prüfer, Curt. 1908. "Drama (Arabic)." In *Encyclopaedia of Religion and Ethics*, edited by James Hastings. Volume IV. New York: Charles Scribner's Sons.

The Queenslander [Brisbane, Queensland, Australia]. 1886. "Our Cairo Letter." 27 February: 336.

Racy, A.J. 2003. *Making Music in the Arab World: The Culture and Artistry of Ṭarab*. Cambridge: Cambridge University Press.

Raymond, André. 1957. "Une Liste des Corporations de Métiers au Caire en 1801." *Arabica* T. 4 (Fasc. 2): 150–163.

Reynolds, Bruce. 1926. *A Cocktail Continentale*. New York: George Sully and Company.

Reynolds-Ball, Eustace A. 1898a *Cairo of To-Day: A Practical Guide to Cairo and Its Environs*. London: Adam and Charles Black.

_____. 1898b. *The City of the Caliphs; a Popular Study of Cairo and Its Environs and the Nile and Its Antiquities*. Boston, London: Estes and Lauriat, T. Fisher Unwin.

Richards, Tazz, editor. 2000. *The Belly Dance Book: Rediscovering the Oldest Dance*. Concord, California: Backbeat Press.

Rizk, Yunan Labib. 2000. "Have a Good Time." *Al-Ahram Weekly Online* (485). http://weekly.ahram.org.eg/Archive/2000/485/chrncls.htm.

Romer, Isabella Frances. 1846a. *A Pilgrimage to the Temples and Tombs of Egypt, Nubia, and Palestine, in 1845–6*. Vol. I. London: R. Bentley.

_____. 1846b. *A Pilgrimage to the Temples and Tombs of Egypt, Nubia, and Palestine, in 1845–6*. Vol. II. London: R. Bentley.

Roushdy, Noha. 2009. "Femininity and Dance in Egypt: Embodiment and Meaning in al-Raqs al-Baladi." *Cairo Papers in Social Science* 32(3).

_____. 2013. "What Is *Baladi* About *al-Raqs al-Baladi*? On the Survival of Belly Dance in Egypt." In *Belly Dance Around the World: New Communities, Performance, and Identity*, edited by Caitlin E. McDonald and Barbara Sellers-Young, pp. 17–32. Jefferson, North Carolina: McFarland.

Sadgrove, P.C. 1996. *The Egyptian Theatre in the Nineteenth Century (1799–1882)*. Berkshire: Ithaca Press.

Said, Edward W. 1979. *Orientalism*. New York: Vintage Books.

_____. 1990. "Homage to a Belly-Dancer." *London Review of Books* 12(17): 6–7.

_____. 1994. *Culture and Imperialism*. New York: Vintage Books.

St. John, James Augustus. 1834a. *Egypt and Mohammed Ali. Volume I*. London: Longman, Rees, Orme, Brown, Green and Longman.

_____. 1834b. *Egypt and Mohammed Ali. Volume II*. London: Longman, Rees, Orme, Brown, Green and Longman.

Saleh, Magda Ahmed Abdel Ghaffar. 1979. "A Documentation of the Ethnic Dance Traditions of the Arab Republic of Egypt." Unpublished Ph.D. dissertation, New York University.

Samia Gamal Interview, Kawakeb Magazine, 1968. n.d. Translation by Priscilla Adum. *All About Belly Dancing, by Shira*. http://www.shira.net/about/interview-samia-gamal-1968-kawakeb.htm.

Savary, M. 1785. *Lettres sur l'Égypte*. Tome 1. Paris: Onfroi.

Scott, Clement. 1894. "Egyptian Dancing." *Evelyn Observer*, and *South and East Bourke Record*. [Australia]. 2 February: 2.

Scott, James Harry. 1908. *The Law Affecting Foreigners in Egypt. Revised Edition*. Edinburgh: William Green and Sons.

Segment of 1928 Interview with Nagib El-Rehani. n.d. Translation by Priscilla Adum. *All About Belly Dancing, by Shira*. http://www.shira.net/about/badia-interview-1928.htm.

Sellers-Young, Barbara. 2013. "Introduction: The Interplay of Dance and the Imagined Possibilities of Identity." In *Belly Dance Around the World: New Communities, Performance, and Identity*, edited by Caitlin E. McDonald and Barbara Sellers-Young, pp. 3–16. Jefferson, North Carolina: McFarland.

Senelick, Laurence. 1998a. "Music Hall: British Traditions." In *International Encyclopedia of Dance, Volume 4*, edited by Selma Jeanne Cohen, pp. 520–523. Oxford: Oxford University Press.

_____. 1998b. "Vaudeville." In *International Encyclopedia of Dance, Volume 6*, edited by Selma Jeanne Cohen, pp. 315–320. Oxford: Oxford University Press.

Shafik, Viola. 2006. *Popular Egyptian Cinema: Gender, Class, and Nation*. Cairo: The American University in Cairo Press.

Shay, Anthony V. 1998. "Iran." In *International Encyclopedia of Dance, Volume 3*, edited by Selma Jeanne Cohen, pp. 513–515. Oxford: Oxford University Press.

_____. 2002. *Choreographic Politics: State Folk Dance Companies, Representation, and Power*. Middletown, Connecticut: Wesleyan University Press.

_____, and Barbara Sellers-Young. 2005. "Introduction." In *Belly Dance: Orientalism, Transnationalism, and Harem Fantasy*, edited by Anthony Shay and Barbara Sellers-Young, pp. 1–27. Costa Mesa, California: Mazda Publishers, Inc.

Siebert, Lauren Marie. 2002. "'All the things that portray us as individuals and as a nation': Reda Troupe and Egyptian National Identity in the Twentieth Century." *Text, Practice, Performance* IV: 51–63.

Sladen, Douglas. 1911. *Oriental Cairo: The City of the "Arabian Nights."* Philadelphia: J.B. Lippincott Company.

South Australian Chronicle. 1893. "Letters to Boys—No. LI. in Egypt." 17 June: 16.

Spiro, Socrates. 1897. *An English-Arabic Vocabulary of the Modern and Colloquial Arabic of Egypt*. Cairo: al-Mokattam Printing Office.

Staff, Frank. 1979. *The Picture Postcard and Its Origins*. Second Edition. London: Lutterworth Press.

Star [Canterbury, New Zealand]. 1902. "The Ghawazee of Cairo: The Picturesque Dancing Women of Egypt." Issue 7512. 20 September: 2.

Steevens, G.W. 1898. *Egypt in 1898*. New York: Dodd, Mead, and Company.

Sullivan, Francesca. 2002. "Sohair Zaki: Singing with Her Body." *Habibi* 19(1).

Tawḥīdah. 1924. *Ṭaqāṭīq al-Sitt Tawḥīdah al-Mughannīyah al-Shahīrah fī Alf Laylah wa-Laylah*. Miṣr: Manṣur 'Abd al-Muta'al Saḥib Maktabat Suq 'Akkaz al-Misriyah.

Taylor, Bayard. 1854. *A Journey to Central Africa; Or, Life and Landscapes from Egypt to the Negro Kingdoms of the White Nile. Tenth Edition*. New York: G.P. Putnam and Company.

Thomas, C.F. 2000. "Dom of North Africa: An Overview." *KURI Journal* 1(1). http://www.domresearchcenter.com/journal/11/domna.html.

Tilke, Max. 1922. *Oriental Costumes, Their Designs and Colors*. New York: Brentano.

Troutt Powell, Eve M. 2001. "Burnt-Cork Nationalism: Race and Identity in the Theater of 'Ali al-Kassar." In *Colors of Enchantment: Theater, Dance, Music, and the Visual Arts of the Middle East*, edited by Sherifa Zuhur, pp. 27–38. Cairo: The American University in Cairo Press.

Tucker, Judith E. 1985. *Women in Nineteenth-Century Egypt*. Cambridge: Cambridge University Press.

U.S. Department of Labor. 1921. *Monthly Labor Review*. Volume XII, Number 4. Washington: Government Printing Office.

University of Chicago Library. 2010. *Underwood & Underwood. Collection 1899–1908*. Chicago: University of Chicago Library.

Van Nieuwkerk, Karin. 1995. *A Trade Like Any Other: Female Singers and Dancers in Egypt*. Austin: University of Texas Press.

Vigarello, Georges. 1989. "The Upward Training of the Body from the Age of Chivalry to Courtly Civility." In *Fragments for a History of the Human Body, Part Two*, edited by Michel Feher, pp. 148–199. New York: Zone.

Villoteau, Guillaume André. 1809. *De l'État Actuel de l'Art Musical en Égypte*. In *Description de l'Égypte*. État Moderne, Tome 1. Paris: l'Imprimerie Impériale.

Vincent, Frank. 1895. *Actual Africa; Or, the Coming Continent; a Tour of Exploration*. New York: D. Appleton and Company.

Voilquin, Suzanne. 1866. *Souvenirs d'une Fille du Peuple; Ou, La Saint-Simonienne en Égypte, 1834 À 1836.* Paris: Chez E. Sauzet.

Von Kremer, Alfred. 1864. "The Gipsies in Egypt." *The Anthropological Review* 2(7): 262–267.

Wade, Peter. 1913. "A Girdle of Film Round the World." *The Motion Picture Story Magazine Volume* 6: 101–107.

Ward, Heather D. 2013a. "The Search for El Dorado ... in Cairo." *The Gilded Serpent.* 3 March. http://www.gildedserpent.com/cms/2013/03/13/nisaa-el-dorado-cairo/.

_____. 2013b. "Desperately Seeking Shafiqa: The Search for the Historical Shafiqa El Qibtiyya." *The Gilded Serpent.* 3 October. http://www.gildedserpent.com/cms/2013/10/03/nisaa-desperately-seeking-shafiqa/.

Warner, Charles Dudley. 1900. *My Winter on the Nile.* Boston: Houghton, Mifflin and Company.

Wehr, Hans. 1976. *A Dictionary of Modern Written Arabic.* Third Edition. Ithaca: Spoken Language Services, Inc.

Wiltshire, A.R.L. 1915–1916. *A.R.L. Wiltshire Diary, 12 December 1915–16 March 1916.* From Mitchell Library, State Library of New South Wales. http://acms.sl.nsw.gov.au/_transcript/2011/D12301/a3357.htm.

Wood, Leona and Anthony Shay. 1976. "Danse du Ventre: A Fresh Appraisal." *Dance Research Journal* 8(2): 18–30.

Worrell, W.H. 1920. "Kishkish: Arabic Vaudeville in Cairo." In *The Moslem World,* Volume X, edited by Samuel M. Zwemer, pp. 134–137. New York: Missionary Review Publishing Co.

Zamora Chamas, Jalilah Lorraine. 2009. "Badia Masabny: Star Maker of Cairo." *The Gilded Serpent.* 16 February. http://www.gildedserpent.com/art47/jalilahbadia.html.

al-Zuhūr. 1913. "al-Raqṣ al-Miṣrī." November: 357–362.

Images, Films and Audio

Aisha Dances Volume II: Dances of the Arab World. 2006. Aisha Ali, director. Associated Research Arabic Folklore. Los Angeles.

'Ala Masraḥ al-Ḥayāt. 1942. Aḥmad Badrakhān, director. Egypt.

Anā Dhanbī Aīh. 1953. Ibrāhīm 'Umārah, director. Egypt.

Anā al-Duktūr. 1968. 'Abbās Kāmal, director. Egypt.

Bambah Kashar. 1974. Ḥassan al-Imām, director. Egypt.

The Bellydancers of Cairo. 2006. Natasha Senkovich, director. NS Enterprises. Los Angeles.

Bint al-Bāshā al-Mudīr. 1938. Aḥmad Jalāl, director. Egypt.

Cairo Unveiled. 1992. Kirk Simon and Karen Goodman, directors. Simon and Goodman Picture Company. New York.

Carte-de-Visite Album of Egypt and Egyptians. 1860. Album of 231 photographs. Ken and Jenny Jacobson Orientalist Photography Collection. Getty Research Institute. Los Angeles. http://hdl.handle.net/10020/2008r3a16.

Concert Égyptien. 1889. Album of 36 anthropological photographs presented at the Exposition Universelle of 1889 in Paris. From the collections of Prince R. Bonaparte. Registered in 1930. Bibliothèque Nationale de France, Département Société de Géographie, SGE SG WE-341. France. http://gallica.bnf.fr/ark:/12148/btv1b7702324n.

Dances of Egypt. 2006. Aisha Ali, director. Associated Research Arabic Folklore. Los Angeles.

L'Expo Universelle de 1900. 1983. Institut National de l'Audiovisuel. France. http://www.ina.fr/video/CAB8301052601/l-expo-universelle-de-1900-video.html.

Fifi Abdo: The Egyptian Star. 2005. Hollywood Music Center. Glendale, CA.

Gilded Serpent Presents Badia Masabni. 2009 [ca. 1934]. Film footage of Badī'ah Maṣābnī credited to Jalilah Lorraine Zamora Chamas and El Hami Hassan. https://www.youtube.com/watch?v=26V9iOEw1co.

In Memory of Sayyid Ahmad al-Baidawi. Moslem Throngs Celebrate Fete of Great Egyptian Saint. 1926. British Pathé. London. http://www.britishpathe.com/video/in-memory-of-sayyid-armad-aka-in-memory-of-sayyid.

Interview to Randa Kamel Ahlan Wa Sahlan Festival. 2008. Interview conducted by Munique Neith. https://www.youtube.com/watch?v=88ThTGQ9Sg8.

al-'Izz Bahdalah. 1937. Tujū Mizrāhī, director. Egypt.

Khafīr al-Darak. 1936. Tujū Mizrāhī director. Egypt.

Khulūd. 1948. 'Izz al-Dīn Dhū al-Fiqār, director. Egypt.

Die Königin der Mohammed-Ali-Strasse. 1991. Raimund Koplin and Renate Stegmüller, directors. Bayerischer Rundfunk. Munich.

Latcho Drom. 1993. Tony Gatlif, director. K.G. Productions. France.

Layla Mumṭirah. 1939. Tujū Mizrāhī, director. Egypt.

Mā Aqdarsh. 1946. Aḥmad Badrakhān, director. Egypt.

Une Marché in Haute-Egypte. 1930. Institut National de l'Audiovisuel. France. http://www.ina.fr/video/VDD10045588/un-marche-en-haute-egypte-video.html.

Music of the Fellahin. 1997. Associated Research Arabic Folklore. Los Angeles.

Music of the Ghawazee. 2004. Associated Research Arabic Folklore. Los Angeles.

Narjis. 1948. 'Abd al-Fattāḥ Ḥassan, director. Egypt.

A Nubian Dancing Girl. Upper Egypt. n.d. Keystone-Mast Collection. UCR/California Museum of Photography, University of California at Riverside. Riverside, California. http://content.cdlib.org/ark:/13030/kt709nd7rz.

Princess Ali. 1895. Thomas A. Edison, Inc. Library of Congress. Washington, D.C., http://www.loc.gov/item/00694136/

Princess Rajah Dance. 1904. American Mutoscope and Biograph Company. *The American Variety Stage: Vaudeville and Popular Entertainment, 1870–1920 (Library of Congress American Memory Collection)*. Library of Congress. Washington, D.C., http://memory.loc.gov/cgi-bin/query/r?ammem/varstg:@field(NUMBER(1821)).

Qaṣr al-Shūq. 1966. Ḥassan al-Imām, director. Egypt.

Randa Kamel Interview at Raqs of Course Festival 2014. 2014. Interview conducted by Yasmina Ramzy. https://www.youtube.com/watch?v=hRkz8K6J2Sg.

Raqṣ al-Ghajariyāt. 2005. Footage of Sūhāj *ghawāzī* dances recorded by Muḥammad Ḥāfiẓ. Egypt. http://www.youtube.com/watch?v=7AM1iv5bIfs; http://www.youtube.com/watch?v=0kxVSTAd2gs; http://www.youtube.com/watch?v=qiou6rvHYaw; http://www.youtube.com/watch?v=Q1uFRXf-yQM.

Raqṣ Shafīqah. 1908. Performed by Bahiyah al-Maḥallāwīyah. Odéon 45032.

Rare Glimpses: Dances from the Middle East, Volume I. 2007. Ibrahim Farrah, director. Distributed by Phyllis Phaedra Saretta. New York.

The Romany Trail. 1992. Jeremy Marre, director. Shanachie Records. Newton, New Jersey.

Sāmī al-Shawwā: Prince of the Violin. 2015. Arab Music Archiving and Research Foundation. Beirut.

Shafīqah al-Qibṭīyah. 1963. Ḥassan al-Imām, director. Egypt.

Shaī' Min Lā Shaī.' 1938. Aḥmad Badrakhān, director. Egypt.

Son of the Sheik. 1926. George Fitzmaurice, director. United Artists. United States of America.

Tamr Ḥinnah. 1957. Ḥusayn Fawzī, director. Egypt.

Turkish Dance, Ella Lola. 1898. Thomas A. Edison, Inc. *The American Variety Stage: Vaudeville and Popular Entertainment, 1870–1920 (Library of Congress American Memory Collection)*. Library of Congress. Washington, D.C., http://memory.loc.gov/cgi-bin/query/r?ammem/varstg:@field(NUMBER(1347)).

Type Arab Dancing Girl. Upper Egypt. n.d. Keystone-Mast Collection. UCR/California

Museum of Photography, University of California at Riverside. Riverside, California. http://content.cdlib.org/ark:/13030/kt0r29q906.
Wedding in Luxor. 2014. Aisha Ali, director. Associated Research Arabic Folklore. Los Angeles.
al-Zawjah al-Thāniyah. 1967. Ṣalāḥ Abū Sayf, director. Egypt.

Index

Numbers in ***bold italics*** indicate pages with illustrations